"In ancient times, friendship was prized as the greatest form of love because it was thought to be free of necessary obligation and therefore the most spiritual bond between human beings. Augustine was no exception to the rule, and we cannot understand him properly without taking that dimension of his life into account. This book opens up the private world of a very public man and deepens our understanding of one of the greatest theologians of all time."

Gerald Bray, research professor, Beeson Divinity School

"In this work, Coleman Ford brings to light the centrality of friendship in St. Augustine's personality, ministry, and theology. He captures this by studying Augustine's letters, which are filled with occasional theology yet do not always receive the attention they deserve. Students and pastors alike will benefit from retrieving Augustine's theology of Christian friendship."

Edward L. Smither, academic dean, Columbia International University

"The great, classical concept of friendship has sadly fallen out of favor in a culture that arrogantly considers its own understanding and re-creation of relationships as being beyond the pale of questioning. This has not always been the case. In fact, the greatest thinkers of the Western tradition spilled much ink analyzing and defining authentic friendship. Augustine of Hippo stands at the pinnacle of that group of greats, and his understanding of friendship deserves our attention. Much can be learned from a man who not only thought deeply about the concept but also put those thoughts into practice, and this work is precisely the right guide for this endeavor. That this work stands as a unique study of Augustine's thoughts on this matter highlights its importance to the field of scholarship. That this work was completed by a pastoral scholar as capable as Coleman Ford highlights its value to the academy and the church. That this work engages both the subject matter and the reader in an accessible—dare I say 'friendly'—fashion highlights its potential for a lengthy legacy."

Jonathan W. Arnold, associate professor of church history and historical theology, Southwestern Baptist Theological Seminary

T0367097

"Patristic theology sometimes has the reputation of focusing solely on transcendent realities. And yet, so much of patristic theology concerns the intersection of the immanent with the transcendent, as in the incarnation. With this excellent work on spiritual friendship in Augustine, Coleman Ford shows how divine grace transforms and lifts up mundane realities of personal relationships. His focus on Augustine's letters allows us not only to encounter Augustine's theology but the incarnation of that theology in practice."

Ben C. Blackwell, director, Houston Theological Seminary

"In this exploration of Augustine's epistolary writings, Coleman Ford has consolidated laudable research. *A Bond Between Souls* is a compelling presentation of the ways that the letters of Augustine described and engaged his varied friendships. Perhaps more than other studies, this book attempts to give a voice to Augustine as a distinctively caring and intentional shepherd, peer, and advocate—in short, as one who saw friendship as a spiritual exercise with eternal bearing. Ford's observations are both insightful and timely. Certainly, this is a worthwhile read."

Megan DeVore, professor of church history and early Christian studies, Colorado Christian University

"It's commonplace to acknowledge that there is a loneliness epidemic currently running rampant through Western society. Coleman Ford provides theological medicine for what ails us by retrieving Augustine's theology of friendship—a theology rooted in Scripture, connected to the whole of Christian dogmatics, conversant with the ancient philosophers, and worked out in relational and pastoral practice. This is a retrieval project for the sake of the spiritual renewal of the church."

Matthew Y. Emerson, professor of religion and dean of theology, arts, and humanities, Oklahoma Baptist University

"For Augustine, friendship is a spiritual friendship that binds two souls together, extols the goodness and virtue in the other, and ultimately hinges upon the Triune God and his love. Dr. Coleman Ford not only displays an Augustinian vision of friendship in his own private life, but as an Augustinian scholar, Ford paints the essential contours of Augustine's spiritual vision of friendship. One's soul will be richly warmed, having feasted upon Augustine's epistolary literature, and upon finishing this book, one may long to have Augustine and a few others as a 'second self.' "

Shawn J. Wilhite, associate professor of New Testament, California Baptist University

"Although abundant attention has deservedly been given to Augustine the theologian, substantially less has been devoted to Augustine the friend. In this extensive, fascinating, and inspiring study of letters Augustine wrote to a multitude of friends, Coleman Ford richly demonstrates how Augustine transformed classical understandings of friendship by considering how friendships could foster growth in the Christian life as together the friends made their way to God. *A Bond Between Souls* not only illustrates the pivotal importance of friendship in the life of Augustine, but is also a gift to any friends wanting to know how their love for one another can deepen their mutual love for God."

Paul J. Wadell, professor emeritus of theology and religious studies, St. Norbert College

"Augustine is known as a bishop, a theologian, and a polemicist. But Coleman Ford reminds us that Augustine would also want to be remembered as a friend. In this study, Ford recovers this overlooked aspect of this momentous figure. He does a fine job of laying out Augustine's theology of friendship, but far importantly, he stirs up a deep desire for godly friendship in the reader. Augustine would be proud of his disciple."

Brian Arnold, president, Phoenix Seminary

"One could hardly find a happier and more fruitful study than the theme of friendship in the letters of St. Augustine. Despite the importance of friendship in ancient literature, few have given sustained attention to it in Augustine's work. Moreover, Augustine's letters have garnered too little scholarly attention over the centuries. Thus, I'm delighted to commend Coleman Ford's timely work, *A Bond Between Souls: Friendship in the Letters of*

Augustine. Ford aptly explores this fertile theme in light of classical models of friendship, giving particular attention to Augustine's sometimes contentious relationship with Jerome. In keeping with the twin loves for God and neighbor so often stressed in Augustine's thought, modern Christians do well to learn from his view of friendship governed by love and integral to our spiritual health and growth."

Benjamin Quinn, associate professor of theology and history of ideas, Southeastern Baptist Theological Seminary

"Augustine had a knack for establishing and cultivating deep relationships. While the early church is often framed as controversy and conflict, this study on friendships and camaraderie is refreshing. From the forms of ancient philosophers to the misunderstandings of his peers, Augustine appreciated the mutual experience of friendship, and no medium in antiquity captures its expression like a letter. Ford shows masterfully how, for Augustine, friendship is rooted in the Triune nature of God to be a communicable attribute among believers, expressing an outflow of Christian love. The author captures the affections of the ancient pastor to instruct the church today on a deeper dimension of reconciliation and harmony. Just like Martinanus and Jerome, perhaps Aristotle and Cicero might have found a friend in this genuine colleague and insightful rhetorician."

W. Brian Shelton, professor of theology, chair of the Christian Studies and Philosophy Department, Asbury University

"Coleman Ford's welcome study of Augustine's letters demonstrates Augustine's wise counsel as a spiritual guide to a broad range of recipients including monastics and virgins, fellow clergy, and civic leaders. The central focus grounded in Christian love overflowed to encourage spiritual transformation and desire for the heavenly city. This highly researched and engaging work not only reveals Augustine's agenda for his letters but challenges contemporary readers to form healthy friendships of integrity that begin and find fulfillment in Jesus Christ. This book needs to speak to our time!"

Tom Schwanda, associate professor of Christian formation and ministry, emeritus, Wheaton College

A BOND
BETWEEN SOULS

Friendship in the Letters of Augustine

STUDIES IN HISTORICAL & SYSTEMATIC THEOLOGY

H
S ☩ S
T

A BOND BETWEEN SOULS

Friendship in the Letters of Augustine

COLEMAN M. FORD

STUDIES IN HISTORICAL AND SYSTEMATIC THEOLOGY

LEXHAM ACADEMIC

A Bond Between Souls: Friendship in the Letters of Augustine
Studies in Historical and Systematic Theology

Copyright 2022 Coleman M. Ford

Lexham Academic, an imprint of Lexham Press
1313 Commercial St., Bellingham, WA 98225
LexhamPress.com

Print ISBN 9781683596509
Digital ISBN 9781683596516
Library of Congress Control Number 2022941541

Lexham Editorial: Todd Hains, Caleb Kormann, Abigail Stocker, John Barach, Mandi Newell
Cover Design: Brittany Schrock
Typesetting: Justin Marr

To Michael Haykin for your ongoing friendship and encouragement

To Shawn Wilhite who has been an "other self" for many years

CONTENTS

—

CONTENTS

ABBREVIATIONS

—

ANF	Ante-Nicene Fathers
Acad.	Augustine, *Contra Academicos* (*Against the Academics*)
Bon. Conj.	Augustine, *De bono conjugali* (*The Excellence of Marriage*)
Conf.	Augustine, *Confessionum libri XIII* (*Confessions*)
CSEL	Corpus scriptorum ecclesiasticorum latinorum
Doctr. chr.	Augustine, *De doctrina christiana* (*Teaching Christianity*)
Enchir.	Augustine, *Enchiridion de fide, spe, et caritate* (*Enchiridion on Faith, Hope, and Charity*)
GRBS	*Greek, Roman, and Byzantine Studies*
Nat. grat.	Augustine, *De natura et gratia* (*Nature and Grace*)
NPNF	Nicene and Post-Nicene Fathers
Nupt.	Augustine, *De nuptiis et concupiscentia ad Valerium comitem* (*Marriage and Desire*)
Off.	Ambrose, *De officiis ministrorum*
Retract.	Augustine, *Retractationum libri II* (*Retractions*)
Serm.	Augustine, *Sermones*
Tract. Ev. Jo.	Augustine, *In Evangelium Johannis tractatus* (*Tractates on the Gospel of John*)
Trin.	Augustine, *De Trinitate* (*The Trinity*)

FOREWORD

—

Michael A. G. Haykin

By any estimation, the experience and concept of friendship was central to the life and thought of the great patristic theologian Augustine. It is surprising, then, that the topic has not been studied in greater detail than it has. Might that be due to the way that friendship has not been an important area of reflection for many twentieth-century thinkers and authors (in recent years this has begun to change)? Numerous works on Augustine recognize its importance for understanding the African theologian, but it has certainly not received the attention it deserves. This new examination of the way that friendship informed Augustine's life and thinking is therefore most welcome. There is far more to this subject than can be easily digested in a monograph such as this. But Dr. Coleman Ford is to be commended for laying out the key elements of friendship in the life of Augustine.

Of course, this was a great topic not only in Augustine's life, but among the ancients in general. Both Plato and Aristotle, for example, regarded it as an essential subject for philosophical reflection, and Ford helpfully orients the reader to these classical perspectives on friendship before he takes us through some of the works of Augustine that relate to a number of his friendships. The range of Augustine's friendships was impressive, from a prickly author like Jerome to significant Roman officials such as Marcellinus and Boniface. A study like this leaves one longing for more and maybe Dr. Ford could use this fine monograph as a vital stepping-stone to a more encyclopaedic work that deals with the entire range of friends in the life of the remarkable African theologian whose works have done so much to shape western thought.

Dundas, Ontario
October 22, 2021

PREFACE

—

My interest in church history blossomed in an introductory class at Dallas Theological Seminary under the tutelage of Jeffrey Bingham. My interest grew with subsequent seminars on specific topics in early Christianity, and even more so while serving as an assistant for Michael Svigel. As I considered the topic for my master's thesis, I couldn't escape my interest in the fourth century and was specifically intrigued by the life and ministry of Ambrose of Milan. Writing my thesis on the history and context of his hymnology, this naturally led me into Augustine and his relationship with Ambrose. Having finished the thesis and looking towards doctoral work, for whatever reason, I shelved my interest in Ambrose and Augustine and turned my sights to other figures and topics. Entering the doctoral program at Southern Seminary, I quickly fell in love with topics pertaining to patristic spirituality under the teaching and guidance of Michael Haykin. In this season, my appreciation for the Cappadocians, including figures such as Macarius Symeon, grew deep. Having entertained the possibility of writing on some aspect of one of these Greek thinkers, I simply could not find a place to land and felt as if I was drifting in an unfamiliar sea, unable to navigate to a safe harbor. This caused me to set my sights back on one of my original loves, Augustine of Hippo. Having continually read *Confessions* for devotional purposes, I simply could not escape his descriptions of friendship. Led by Michael Haykin, the notion of friendship in Augustine was refined and grew into a full-fledged research project which resulted in this book. It has been a labor of love.

With this in mind, there are many friends who have brought encouragement in the process of writing. First, I must thank Michael Haykin for the mentorship and friendship he has provided me in the course of my doctoral work. His desire for academic excellence is only matched by his grace and charity which he has consistently demonstrated to me as a student. Second, I must thank men such as Timothy Paul Jones, Jonathan Pennington, and Michael Wilder, who gave me a chance to work and serve alongside them while "training me up in the way I should go" when it came to ministry, whether academic or pastoral. Next, the numerous peers and friends who have encouraged and challenged me along the way must not go unmentioned. One group, my personal Cassiciacum cohort, includes friends like Garrick Bailey, Dustin Bruce, Jonathan Kiel, Brian Renshaw, Sam Tyson. I continue to go back to this group for spiritual sustenance and would not have come to this point without their friendship. I must also thank the various staff and members at The Village Church who encouraged me along the way as I have ministered amongst them while simultaneously writing my dissertation. Thank you for helping me see the beauty and grace of the gospel in new and refreshing ways. I also want to thank my colleagues and friends at Southwestern Seminary and Texas Baptist College who encourage and challenge me. In particular, Madison Grace has become an "other self" to me. Most especially, Shawn Wilhite has been the epitome of an "other self" in this journey and I will cherish the friendship we have though separated by fourteen hundred miles.

Finally, I must thank my family who have supported me spiritually, emotionally, and financially along the way. From my first day of seminary until now, you have been steady and unwavering in your consolation and reassurance. This, of course, includes my wife Alex who has walked alongside me in this journey from day one. Having been a steady friend who has seen my flaws and knows my weaknesses, she has continued to show Christlike grace, love, and kindness and has been the greatest encouragement of all. You have helped me define spiritual friendship because you have modeled it so well with your life. Thank you for helping make this possible.

Coleman M. Ford
Fort Worth, Texas
June 2022

1

—

INTRODUCTION

In his biography on Augustine, Possidius (fl. fifth century AD) recounted the regular judicial duties of his subject. He executed his obligations with care and, when possible, "he taught both parties the truth of divine Law" and "stressed its importance, and suggested means of obtaining eternal life."[1] While Augustine discharged this duty willingly, according to Possidius, "this work … took him away from better things. … His greatest pleasure was always found in the things of God, or in the exhortation or conversation of intimate brotherly friendship."[2] Here Possidius provided his readers with a portrait of a man who, among handling theological controversies and performing pastoral duties, demonstrated a deep love for divine reflection and friendly conversation. These two activities were rarely separated in the mind of Augustine. For Augustine, friendship was no mere casual relationship—true friends brought each other nearer to the face of God.

Augustine of Hippo (354–430) lived and moved within the context of Roman North Africa. Born to a father of Roman heritage and disposition and a mother of Berber descent with Christian commitments, Augustine's pedigree exhibited a multicultural blend and reveals a man who paved the way for both doctrine and practice for the next millennium following his death. He lived at a key turning point in history and witnessed a cultural shift while embodying such a shift as well. Justo González rightly notes that Augustine served as a "bridge between the former Christian tradition and the new context and cultures."[3] He

---

1. Possidius, *Life of St. Augustine* in *Early Christian Biographies: Lives of St. Cyprian, St. Ambrose, St. Augustine, St. Anthony, St. Athanasius, St. Paul the First Hermit, St. Jerome, St. Epiphanius, with a Sermon on the Life of St. Honoratus*, ed. Roy J. Deferrari, trans. Roy J. Deferrari et al., Fathers of the Church 15 (Washington, DC: Catholic University of America Press, 1954), 19. Unless otherwise noted, citations from this text will come from this translation.

2. Possidius, *Life of St. Augustine*, 19.

3. Justo González, *Mestizo Augustine: A Theologian Between Two Cultures* (Downers Grove, IL: IVP Academic, 2016), 13.

is one of the most explored figures within history in terms of theology, psychology, philosophy, and biblical interpretation (among other subjects), yet much remains to be explored in regard to his personal, pastoral, and spiritual life.[4]

Possidius's remark noted earlier is a profound observation revealing the heart within such a multifaceted character. At the conclusion of his work he says, "[May] I emulate and imitate in this world that man, now dead, with whom by God's grace, I lived intimately and pleasantly without any bitter disagreement for almost forty years. Having done this, I will enjoy with him in the world to come the promises of almighty God. Amen."[5] This remark demonstrates the profound impact of Augustine's piety and friendship. It would seem that this intimate friendship motivated Possidius toward imitation of Augustine's devotion to God. Friendship, therefore, was the channel in which piety was both to be pursued and modeled.

Now, significant reflection on friendship existed in antiquity. Aristotle's *Nicomachean Ethics* contains two books on the topic of friendship. At the outset of book 8, he asserts, "For friendship is a virtue, or involves virtue; and also it is one of the most indispensable requirements of life. For no one would choose to live without friends, but possessing all other good things."[6] With regard to friendship, Augustine would certainly agree with many of the classical thinkers who preceded him. It is certain that his understanding of friendship was shaped in many ways by this classical foundation. His perception of and motivation for friendship, however, differed significantly from the classical ideal.

UNDERSTANDING AUGUSTINE AS
FRIEND AND LETTER WRITER

James O'Donnell has remarked, "Least well represented in modern readings of Augustine are his letters."[7] Most revealingly, Peter Brown has noted how the letters of Augustine discovered by Johannes Divjak in 1969 caused him to

---

4. Peter Brown notes, "One of the greatest gains in recent scholarship is that it is now possible to see Augustine's life as a bishop as no longer reduced to his role in [various] mighty upheavals." Peter Brown, *Augustine of Hippo: A Biography*, 2nd ed. (Berkeley: University of California Press, 2000), 498.

5. Possidius, *Life of St. Augustine*, 31.

6. Aristotle, *Nicomachean Ethics* 8.1.1, trans. H. Rackham, 2nd ed., Loeb Classical Library 73 (Cambridge, MA: Harvard University Press, 1934), 451.

7. James O'Donnell, "Augustine: His Times and Lives," in *The Cambridge Companion to Augustine*, ed. Eleonore Stump and Norman Kretzmann (Cambridge: Cambridge University Press, 2001), 11.

rethink his view of Augustine.[8] Robert Eno observed, "Letters were of vital importance for Augustine because friendship was essential to him."[9] The letter in antiquity served as a vehicle, or "living example," wherein "the shared lives of teacher and student could best be communicated."[10] As Stanley Stowers notes, the letter bears the mark of the writer's soul, especially as it developed in the fourth and fifth centuries among Christian writers.[11] Augustine, along with Jerome, represents a "synthesis of classical rhetoric and Christian traditions" in regard to letter writing. The fourth and fifth centuries could rightly be called "the golden age of Christian letter writing."[12] Based on its necessity for communicating one's soul to another, the letter was rightly seen as a natural means for developing and maintaining friendships. With this in mind, how should one see Augustine both as friend and letter writer?

AUGUSTINE AS FRIEND

As one considers friendship in Augustine, the mid-twentieth century marks the beginning of English scholarship on the topic.[13] Reflecting on a large swathe of Augustine's work, the earliest work focused more on his philosophy of

---

8. For an assessment on the Divjak discovery of twenty-nine additional letters of Augustine, see Henry Chadwick, "New Letters of St. Augustine," *Journal of Theological Studies* 34, no. 2 (October 1983): 425–52; W. H. C. Frend, "The Divjak Letters: New Light on St. Augustine's Problems, 416–428," *Journal of Ecclesiastical History* 34, no. 4 (October 1983): 497–512. Brown notes how the Divjak letters have influenced his view on Augustine and his pastoral heart, particularly in his later years. While not directly related to the concept of friendship in Augustine, this realization from an accomplished scholar such as Brown is revealing in understanding the need for additional scholarship in Augustine's epistolary literature. Brown states, "The Dolbeau sermons and the Divjak letters have shown me that my forebodings were exaggerated. I had allowed the undoubted, stern element in Augustine and his legacy to future ages to occupy the foreground of my narrative. I had not caught the more muted, background tones of his day-to-day life as a bishop." He goes on to note, "It is, above all, the Divjak letters that have made me change my mind. ... The letters make plain that the old Augustine was prepared to give his unstinting attention to any problem that might trouble the faithful, no matter how busy he was, no matter how trivial or how ill-framed the problem seemed to be, and no matter how remote from Hippo, or how eccentric, its proponents were." Brown, *Augustine of Hippo*, 466–67.

9. Robert B. Eno, "Epistulae," in *Augustine through the Ages: An Encyclopedia*, ed. Allan D. Fitzgerald (Grand Rapids: Eerdmans, 1999), s.v. "Epistulae."

10. Stanley K. Stowers, *Letter Writing in Greco-Roman Antiquity*, ed. Wayne A. Meeks, Library of Early Christianity (Philadelphia: Westminster, 1986), 38.

11. Stowers, *Letter Writing in Greco-Roman Antiquity*, 67. As Stowers notes, the motif of letter as bearer of the writer's soul developed primarily in a Christian context of letter writing in the late fourth and fifth centuries.

12. Stowers, *Letter Writing in Greco-Roman Antiquity*, 45.

13. Marie Aquinas McNamara, *Friends and Friendship for St. Augustine* (Staten Island, NY: Alba House, 1964).

friendship, including its theological and biblical emphases. Individual relationships were discussed, but only insofar as they contributed to the larger
framework of Augustine's thought. The nature of Christian friendship within
the fourth century received a fuller treatment in the late twentieth century,
with friendship in Augustine receiving a significant portion of reflection.[14]
Augustine and his specific relationships were now beginning to enter the conversation. The concept of friendship was also being wedged into the larger
fabric of Augustine's ethical and social thought, specifically how Augustine's
thought on friendship intersects with the related topics of family and the state.[15]

Within these discussions authors have also been concerned with how
Augustine's thought fits into the larger mold of philosophies of friendship.
Authors over the past three or four decades have sought to relate Augustine's
concept of friendship to the broader Roman tradition, in particular, to
Cicero's On Friendship.[16] Within this discussion too has arisen reflection on
the political dynamics of friendship.[17] Donald Burt has stated that Augustine
"believed that our social nature is a true good. We are perfected as humans by
our love for other humans. We are made happy when that love is returned,
and the most important expression of such reciprocal love is the love of
friendship."[18] It is true that Augustine's notion of friendship was thoroughly
influenced by the Roman tradition, yet with clear distinctions. Carolinne
White noted that Augustine's early concept of friendship was influenced by
Ciceronian notions found particularly in On Friendship.[19] In a letter written

14. Carolinne White, *Christian Friendship in the Fourth Century* (Cambridge: Cambridge University Press, 1992).

15. Donald X. Burt, *Friendship and Society: An Introduction to Augustine's Practical Philosophy* (Grand Rapids: Eerdmans, 1999).

16. Luigi Franco Pizzolato, "L'amicizia in Sant'Agostino e il 'Laelius' Di Cicerone," *Vigiliae Christianae* 28, no. 3 (September 1974): 203–15; Wilhelm Geerlings, "Das Freundschaftsideal Augustins," *Theologische Quartalschrift* 161, no. 4 (1981): 265–74; Tamer Nawar, "Augustine on the Dangers of Friendship," *Classical Quarterly* 65, no. 2 (December 2015): 836–51; Jean-François Petit, "Sur Le 'Phénomène Amical': L'expérience de l'amitié chez Saint Augustin," *Transversalités* 113 (January 2010): 47–63.

17. Frank Vander Valk, "Friendship, Politics, and Augustine's Consolidation of the Self," *Religious Studies* 45, no. 2 (June 2009): 125–46. While Augustine retains much of the language of Greco-Roman notions of friendship, Vander Valk argues that Augustine reinterprets the relationship between individual and society in his view of friendship, eventually leading to the primacy of the individual.

18. Burt, *Friendship and Society*, 56.

19. White, *Christian Friendship in the Fourth Century*, 187.

to an old friend, Martianus, Augustine explained how their friendship fulfills the Ciceronian description of "agreement on things human and divine
along with good will and love."[20]

According to Koenraad Verboven, "Friendship loomed large in the Roman
mind, and was much reflected upon."[21] Augustine inherited a tradition of
friendship within the genre of epistolography, particularly in the Latin West
from Cicero up to his own time. While there is continuity with earlier traditions, there are also adaptions of ancient views of friendship found within
Augustine's letters. The *lingua* of friendship was thus adopted and then significantly adapted by Augustine to fit his specific Christian definition. Specifically,
the Roman idea of patron-client relations informs much of the language of
friendship in Roman era epistolography. Such friendships were "very unequal"
and involved one being "morally bound" to another.[22] Particularly within the
late Republic and early Imperial Roman tradition, the notion of patron and
client could still be considered a type of friendship or *amicitia*. That said, the
ideal Roman friendship (*amicitia*) was a "voluntary relationship between two
persons ideally based on affection but strongly regulated by ethical norms and
social expectations."[23] A friendship could last for many years, even if a significant gap in wealth, status, and influence existed between a patron and his
client.[24] The language of friendship did not necessarily imply social or political
equality, but was often preferred to that of patronage to avoid implications of
"inferiority and dependency."[25] The idea of *amicitia* also had political under-
tones.[26] The idea of *amicitia* and Roman friendship, particularly as it pertains
to Cicero, will be explained more in chapter 2.

Augustine demonstrates his inheritance of the Roman *lingua* of friendship
at various points within his letters, though he is quick to redefine such language
in particularly Christian ways. As will be shown, Augustine presents a notion
of Christian friendship as extending to all based on the dual command of love,

---

20. *Epistula* 258.1.

21. Koenraad Verboven, "Friendship among the Romans," in *The Oxford Handbook of Social
Relations in the Roman World*, ed. Michael Peachin (New York: Oxford University Press, 2011), 404.

22. Verboven, "Friendship among the Romans," 412.

23. Koenraad S. Verboven, "*Amicitia*," in *The Encyclopedia of Ancient History*, ed. Roger S.
Bagnall et al., vol. 1. (Malden, MA: Wiley-Blackwell, 2012), 362.

24. Verboven, "Friendship among the Romans," 413.

25. Verboven, "Friendship among the Romans," 413.

26. Verboven, "Friendship among the Romans," 414–15.

and specific friendships as fulfilling the Ciceronian distinction of agreement in "all things human and divine," yet transformed by grace and given a new eternal perspective based on mutual faith in Christ.[27] In other words, Augustine perceives the obligation of friendship extended toward all humankind but the fulfillment of friendship among only those who share a common commitment to Christ.

AUGUSTINE AS LETTER WRITER

The first modern work on Augustine and his letters appeared in 1935.[28] Information gleaned from Augustine's letters pertaining to social life, economic realities, political movements, and life in Christianized Roman society in general was used as literary evidence to produce a more robust image of Augustine and his context. This study, however, amounts to social data rather than drawing connections to the greater matrix of Augustine's thought. Later in the twentieth century, authors began looking to Augustine's letters in order to demonstrate how he used them as a means of discipline.[29] The idea of *disciplina* emerged as an operative factor in his pastoral leadership, as discerned from his letters. Augustine, in this reckoning, embraced the doctrine of the church as the standard for Christian conduct, including how to address misconduct. Other studies followed, shedding additional light upon Augustine's letters as a corpus of work and how they functioned within doctrinal controversy.[30] Assessing particular situations such as the Donatist schism as well as issues pertaining to Jerome and Augustine's relationship showed Augustine as one concerned primarily with correcting error in his letter writing, a tactic unique in late antique epistolary communication. With these contributions in view, yet more work remains in using Augustine's letters to understand particular facets of his thought, particularly his spirituality.

These studies affirmed the fact that letters in late antiquity often functioned as pieces of oratory, pieces of "public intimacy" often to be published and read

---

27. More on the Ciceronian definition of friendship will be explored in chapter 2.

28. Mary Emily Keenan, *The Life and Times of St. Augustine as Revealed in His Letters* (Washington, DC: Catholic University of America Press, 1935).

29. Daniel Edward Doyle, *The Bishop as Disciplinarian in the Letters of St. Augustine* (New York: Peter Lang, 2002).

30. Jennifer Ebbeler, *Disciplining Christians: Correction and Community in Augustine's Letters* (New York: Oxford University Press, 2012).

aloud.[31] Though the epistolary genre is somewhat difficult to define, in general letters were distinct from other texts in that they were written messages conveyed between a sender and recipient.[32] The fact that Augustine's letters were collected and preserved—both during his life and especially after his death—demonstrates their inherent value to the Christian community.[33] Augustine himself was aware of how his letters would be a crucial component of his literary and theological legacy.[34] As the earliest studies have noted, Augustine's corpus of letters provide a wealth of biographical, social, historical, and theological information. As noted previously, he wrote as one who bared his soul to his recipient, yet he also did so as one trained in rhetoric. The art and practice of rhetoric was inherent in the Roman world, and thus it is not surprising that Augustine was deeply committed to the art of speaking, and hence writing, well. Augustine's famous work on Christian teaching and doctrine, *Teaching Christianity*, demonstrates Augustine's desire to see rhetoric transformed for the purpose of a convincing and compelling Christian oratory. Hence Charles Baldwin notes:

> [The] great Christians of the fourth century, if they could not escape sophistic, at least redeemed it by curbing its extravagance and turning it to nobler uses. But Augustine did much more. He set about recovering for the new generation of Christian orators the true ancient rhetoric. He saw that for Christian preaching sophistic must not only be curbed; it must be supplanted.[35]

---

31. Pauline Allen, Bronwen Neil, and Wendy Mayer, *Preaching Poverty in Late Antiquity: Perceptions and Realities* (Leipzig: Evangelische Verlagsanstalt, 2009), 44–45.

32. Roy K. Gibson and A. D. Morrison, "What Is a Letter?" in *Ancient Letters: Classical and Late Antique Epistolography*, ed. Ruth Morello and A. D. Morrison (Oxford: Oxford University Press, 2007), 2–4. Gibson and Morrison note that the epistolary genre itself is somewhat difficult to define and assert that a "phenomenology" rather than a "watertight definition" for the genre of letters is more appropriate. Gibson and Morrison, "What is a Letter?" 3.

33. For a helpful analysis and overview of scholarship regarding the theory and methodology of letter-collecting, see Bronwen Neil, "Continuities and Changes in the Practice of Letter-Collecting from Cicero to Late Antiquity," in *Collecting Early Christian Letters: From the Apostle Paul to Late Antiquity*, ed. Bronwen Neil and Pauline Allen (Cambridge: Cambridge University Press, 2015), 3–17.

34. Although Augustine does not allocate a specific section in *Retract.* for his letters, he recounts them as separate *libri* on specific topics. For more on Augustine's reflections of his letters in *Retract.*, see Augustine, *The Retractions*, trans. Sister M. Inez Bogan, Fathers of the Church 60 (Washington, DC: Catholic University of America Press, 1968, xiii–xviii.

35. Charles Sears Baldwin, "Saint Augustine on Preaching," in *The Rhetoric of St. Augustine of Hippo: De Doctrina Christiana and the Search for a Distinctly Christian Rhetoric*, eds. Richard Leo

Augustine maintained the value of classical education, particularly rhetoric, yet desired to promote such learning for the distinct calling of Christian oratory. This desire for a particularly Christian rhetoric was also promoted within the pages of his numerous letters.

Calvin Troup notes that Augustine "never abandons rhetoric qua rhetoric in practice, but rejects only the abuses."[36] Augustine's formation in and dedication to rhetoric is important to note as Augustine was not immune to rhetorical tropes such as hyperbole and allusion in order to demonstrate literary erudition. There was also a stock vocabulary of epistolography within late antiquity that Augustine freely accessed. Éric Rebillard notes the various "epistolary rituals" that Augustine observed as he undertook to write to various individuals.[37] Similarly, Jaclyn Maxwell highlights the rhetorical culture of late antique Christian letter writers who "followed the conventions of letter writing, often including classical as well as Christian references."[38] Augustine was aware that his letters would have been read out loud as "[ancient] letters were not considered to be private correspondence."[39]

In *Teaching Christianity*, Augustine commended traditional rhetorical training for Christian orators in order "to teach, to delight, and to sway."[40] Augustine's letters must not be treated as if they were only candid portraits of personal biography, but as literary texts with rhetorical devices and complex contextual layers. As George Kennedy notes, Augustine encouraged Christian orators "to delight listeners in order to retain them as listeners and move them in order to impel them to do what is right."[41] This need to delight readers was not opposed to honesty, as a Christian orator was to live in accordance with the Scriptures that they expounded upon. Thus, Christian virtue must accompany and complement the orator.[42] This dedication to

Enos et al. (Waco, TX: Baylor University Press, 2008), 188.

36. Calvin Troup, *Temporality, Eternity, and Wisdom: The Rhetoric of Augustine's Confessions* (Columbia, SC: University of South Carolina Press, 1999), 4.

37. Éric Rebillard, *Transformations of Religious Practices in Late Antiquity* (London: Routledge, 2013), 89.

38. Jaclyn Maxwell, "Letter Writing and Preaching," in Tarmo Toom, ed., *Augustine in Context* (Cambridge: Cambridge University Press, 2018), 113.

39. Maxwell, "Letter Writing and Preaching," 117.

40. *Doctr. chr.* 4.17.34.

41. George A. Kennedy, *Classical Rhetoric and Its Christian and Secular Tradition from Ancient to Modern Times*, 2nd ed. (Chapel Hill: University of North Carolina Press, 1999), 179.

42. *Doctr. chr.* 4.59–63.

virtuous character within the rhetorical act applied to Augustine's epistolary life as well.

Even with this rhetorical and literary framework working within his
thought, Augustine's letters demonstrate a consistent inclination toward
personal and spiritual connection. While Augustine was certainly a promoter
of oratory and literary eloquence, his was an eloquence in service to truth
and spiritual encouragement. Augustine would not tolerate eloquence for
eloquence's sake, for such a presentation focused attention on the speaker of
the words rather than the words themselves. Thus, Augustine's letters aim at
spiritual motivation in service to the truth of Scripture and therefore range
from occasional exchanges, to deeply personal exchanges, to book-length
theological treatises. For Augustine, a letter was a conduit for spiritual conversation of all sorts.[43]

While Augustine remains a prominent figure in the history of the church,
his concept of friendship in his epistolary literature remains relatively unex-
plored. Indeed, scholars have much more to understand from the bishop of
Hippo from his letters alone. Though recent work has been done in this area,
more can be said as to the specific nature of his relationships as expressed
in his epistolary exchanges.[44] Hence, this work seeks to fill the gap in understanding Augustine's view of friendship as it is expressed, promoted, and
practiced within his letters.

THESIS

In his letters, Augustine conceived of friendship as an outflow of Christian
love, integral to the Christian life for the purpose of building Christlike
virtue, yet shaped differently based on context and person. Specifically,
the purpose of this work is to answer the following question: is there a
relationship between friendship and spirituality in Augustine's epistolary

---

43. In a letter to the imperial official Marcellinus, Augustine refers to their exchange as a
"conversation by letter" and adds that their dialogue with one another amounts to a thorough
discussion. See *Epistula* 138.1.

44. For a recent dissertation, see Joshua Jay Congrove, "Authority, Friendship, and Rhetoric
in the Letters of St. Augustine of Hippo" (PhD diss., Indiana University, 2011). Congrove's eval-
uates the relationship between authority, friendship, and rhetoric in the letters of Augustine.
His goal is to reveal how friendship and authority function within Augustine's epistolary and
rhetorical structures. He suggests that both friendship and authority maintain a careful balance
in Augustine's letters, one feeding off the other with positive, or sometimes deleterious, effects.

literature? Additionally, how did Augustine conceive of friendship as a means
to spiritual growth? What was the spiritual essence of friendship according
to Augustine? More specifically, how did this "spiritual friendship" play out
in specific relationships? In a series of letters between Jerome and himself,
the bishop of Hippo expressed the vital importance of developing friendship:

> Oh, if I were only permitted, even if not living in the same house, at
> least nearby, frequently to enjoy in the Lord a pleasant conversation
> with you. But since God has not granted this, I ask that you strive to
> preserve, increase, and make perfect our being together in the Lord
> as much as we can be and not disdain to reply, however rarely.[45]
>
> But it is a real reason for reproach among friends if we do not see
> our own satchel and fix our eyes on the knapsack of others, as Persius
> says. There remains for you only that you love one who loves you and
> that you, a youth in the field of scripture, do not challenge an old man.
> ... Would that we deserved your embraces and that by conversation
> with each other we either learned something or taught something![46]

In answering the primary research question, this book also addresses the
following related questions: first, to what extent did Augustine hold to classical notions of friendship? Second, what is the nature and role of friendship
in the spiritual life of Christians? Third, what makes the epistolary format
unique to the development of friendship? Finally, what role do Scripture
and the Spirit play in Augustine's notion of friendship? Friendship was not
static but dynamic and encompassed numerous facets since love necessitated different approaches to different situations. Despite its various man-
ifestations, the core of friendship—a mutual desire for virtue and wisdom
found in Christ—remained consistent. Thus, friendship for Augustine was a
profoundly spiritual exercise. In this way, Augustine uniquely transformed
classical notions of friendship in service to the Christian life. The letters are

---

45. *Epistula* 67.3. Unless otherwise noted, quotations from Augustine's letters will come from
the following: *Letters 1–99*, ed. John E. Rotelle, trans. Roland Teske, *Works of Saint Augustine* II/1
(Hyde Park, NY: New City Press, 2001); *Letters 100–155*, ed. John E. Rotelle, trans. Roland Teske,
Works of Saint Augustine II/2 (Hyde Park, NY: New City Press, 2002); *Letters 156–210*, ed. Boniface
Ramsey, trans. Roland Teske, *Works of Saint Augustine* II/3 (Hyde Park, NY: New City Press, 2005);
Letters 211–270, 1*–29*, ed. Boniface Ramsey, trans. Roland Teske, *Works of Saint Augustine* II/4
(Hyde Park, NY: New City Press, 2005).

46. *Epistula* 68.2–3.

the foremost place to turn to in Augustine's works to best understand his view and practice of spiritual friendship.

METHODOLOGY

The study will be an inductive analysis of Augustine's epistolary literature, supplemented by other primary sources from Augustine, and further supplemented by relevant secondary sources. Particular attention will be given to topics of friendship, sanctification, and spirituality as they relate to Augustine. The *Corpus Scriptorum Ecclesiasticorum Latinorum* (CSEL) remains the primary Latin text of Augustine's letters and will be cited occasionally when the Latin meaning bears weight upon the discussion.[47] The *Letters* of Augustine, published within the Works of Augustine series by New City Press, will serve as the standard English translation for this project, though other translations will be consulted as needed.[48] Other primary sources such as Augustine's *Confessions, On Christian Doctrine, On the Trinity, City of God*, as well as his sermons will also be consulted. Additionally, Possidius's biography of Augustine will provide helpful and occasional reflection.[49] Along with other pertinent secondary sources, Brown's definitive biography is also consulted regularly throughout.[50]

With respect to understanding friendship in antiquity, numerous primary sources will be consulted, including relevant works from Aristotle, Plato, Cicero, and Seneca. Specifically, Plato's *Lysis*,[51] Aristotle's *Nicomachean Ethics* (particularly book 8)[52] and Cicero's *On Friendship*[53] will be pivotal in understanding classical notions of friendship. Scholarly sources related to friendship in antiquity will also be consulted.

Chapter 2 on Augustine and spiritual friendship draws from studies mentioned previously and offers some new insights focused primarily in

---

47. Augustine, *Epistulae*, ed. A. Goldbacher, CSEL, vols. 34, 44, 57, 58 (Vienna: F. Tempsky, 1895–1923).

48. Augustine, *Letters 1–99; Letters 100–155; Letters 156–210; Letters 211–270,1*–29**.

49. Possidius, *Life of St. Augustine*, 69–126.

50. See Brown, *Augustine of Hippo*.

51. Plato, *Lysis, Symposium, Gorgias*, trans. W. R. M. Lamb, Loeb Classical Library 166 (Cambridge, MA: Harvard University Press, 1925).

52. Aristotle, *Nicomachean Ethics*.

53. Cicero, *On Old Age, On Friendship, On Divination*, trans. W. A. Falconer, Loeb Classical Library 154 (Cambridge, MA: Harvard University Press, 1923).

his letters. This chapter will establish the framework for understanding the dynamics of friendship in Augustine's letters as seen in subsequent chapters. New attention will be given to the nature of spiritual friendship in Augustine, and how it differs from classical ideas of friendship. This chapter also draws from other texts of Augustine so as to understand his spirituality as it relates to friendship. Thus, I will consult works pertaining to Augustine's spirituality in general. Other chapters focusing on specific exchanges between Augustine and his friends draw mainly upon the primary source material and consult relevant secondary works where necessary.

2
—

AUGUSTINE AND SPIRITUAL FRIENDSHIP

"'For now we have an agreement on things human and divine along with good will and love in Christ Jesus, our Lord, our truest peace."

—Augustine to Martianus[1]

INTRODUCTION

Joseph Lienhard notes, "Augustine was the first Christian writer to elaborate a theory of Christian friendship."[2] Thus, friendship was to always play an important role in Augustine's life. Peter Brown observes, "Augustine will never be alone."[3] John O'Meara indicates that "one of the remarkable features of Augustine's character" was his ability to make and retain friends.[4] Friends were highly valued and cherished, as his life and correspondence clearly demonstrate. His friendships were part of his story, with friends playing different parts within their mutual experiences.[5] Again Brown can state, "Augustine was an imperialist in his friendships. To be a friend of Augustine's

---

1. *Epistula* 258.4.

2. Joseph T. Lienhard, "Friendship, Friends," in *Augustine through the Ages: An Encyclopedia*, ed. Allan D. Fitzgerald (Grand Rapids: Eerdmans, 1999), s.vv. "Friendship, Friends."

3. Brown, *Augustine of Hippo: A Biography*, 50.

4. John J. O'Meara, *The Young Augustine: The Growth of St. Augustine's Mind up to His Conversion* (London: Longmans, Green, 1954), 86.

5. Vernon J. Bourke, *Augustine's Quest of Wisdom: Life and Philosophy of the Bishop of Hippo* (Milwaukee, WI: Bruce, 1945), 148.

meant only too often becoming a part of Augustine himself."[6] This "impe-
rialism" was not however focused only on what his friends could provide
for him, but his desire was for mutual encouragement in the Christian life.

This friendship played out in different ways, but always with the under-
lying goal of seeing Christian virtue further formed in the other as a demon-
stration of Christian love. This is what it meant to be one with another soul,
to see the love of Christ formed in the other as he would want it formed in
himself. This was not the case earlier in his life prior to conversion. Though
his thought was always evolving, most noticeably upon his conversion to
Christianity, the notion of friendship was something that Augustine never
left behind. As Carolinne White notes, "[Augustine] remained true to the ideal
of friendship, in one way or another constantly giving it a central place in
his way of life and his theology."[7] His early relationships certainly displayed
classical ideals inherited from Cicero, and he realized later that some of his
early relationships were unhealthy based on a lack of Christian perspective.
The famous example in Augustine's life was the death of his unnamed friend
described in Confessions book 4. This friend was like a "second self" and the
loss of him created a significant hole which Augustine struggled to fill.[8] In his
post-conversion relationships, particularly those contained within his epistolary literature, Augustine's primary void had been filled; yet he longed to see
friendship extended to others as a means of further filling up his heart and
theirs with Christian love. Christ had entered in and had created a longing to
see others be encouraged in the hope and love of Christ. These "other selves"
were so because of the indwelling Spirit which had mutually been poured forth
in their hearts. If this were not yet the case, Augustine prayed that it would be
that which informed his desire to extend friendship.

Thus, for Augustine, letters served as not only vehicles of dialogue, but as
a stimulus for friendship. Letters as an aid to friendship were certainly nothing new within the classical world. The review of classical notions of friendship in chapter three demonstrates a wealth of reflection prior to Augustine.
Both in theory and in practice, classical conceptions of friendships were a

6. Brown, *Augustine of Hippo*, 52.

7. White, *Christian Friendship in the Fourth Century*, 183.

8. *Conf.* 4.6.11. All quotations of Augustine's Confessions are from Augustine, Confessions, trans. Carolyn J.-B. Hammond, Loeb Classical Library 26–27 (Cambridge, MA: Harvard University Press, 2014–2016).

significant influence upon Augustine. Regarding the influence of classical renderings of friendship, Marie Aquinas McNamara notes, "[Using] it as a scaffolding he arrived at a notion of friendship which is entirely Christian and reaches beyond time to eternity itself."[9] As will be seen below, Augustine was very much dependent upon classical (specifically Ciceronian) understanding of friendship. Augustine found much agreement with Cicero's definition of friendship. Friends think alike on a number of issues both earthly and divine, as Cicero maintained. Yet for Augustine, there was much more than mere agreement. Friendship is a union of hearts (*concordia*).[10] This union had its foundation in humanity's created origin.[11]

Joseph Clair concludes his study on Augustine's notion of the good within his letters and sermons with this observation:

> To help others discern the good requires that one become a friend—to welcome others within the sphere of one's self-love, and to experience others' questions and problems as one's own. Morality is ultimately about friendship, for Augustine. For it is the temporal good of genuine friendship that is the greatest foretaste of eternal good—the singular site where the unchangeable good appears within human existence.[12]

Thus, friendship was a multivalent relationship embarked upon for the purpose of helping the other discern the good. At the center was love. It was a transforming love, seeking to make an enemy into a friend. It was a sustaining love, tending to the flame of love long present within a dear friend. It was a refining love, contending with a like-minded soul in order to build and preserve a fragile friendship. Friendship expressed itself in Augustine's many relationships as a robust and, at times, demanding lattice of love. Spiritual friendship, as I have demonstrated and shall further explore, was singularly focused on one task: building and helping maintain Christlike virtue. This required a different approach with each person, or group of people, in order to meet their spiritual needs.

---

9. Marie Aquinas McNamara, *Friendship in St. Augustine* (Fribourg, Switzerland: University Press, 1958), 196.

10. *Epistula* 258.1; *Acad.* 3.6.13.

11. *Bon. Conj.* 1.1.

12. Joseph Clair, *Discerning the Good in the Letters and Sermons of Augustine* (Oxford: Oxford University Press, 2016), 172.

THE SPIRITUALITY OF AUGUSTINE

Pivotal to understanding spiritual friendship in Augustine's letters is the way in which he viewed the Christian life in general. Humility and love—for God and for neighbor—were the essential components of Augustine's spirituality. In writing to a student named Dioscorus, Augustine asserted, "that first way [to truth] … is humility; the second way is humility, and the third way is humility."[13] For Augustine, practicing true humility meant that one's heart must be focused in the proper direction. It was a life of "radical dependence."[14] Humility, therefore, was impossible to achieve without love. Love and humility are inseparable in that true humility guarantees the practice of true love.

Thomas Martin notes that for Augustine, "Love transforms humility, making it redemptive; humility transforms love, making it universal."[15] Humility opens us to God; pride removes our capacity to love God. The grace of God is necessary to transform our wills, making us able to choose God's will out of love and with joy.[16] Christian love is inspired by divine love and seeks to mirror it. Love as a gift of God endows the human will with a new desire, a striving for the things of God including truth, wisdom, and the virtues of Christ. Such love excludes possessive or egotistic love, pretension, and self-glorification. From this transformation, spiritual practices such as prayer and loving others seek to further instill God's love while one continually humbles oneself before him. The Holy Spirit propels people to the love of their neighbor. A human being's capacity to love God comes from God alone, and by this divinely inspired love one should love the neighbor.[17] All such attitudes are furthered through humility, knowing that love for others demands that one cast aside one's own desires for the sake of the other. True love consists in loving others with God's love given by the Holy Spirit.[18]

---

13. Augustine, *Letters (Epistulae) 100-155*, ed. Boniface Ramsey, trans. Roland Teske, *Works of Saint Augustine* II/2 (Hyde Park, NY: New City Press, 2003), 116.

14. Kent Dunnington, "Humility: An Augustinian Perspective," *Pro Ecclesia* 25, no. 1 (2016): 18.

15. Thomas F. Martin, *Our Restless Heart: The Augustinian Tradition*, Traditions of Christian Spirituality (Maryknoll, NY: Orbis, 2003), 46.

16. *Nat. grat.* 67.81; *Enchir.* 32.

17. *Trin.* 15.17.31-15.18.32.

18. *Tract. Ev. Jo.* 83.3.

FRIENDSHIP AS CHRISTIAN LOVE

Paul Wadell describes Christian friendship according to Augustine as a "school in Christian love."[19] While Augustine believed that he experienced friendship with his unnamed friend in book 4 of the *Confessions*, the fact that it was neither centered on Christ nor directed toward God made it an incomplete friendship. Romans 5:5 serves as a defining passage for Augustine's view of friendship. Reflecting on the death of this friend Augustine stated, "But in childhood he was not such a friend as he became later on, and even later on ours was not a true friendship, for friendship cannot be true unless you solder it together among those who cleave to one another by the charity poured forth in our hearts by the Holy Spirit, who is given to us."[20] Thus for Augustine, true friendship occurred when one loved the good in another person, with the good being a reflection of God in that person.[21] This sort of love gravitates toward the other because of the inherent good they contain as creatures made in God's image.

That Augustine owes much to the classical tradition for his conception of friendship will be explained in the following chapter. As White relates, he demonstrated a "continued attachment to such ideas and shared interests, and by his persistence in using the traditional, classical language relating to friendship."[22] This classical influence, though never fully jettisoned, received a thorough Christian immersion, with friendship given a new orientation within the Christian's journey to God. McNamara has helpfully provided the categories in which Augustine views friendship.[23] Unique to Augustine was his view that friends and friendship are a gift from God. Whereas Aristotle would assert that people choose friends based on the virtue they see in others, Augustine viewed friends as those who are placed in one's lives for the purpose of seeking God together. With this in mind, friendships that have their genesis with God must find their source in God, be conformed to his will, and be mutually seeking his face. Friendship is infused with grace based on the pouring out of the Spirit's love. It originates with the Spirit and propels the

---

19. Paul J. Wadell, *Friendship and the Moral Life* (Notre Dame, IN: University of Notre Dame Press, 1990), 97.

20. *Conf.* 4.4.7.

21. *Epistula* 130.7.14, *Epistula* 155.4.15.

22. White, *Christian Friendship in the Fourth Century*, 189.

23. McNamara, *Friendship in St. Augustine*, 196–97.

friends on toward friendship in God's kingdom where all will be friends as
they share in true friendship with God.

LOVE AND AMICITIA

Augustine asserted that a friend was loved based on God's presence within
them.[24] White has noted how Augustine retains the classical notion of *amicitia*
in his idea of friendship. That said, the ideas of *caritas* and its related words
of *amor* and *dilectio* are evident throughout Augustine's letters. However, the
relationship between *caritas* to *amicitia* is not always clear in notions of friendship. Can *amicitia*, with its particular nature, accommodate the more universal notion of *caritas* in Christian conception? Lienhard remarks, "Augustine
never made his ideas simple by ignoring his experience, and his experience
taught him that friendship meant a good deal more than fraternal charity."[25]

Caritas is granted by the Holy Spirit through grace. It is thus the binding
agent for friendship. This reflection describes the second period of Augustine's
conception of friendship, the first being the period from Cassiciacum up until
the *Confessions* where "human sympathy" is seen as the source of friendship.[26]
This second period applies to Augustine's epistolary interaction, wherein love
is the central "fact at the heart of Augustine's view of friendship."[27] Thus the
relationship of *caritas* to *amicitia* is melded together in Augustine's letters, *caritas* being the lived component of *amicitia*, which in turn is extended to all in
an effort of exhibiting the transforming love of God. Sometimes this connection was more generic, as in the love due to all mankind which is expressed in
friendship.[28] Other times, the connection was much more precise.[29] In writing to Martianus, he consistently related the idea of goodwill and mutual love
from Cicero (*benevolentia et caritate consensio*) to the notion of *amicitia*.[30] But
Augustine's notion of love derived from God and, specifically, was Trinitarian
in shape.

---

24. McNamara, *Friendship in St. Augustine*, 218; *Conf.* 4.4.7; *Solil.* 1.20.

25. Joseph T. Lienhard, "Friendship in Paulinus of Nola and Augustine," in *Collectanea
Augustiniana: Mélanges T. J. van Bavel*, ed. B. Bruning, M. Lamberigts, and J. Van Houtem,
Bibliotheca Ephemeridum Theologicarum Lovaniensium 92 (Leuven, Belgium: Leuven
University Press, 1990), 296.

26. Lienhard, "Friendship, Friends," 372.

27. White, *Christian Friendship in the Fourth Century*, 197.

28. *Epistula* 130.6.13.

29. *Epistula* 258.

30. *Epistula* 258.1.4 (CSEL 57:605–6).

Triune Love

This also demonstrates that friendship is necessarily rooted in the Triune nature of God. Whereas Cicero would define friendship as agreement in all things human and divine, Augustine would further define the divine character of friendship based on the inner relations of the Triune God. Human friendship can only properly begin from the perspective of Trinitarian love. The center of Christian friendship is the Spirit, that Trinitarian bond of love, which is available to believers since the Spirit has been poured forth in their hearts.[31] This love binds friends together and is the means of mutual transformation. As McNamara notes, "God is the end as He is the beginning of all true friendship."[32]

Grace is essential within Christian friendship according to Augustine. This quality sets Christian friendship apart from pagan ideals centered on the value of natural virtue. Thus, simply agreeing on human things a true friendship does not make. This transforming grace is focused heavenward. While grace produces an experience of temporal love, its primary purpose is to carry one along and prepare one for God's eternal city. This makes Christian friendship the only true friendship as it provides the pathway toward the "telos for which everyone is made."[33] The perfect love and benevolence experienced at the culmination of all things when God will be all in all is both the goal and example for authentic friendship. Friendship, for Augustine, is the context where this eternity-focused love is learned and practiced. Christian friendship is not a hindrance but a vehicle toward obtaining this eternal love. Friendship has always been connected to community, whether that is the *polis* in classical rendering or a philosophical community represented by a group such as the Epicureans or Stoics. Similarly, Augustine views friendship in communal terms, with its ultimate fulfillment in the eschaton.

A Debt of Love Owed to All

Numerous times throughout his letters, Augustine expressed an idea of mutual love shared between him and his friends. He often described this as a "debt" that each one owed to the other. Evodius wrote Augustine to

---

31. For a thorough exploration of Augustine's understanding of the Spirit's love as the unity agent within the Trinity, see Lewis Ayres, *Augustine and the Trinity* (Cambridge: Cambridge University Press, 2010), 251–72.

32. McNamara, *Friendship in St. Augustine*, 206.

33. Wadell, *Friendship and the Moral Life*, 99.

collect on this "debt."[34] In his letters to the deacon and eventual bishop of Rome, Celestine, Augustine described a certain "debt of love" that was owed based on a mutual affection for the other person.[35] This kind of love recognizes that love is owed to another based on their innate qualities as a human, and hence love is owed to friends but also to enemies. This love, Augustine asserted, seeks to transform one's enemy "whom we truly love to become a friend."[36]

The idea of transforming love is similar to the idea expressed to his friend Proba. Though Augustine recognized that friendship is most intimately expressed between two who share the same love for God, this did not mean that friendship should be reserved for an elite few. There must be an openness to friendship, even to those who we may deem enemies, for love is due all. For Augustine, extending friendship to all was a gesture which acknowledged our common human nature. It was a call to join the journey toward the eternal city of God where friendship finds its culmination. The idea of universal friendship is expressed in his letter to Proba. He asserted,

> The health and friendship of a human being are sought for their own sake. ... Likewise, friendship should not be bounded by narrow limits, for it embraces all to whom we owe affection and love, though it is inclined more eagerly toward some and more hesitantly toward others. It, however, extends even to enemies, for whom we are also commanded to pray. Thus there is no one in the human race to whom we do not owe love, even if not out of mutual love, at least on account of our sharing in a common nature.[37]

Friendship is the means by which we can demonstrate the love which Christians are called to exhibit.

Noting the "practical impossibility" of being friends with all, Donald Burt says that for Augustine this means that one should desire universality as a goal. While it is impossible to meet every human in one's lifetime, "we can strive to make every human we meet a friend."[38] This was Augustine's

---

34. *Epistula* 158.1.
35. *Epistula* 192.1.
36. *Epistula* 192.1.
37. *Epistula* 130.6.13.
38. Burt, *Friendship and Society*, 67.

posture and his encouragement to his friends. Augustine extended the hand of friendship as a means to love and bring others to the truth. Those who are not yet true spiritual friends, Augustine believed, one should love and befriend with the hope that they will one day be counted among the true friends in the eternal city of God.

Friendship as a debt of love to all is also evident in the way Augustine viewed friendship in its eternal perspective. Friendship in Augustine, according to McNamara, was a sign of the love that is to come in God's eschatological kingdom. The coming kingdom is a realized state, not a termination, of friendship. McNamara notes, "His ideal was to have the unity which is an integral part of individual friendship reign among all men joined in fraternal charity."[39] This concept comes out in numerous ways throughout Augustine's letters, especially those written to civic officials. Augustine encouraged those in public office to view their work as reflective of their commitment to God's heavenly city. Due to their friendship with God, they were better equipped to befriend others and work for the common good of the earthly city.

LOVING GOD AND OTHERS

As mentioned previously, much of Augustine's spirituality has to do with how to integrate the dual command to love into the Christian life. Our love for others, the foundation of friendship, is grounded in the love of God.[40] In writing to Proba, Augustine framed the universal love owed to all as the basis of Christian friendship. This was a transforming type of love, based on common human nature, which sought to turn enemies into true friends who would in turn be transformed by the effects of God's love. Augustine asserted, "In him we, of course, love ourselves if we love God, and by the other commandment we truly in that way love our neighbors as ourselves if we bring them, to the extent we can, to a similar love of God. We, therefore, love God on account of himself and love ourselves and our neighbors on account of him."[41]

---

39. McNamara, *Friendship in St. Augustine*, 221.
40. White, *Christian Friendship in the Fourth Century*, 196–204.
41. *Epistula* 130.7.14.

FRIENDSHIP AS NECESSARY FOR HAPPINESS

Burt observes, "Augustine was convinced that human beings cannot enjoy the fullness of happiness in this life and in the next if they are by themselves, if there is no one they care about or anyone cares for them."[42] Indeed, as Augustine once remarked, "It is hard to laugh when you are by yourself."[43] With this in mind, Augustine views friendship as essential for happiness. Indeed, friendship indicates the type of relationship that all humanity will have in heaven with one another and with God.[44] Friendship in a temporal sense is a foretaste of this heavenly friendship and contributes to our earthly happiness as it prepares us for eternal bliss. This design of friendship is woven into the fabric of our being. In his treatise *The Excellence of Marriage*, Augustine begins by stating the vitality of friendship within society: "Every human being is part of the human race, and human nature is a social entity, and has naturally the great benefit and power of friendship. For this reason, God wished to produce all persons out of one, so that they would be held together in their social relationships not only by similarity of race, but also by the bond of kinship."[45] That initiating relationship of husband and wife is first and foremost one of friendship. God ordained such a relationship as it contributed to happiness and human flourishing, increasing our joy.

FRIENDS ENCOURAGING HAPPINESS

Human beings exist with a desire for happiness. This desire must be "good" according to Augustine, since it was clear God made humanity this way and God only creates that which is good.[46] Happiness was related to friendship in that friendship was a component of Christian love. Love and happiness were thus inseparable in the mind of Augustine. This included one person loving another, but chiefly meant one's love of God. Happiness was thus achieved when one had rightly-ordered love toward things and others in light of his or her love of God. In many of Augustine's letters, his friendship was meant to guide others along this path toward happiness. Augustine encouraged

---

42. Burt, *Friendship and Society*, 59.

43. *Conf.* 2.9.17.

44. For numerous places where Augustine makes this connection in his writings, see White, *Christian Friendship in the Fourth Century*, 206–8.

45. Augustine, *Letters 1–99*, ed. John E. Rotelle, trans. Roland Teske, *Works of Saint Augustine* I/9:33.

46. *Epistula* 140.2.4.

his friend Macedonius to seek God as the highest good which would bring full realization to his happiness.[47] In his letters to both Proba and Demetrias, he encouraged them in their pursuit of rightly-ordered loves which would lead to happiness. To Proba, having noted the need to extend friendship to enemies as an act of Christian love, he states, "But these persons by whom we are loved in return by a holy and chaste love are a great source of delight, and rightly so. We ought to pray that, when we have these goods, we may retain them and that, when we do not have them, we may acquire them."[48]

In Letter 150, written to Proba regarding Demetrias's choice to pursue the consecrated life, Augustine rejoiced, "[Demetrias has] chosen more generously to bring happiness to so illustrious a family. ... It is a richer and more fecund happiness not to become heavy in the belly but to become great in the mind ... to become resplendent in heart, to bear not earthly children in the womb but heavenly children in prayer."[49] In loving God and others, our happiness is increased, though it is still an incomplete happiness. Again, to Proba, "And when we live in that way, we should not suppose that we are already situated in the happy life itself, as if there were nothing for to pray for. For how do we already live happily when there is still lacking the one thing on account of which we are living a good life?"[50] Part of Augustine's friendship to Proba, therefore, was to encourage her to remain steadfast in praying, which was a preparation for obtaining the full extent of the happy life.

Prayer was an essential component of happiness, and Augustine encouraged his friends to exercise prayer for the sake of obtaining happiness. Prayer would help put one's life in perspective of eternity. Proba's station in life has afforded her much consolation, however, such comforts are ridden with "the fear of their loss" and mankind does not "become good because of such goods."[51] Augustine asserted, "True consolation, then, is not found in these, but is rather found where there is true life."[52] What then is the true consolation that Proba should seek? In this life of darkness, one should turn to the light of "the divine and holy scriptures, as if to a lamp set in a dark place,

---

47. *Epistula* 155.3.12.
48. *Epistula* 130.6.13.
49. *Epistula* 150.
50. *Epistula* 130.7.14.
51. *Epistula* 130.2.3.
52. *Epistula* 130.2.3.

until the day dawns and the morning star rises in our hearts."[53] The "ineffable source" of this lamp, that is Christ, can only be perceived through the eyes of faith, and it is this source which offers stimulus for prayer.[54] Consequently, Augustine encouraged Proba to rely upon Scripture for rest and encouragement. His desire was for Proba to be shaped by the light of Scripture for the purpose of prayer in order to seek true happiness. One day our prayer will be obsolete as "there will be no temptation. ... [and] no expectation of the good that was promised, but the contemplation of the good that has been received."[55] Prayer, therefore, acts as a preparation for such a day, recognizing the desolations of this life and eagerly seeking the true consolation (happiness) of the life to come. Since the consolation of eternity has not yet come, one must persist in prayer.

FRIENDS AS ADDING TO HAPPINESS

Throughout all his letters to friends, Augustine expressed the notion that such relationships greatly added to his happiness. There can be no happiness without friendship.[56] Augustine reminded Proba that happiness included friendship, and such friendship should be extended to all.[57] Wilhelm Geerlings has noted, "[Augustine] was in accord with the classical philosophical tradition, which emphasized the close connection between the happy life and friendship."[58] Channeling Cicero, Augustine believed agreement on the things of God was necessary in order to have true friendship and hence experience true happiness. Augustine often lamented that he could not spend time with his friends face-to-face, but this fact did not diminish the joy he gained in their exchange. If anything, it caused him to yearn more for the complete happiness that would be present in the eternal city. For example, with his friends Paulinus and Therasia, Augustine was willing "to cross the sea for the sole purpose of enjoying [their] presence."[59]

---

53. *Epistula* 130.2.5.
54. *Epistula* 130.2.5.
55. *Epistula* 130.2.5.
56. *Conf.* 6.16.26.
57. *Epistula* 130.6.13.
58. Geerlings, "Das Freundschaftsideal Augustins," 266.
59. *Epistula* 95.1.

Wadell notes that Augustine saw a "continuity between the happiness we enjoy now and the happiness we will have in heaven."[60] That said, temporal happiness only comes when others share in the "love and goodness of God."[61] It was this mutual participation in God's love and goodness which informed Augustine's view of happiness among his friends.[62] Though his relationship with Jerome was filled with disagreement, Augustine believed that their mutual love for one another would lead to a greater love for God. Augustine wished to "abandon [his] whole self to the love" for Jerome because he perceived that he was "aflame with Christian love."[63] Hence, happiness would increase as love was extended to a friend in their mutual pursuit of love for God.

SPIRITUAL FRIENDSHIP AS EXHORTATION

Jennifer Ebbeler has helpfully noted the nature of epistolary correction in Augustine.[64] Augustine sought more from epistolary exchanges than was typically expected in prior generations. That said, such correction (I prefer the idea of exhortation) was fundamental to Augustine's epistolary exchange because it was central to his understanding of friendship. Another way of describing this friendship trait is frankness. If friendship is based on the pursuit of truth, then the notion of exhortation toward truth, and correction when not moving in that direction, is indispensable to a proper friendship. Such was the case with his friend Macedonius. He asserted, "Sure I may be more respectful when I intercede with you on behalf of others, but when I interceded on your own behalf I am franker to the extent that I am more your friend because I am more your friend the more loyal I am."[65] This trait is even more necessary in Augustine's conception of spiritual friendship as many of his correspondents he never met face to face.

60. Paul J. Wadell, *Happiness and the Christian Moral Life: An Introduction to Christian Ethics*, 3rd ed. (Lanham, MD: Rowman & Littlefield, 2016), 12.

61. Wadell, *Happiness and the Christian Moral Life*, 12.

62. White, *Christian Friendship in the Fourth Century*, 198.

63. *Epistula* 72.3.10.

64. Ebbeler, *Disciplining Christians*, 8–10.

65. *Epistula* 155.3.11.

Such is the case with Jerome, but he is only the more famous example among a host of other epistolary exchanges. As Burt relates, "[Frankness] enables us to dare to pour out all of our plans and gives us the freedom to tell our friends what bothers us about them."[66] David Konstan notes that for the ancients "candor is the sign of the genuine friend."[67] This said, the idea of frankness can easily turn abusive. Noting Plutarch's discussion of this idea, Konstan observes, "Timing (kairos) is of the essence. ... Thus, one must recognize the season when a friend is open to correction ... [and] criticism must be tempered with praise."[68] Frankness, therefore, is all about balance. One must be able to share the good with the bad, or to use a more biblical phrase, to speak truth in love.[69]

This necessary component of friendship was expressed in multiple ways in Augustine's various epistolary friendships. The idea of frankness was most expressed in the form of exhortation, challenging his friends toward specific spiritual activity or a more spiritually sound frame of mind. This, as Augustine laments, will be imperfect in this life. Such frankness in the form of exhortation relates to Augustine's notion that people need assistance from others in order to help them understand themselves, to shine a light inside the "well of darkness surrounded by thick walls."[70] A friend should endeavor to know the will of the other and desire to be known by them as well. Though one will never be able to plumb the depths of his or her heart completely, the only hope we have at all is to do so together. In writing to Jerome, Augustine lamented and wished to know his heart better, yet understood the reality of his finite nature making such a task impossible. He confessed,

What trusting hearts will safely pour themselves out to one another? To whose minds will love wholly entrust itself in security? ... Oh, our wretched and pitiable state! Oh, how unreliable is our knowledge of

---

66. Burt, Friendship and Society, 64.

67. David Konstan, "Friendship, Flattery, Frankness," in Friendship, Flattery and Frankness of Speech: Studies on Friendship in the New Testament World, ed. John T. Fitzgerald (New York: Brill Academic, 1997), 7.

68. David Konstan, Friendship in the Classical World (Cambridge: Cambridge University Press, 1997), 103. Konstan refers to Plutarch's Moralia, vol. 1, which is his treatise wherein he describes the differences between a friend and a flatterer. For a more in-depth discussion of this text, see D. A. Russell, "On Reading Plutarch's 'Moralia,'" Greece and Rome 15, no. 2 (1968): 130–46.

69. See Eph 4:15.

70. Burt, Friendship and Society, 64.

the wills of present friends where there is no foreknowledge of their future! But why should I suppose that I should lament this to one person about another when a man's own future is not even known to himself. For each of us knows somehow, perhaps hardly at all, the person he now is, but he does not know what he will be afterward.[71]

Though he expressed a certain heartache at the impossibility of truly knowing the other, Augustine's practice of exhortation in friendship assumed that there was necessary positive ground to be gained.

Exhortation was necessary if one truly believed in Christian love and desires to see one grow in Christlike virtue on the way to the eternal city. One of the more prominent examples of exhortation in his epistolary friendships was with Jerome. Augustine expressed a certain freedom of speech (*libertas amicitiae*) that should be present in any good relationship.[72] This "freedom of friendship" was meant to draw out what weaknesses each might have seen in the other. This relates to the biblical notion of "speaking truth in love" and specifically as Augustine saw it, "this [is done] in fraternal love with a spirit that is not displeasing in the eyes of God."[73] This sort of freedom was also expressed to Proba as he exhorted her to cherish the spiritual life more than what was earthly. Augustine exhorted, "Remember that you are desolate in order that you may persist night and day. ... Disdain and scorn [pleasures] utterly in yourself so that you do not seek anything in them but full well-being of the body."[74] Exhortation was meant to remind his recipient that there was a greater goal of Christlikeness. Indeed, exhortation was fundamental to growth in virtue and this was expressed variously yet consistently all throughout his letters.

LETTER 258 FROM AUGUSTINE TO MARTIANUS

At some point later in life, Augustine wrote to his old friend Martianus, whom he had known before his baptism. In this letter he described the history and progression of their friendship. Augustine first cited Cicero as an expert on

---

71. *Epistula* 73.3.6.
72. *Epistula* 82.5.36 (CSEL 32.2:387).
73. *Epistula* 82.5.26.
74. *Epistula* 130.3.7.

friendship: "'Friendship is an agreement on things human and divine along with good will and love.'"[75] At one point in their friendship, Augustine and Martianus only agreed on things human, when they "enjoyed them in the manner of the crowd."[76] Martianus had "filled the sails" of Augustine's desires with "the wind of praise."[77] They enjoyed the trappings of society, things of which Augustine had now repented. Because they previously did not have the proper view on "things divine" because the truth had not yet "shone forth" in Augustine, the result was that their friendship "limped along."[78] Even though their agreement on things human was filled with good will and love, the lack of agreement on things divine meant their friendship was incomplete.

Their friendship, however, went through a transformation. Though they had "to some extent a benevolent and loving agreement on things human," the agreement on things divine eventually came. Augustine rejoiced over Martianus as a "true friend" who had come to share with Augustine "the hope of eternal life."[79] This did not annul their disagreement on human things— it set it aright. Their agreement on human things was no longer based on temporal desires but based on their divine agreement so that such human things would not be given more weight than they were due.[80] Agreement on things divine meant they were able to view temporal things as given by their Creator. Augustine concluded, "Thus it turns out that between friends who do not agree on things divine there cannot be a full and true agreement on things human either."[81] Thus, Augustine admitted that their friendship was incomplete. Though incomplete, for Augustine, extending friendship was part of a goal and vision to see true spiritual friendship flourish. Friendship must begin somewhere, and one can look back and recognize that it was perhaps incomplete until there was full agreement on things divine.

To this end, Augustine encouraged his friend not to feel as if their friendship was a complete sham while Augustine was "passionately seeking the vanities of this world."[82] The reality was that Augustine was unable to be

---

75. *Epistula* 258.1.
76. *Epistula* 258.1.
77. *Epistula* 258.1.
78. *Epistula* 258.1.
79. *Epistula* 258.2.
80. *Epistula* 258.2.
81. *Epistula* 258.2.
82. *Epistula* 258.3.

a friend even to himself. By loving iniquity, he was actually his own worst enemy and it would be absurd to think that one would truly wish to encourage such false love. Hence, Martianus could not truly have been his friend were he encouraging such pursuits, however unknowingly. Additionally, since Augustine's salvation was based completely on God's mercy, Martianus further could not share in friendship since he was at that time "completely ignorant" of why Augustine had come to be so happy.[83] Augustine admitted, "How could you be my friend when ... you did not love me in him in whom I myself had somehow become a friend to myself?"[84] Augustine, therefore, was able to experience the joy of true friendship while his friend Martianus could not yet do the same.

Though this was once the case, Augustine now rejoiced over their full spiritual friendship which was wrought entirely by God's grace. The Ciceronian definition was complete for them "in Christ Jesus, our Lord, our truest peace."[85] The biblical correspondent to this definition was Jesus's dual command of love in Matthew 22:39–40. The first commandment deals with agreement on things pertaining to the divine in loving the Lord, and the second commandment spoke to agreement on things human. These commands were the basis for true spiritual friendship. Augustine implored Martianus toward mutually upholding these commands so that their friendship would be "true and everlasting," uniting them "not only to each other but also to the Lord."[86] Though the Ciceronian definition of friendship was adequate, it was the biblical command of love that truly cemented spiritual friendship.

This blossoming of spiritual friendship, it seemed, was a recent event. Thus Augustine encouraged Martianus toward further spiritual growth. This included participating in the life and worship of the church. This necessitated his reception of the "sacraments of the faithful," including baptism and then the Eucharist. The time had come, having received the grace of God, to seal such grace in baptism. Augustine closed his letter with a series of encouragements to his friend. He wished to receive a reply in order to know whether Martianus proceeded with his baptism. He also concluded his letter with a benediction that the Lord whom he had recently come to believe

---

83. *Epistula* 258.3.
84. *Epistula* 258.3.
85. *Epistula* 258.4.
86. *Epistula* 258.4.

would sustain him "both in this life and in the world to come."[87] Augustine closed with an affectionate word to his friend who was "most beloved and worthy of affection in Christ."[88]

AUGUSTINE, MARTIANUS, AND SPIRITUAL FRIENDSHIP IN THE LETTERS OF AUGUSTINE

Letter 258 is a perfect summation of spiritual friendship in the letters of Augustine. In this letter, Augustine encapsulates his entire view of spiritual friendship. In his letters to other Christians, whether to one like Jerome or to Marcellinus, true friendship existed on the basis of their agreement on things human and divine in light of the dual command of love. Friendship was established and perpetuated by grace, and the act of friendship served to bring mutual encouragement toward Christlike virtue. Likewise, Augustine recognized that true happiness was impossible without spiritual friendship, for each one sought only those things which were temporal, hence leading to an incomplete friendship. Spiritual friendship must have Christ at its center and have eternity as its guiding perspective. As friends mutually encourage each other toward Christlike virtue, they do so because they have a heavenly outlook. This outlook informs their spiritual life, including how they view temporal things, but specifically how they view their life of prayer. Spiritual friendship seeks to mutually perpetuate each one's spiritual growth. Since the work of God is the driving force, spiritual friendship can be experienced with another Christian regardless of physical proximity. As was the case with many of Augustine's friends, spiritual friendship was sustained despite physical distance.

CONCLUSION

In this chapter, I have summarized spiritual friendship according to Augustine. Drawing from the spirituality of Augustine, with special attention to his letters, Augustine's view and practice of spiritual friendship comes into focus. Augustine, prioritizing humility and the dual-command of love, encouraged these Christlike virtues with numerous people with whom he corresponded. Whether he had met them in person or not, Augustine extended the hand

---

87. *Epistula* 258.5.
88. *Epistula* 258.5.

of friendship for the purpose of helping his friends grow in their practice of virtue and love of God. This encouragement was founded upon a vision of the city of God and a conviction that friendship should be offered to all. Spiritual friendship was focused on eternity and the desire for mutual growth in Christlike virtue in preparation for God's eternal city. Though the goal was the same, each friendship warranted a nuanced approach based on vocation. Thus for Augustine, the way in which he motivated fellow clerics differed slightly from how he encouraged civic officials.

3
—

ASSESSING CLASSICAL MODELS OF FRIENDSHIP

We have not yet been able to discover what a friend is.

—Socrates[1]

Having explored the main themes of spiritual friendship present in Augustine's letters, we need to take a step back to admire the landscape of friendship prior to Augustine. An overview of classical models of friendships will greatly enhance our appreciation for Augustine's unique contribution and help us understand why his reformulation in theological terms was such an advanced step forward. While Augustine acknowledged the Ciceronian definition of friendship (more below), he would redefine it in biblical and theological terms based on his understanding of the work of the Holy Spirit upon human hearts. Augustine's view of friendship in terms of growth in virtue based on divine love had no parallel in antiquity.

Friendship, as a philosophical concept, was given extensive treatment within the writings of significant thinkers throughout antiquity. By reflecting on the philosophical reflection on friendship prior to Augustine, readers gain a greater sense of the ways and to what degree Augustine was influenced by prior friendship traditions. Readers will also understand the departure Augustine took in formulating and practicing spiritual friendship. While historical and contextual particularities undoubtedly influenced thinkers in regard to their views of friendship, the theme of friendship as an intimate relationship based upon mutual devotion is woven throughout the ancient

---

1. Plato, *Lysis* 223b7–8, in *Other Selves: Philosophers on Friendship*, ed. Michael Pakaluk (Indianapolis: Hackett, 1991), 27.

world.[2] Reflections on friendship fall into four broad traditions: Platonic, peripatetic or Aristotelian, Stoic, and Epicurean.[3] These philosophical schools share many commonalities with one another, though they diverge in various areas. This overview of friendship in antiquity demonstrates the unique contribution of each school and reveals different levels in which friendship was experienced among key thinkers in the classical tradition.

DEFINING FRIENDSHIP IN ANCIENT PERSPECTIVE

The concept of friendship is prominent within all of the main philosophical traditions of antiquity. The consistent term for "friend" in classical Greek was *philos*. This term was associated with a voluntary relationship of affection. This relationship contrasted with kin relationships (as they were involuntary) and distant acquaintances (as they did not necessarily involve fondness). Though concepts of friendship can be discerned in earlier writings, Plato appears to have been the first thinker to give friendship significant exposure within ethical reflection.[4] It is often presumed that Aristotle represents a more mature reflection on friendship; however, Plato provides a richer heritage than is often recognized. Dimitri El Murr notes how Plato's conception of friendship (*philia*) was often overshadowed by discussions of love (*erōs*). This "exegetical imbalance," according to El Murr, results from a philosophical priority given to Aristotle's "grander and supposedly more

2. In his overview of friendship in antiquity, David Konstan notes, "The functions of friendship undoubtedly responded to historical exigencies and possibilities, but it is not assumed that social changes condition a development, as opposed to inflections, in the notion of friendship. What is more, there is no guarantee of uniformity among the conceptions of friendship disseminated in a single era. Commonplaces persist for a thousand years despite vast social changes." Konstan, *Friendship in the Classical World*, 19.

3. Within antiquity, friendship is discussed in numerous philosophical streams. The pre-Socratic traditions have provided some reflection, as has the Pythagorean tradition. While these may provide some useful background information, for the purpose of this chapter, I will focus only on the main streams wherein influential reflection on friendship was developed. This is not to diminish the importance of other ancient thinkers; yet the main influences upon Augustine and later antique notions of friendship are found in the main philosophical traditions discussed in this chapter. For more consideration on Greco-Roman reflection of friendship, see John T. Fitzgerald, ed., *Greco-Roman Perspectives on Friendship*, SBL Resources for Biblical Study 34 (Atlanta: Scholars, 1997).

4. For an overview of Greek expressions of friendship prior to Aristotle, see John T. Fitzgerald, "Friendship in the Greek World Prior to Aristotle," in Fitzgerald, *Greco-Roman Perspectives on Friendship*.

stimulating account of friendship."[5] Additionally, Plato's specific work on the nature of friendship, *Lysis*, is often overshadowed by the "greater splendor" of his *Symposium*.[6]

Reflection on friendship in Plato represents the vague distinction made within Greek culture between *philia* and *erōs*. This ambiguity is prominent in Plato's *Lysis*, a dialogue primarily focused on *philia*. In the *Lysis*, the outcome of Plato's discussion on friendship demonstrates that "desire is cause of friendship, and that what desires is friend to that thing it desires and at such time that it desires it."[7] El Murr further argues that Plato's *Laws* provides the completing thought introduced in the *Lysis*. Whereas in the *Lysis*, Socrates proposed that friends must be alike in all things ("like loves like"), the more developed discussion in his *Laws* demonstrates that differences can be present so long as a matching desire for virtue propels each friend.

Following Plato, Aristotle represents the next development in discussions upon *philia*. Aristotle elucidated the various forms of friendship within books 8 and 9 of his *Nicomachean Ethics*. His main concern was relating virtuous activity and friendship. Since Aristotle conceived of happiness as virtuous activity, discussions of friendship revolved around the sorts of relationships that a virtuous person should expect to cultivate.[8] Aristotle conceived of friendship along three lines: seeing another as truly good, seeing another as useful, or seeing another as pleasant. Friendship, according to Aristotle, is both a necessary good and a form of virtue. Friendship is necessary to both rich and poor alike.[9] The key difference between those who are capable of obtaining true friendship and those who are not is a virtuous character or disposition. The virtuous subject will always choose the good, rather than looking at the object

---

5. Dimitri El Murr, "*Philia* in Plato," in *Ancient and Medieval Concepts of Friendship*, ed. Suzanne Stern-Gillet and Gary M. Gurtler (Albany: State University of New York Press, 2014), 3.

6. James Haden, "Friendship in Plato's *Lysis*," *Review of Metaphysics* 37, no. 2 (1983): 329.

7. Plato, *Lysis* 212d2–4, in *Plato's Lysis*, ed. Terry Penner and Christopher Rowe, Cambridge Studies in the Dialogues of Plato (Cambridge: Cambridge University Press, 2009), 349.

8. The relationship between virtue and happiness in Aristotle is a well-explored theme, with various perspectives represented within the scholarship. For specific works that develop this theme, see Howard J. Curzer, "The Supremely Happy Life in Aristotle's *Nicomachean Ethics*," *Apeiron* 24 (1991): 47–69; Anna Lännström, *Loving the Fine: Virtue and Happiness in Aristotle's Ethics* (Notre Dame, IN: University of Notre Dame Press, 2006).

9. Aristotle, *Nicomachean Ethics* 8.1.

itself as good, useful, or pleasurable.[10] Aristotle also asserted that a friend was a form of another self. In other words, we love the other because in them we see ourselves.[11] Friendship is related to happiness in that a friend works to see the other flourish, sharing joys and bearing sorrows. The relationship between friendship and happiness will be explored in more detail below.

Following Aristotle, Epicurean philosophy provides considerable reflection on friendship. Though founded upon the teachings of Epicurus, much of what is known about Epicurean friendship comes from sources other than Epicurus. One source for the transmission of Epicurean philosophy is Diogenes Laertius. The famed poet Lucretius also represents a significant source of Epicurean thought, though the degree to which he transmits the original philosophy of Epicurus is debated.[12] From the writings we possess, it is clear that Epicurus distinguished between the usage of "friends" and "friendship."[13] Believing that humanity did not originally have need of each other, Epicurus posited that initial affection arose out of the need for mutual aid and benefit.[14] Friendship was now an essential component of life. Epicurus declared, "The wise man feels no more pain by being tortured himself than by seeing a friend being tortured."[15] Elsewhere he stated, "Friendship dances around the world proclaiming to us all to rouse ourselves to give thanks."[16]

While *erōs* and *philia* fluctuated in the writings of Plato, Epicurean thought distinguished between the two. For Epicurus, and to some extent his poetic conduit Lucretius, *erōs* related to the love that the wise man practices as he marries and produces a family. This type of love does not go outside the bounds of prescribed laws, that is, engage in deviant sexual behavior. *Philia* was more specifically applied to those relationships which bring value and

---

10. Aristotle, *Nicomachean Ethics* 8.2.1155b26–27.

11. Aristotle, *Nicomachean Ethics* 9.4.1166a31–32, 9.1170b6–7.

12. Harry Lesser notes that the language of love and friendship in Lucretius may not exactly be that of an "orthodox Epicurean." For more on Lucretius's depiction, see Harry Lesser, "*Erōs* and *Philia* in Epicurean Philosophy," in Stern-Gillet and Gurtler, *Ancient and Medieval Concepts of Friendship*, 117.

13. For more on Epicurean distinction between "friend" and "friendship," see David K. O'Connor, "The Invulnerable Pleasures of Epicurean Friendship," *GRBS* 30 (1989): 185.

14. Konstan, *Friendship in the Classical World*, 110.

15. Epicurus, *Vatican Sayings* 56, in *The Essential Epicurus: Letters, Principal Doctrines, Vatican Sayings, and Fragments*, trans. Eugene M. O'Connor (Buffalo, NY: Prometheus, 1993), 82. Unless otherwise noted, O'Connor's translations are used for citations of Epicurus.

16. Epicurus, *Vatican Sayings*, 52.

pleasure to one's life, having specific relationships wherein that pleasure is experienced with a high level of confidence in the other's ability to bring mutual benefit and satisfaction.[17] Thus, for Epicureans, *philia* was a universal good and *philoi* represent specific intimate relationships.[18]

The Stoic tradition likewise contributed to ancient reflection on friendship. Stoics recognized that friendship was "a kind of knowledge of a most general type" and that there was "a virtue and an art of how to make friends."[19] According to Bernard Collette-Dučić, in the Stoic conception, friendship was the "aim and effect of love."[20] In strict Stoic understanding, true friendship occurred solely among sages. The attainment of wisdom, therefore, was a prerequisite for friendship. For example, Epictetus discouraged his disciples from association with laymen or former acquaintances.[21] Later Stoic philosophers may have exerted less stringent stipulations upon friendship. For instance, the Stoic influence upon Cicero's conception of friendship, seen in his *On Friendship*, appears to be less strict.[22] Similar to friendship in Aristotelian or Epicurean renderings, friendship in Stoic thought "is the condition of happiness and one of its fundamental components."[23]

In many ways, the previously mentioned schools of thought are represented in later Roman writers reflecting on friendship. Thus, friendship in Roman perspective is the product of complex interaction between Hellenistic and Roman

---

17. John M. Rist, "Epicurus on Friendship," *Classical Philology* 75, no. 2 (1980): 121–29.

18. The understanding of friendship as a universal good comes from Epicurus, *Vatican Sayings*, 23. The exact nature of how Epicurus conceives of this good has been recently challenged by Eric Brown who states, "[Contrary to the orthodox reading] Epicurus must think that every friendship is choiceworthy only for the sake of pleasure, for he clearly holds that every choice should be referred to pleasure, that is, to the absence of mental disturbance (ἀταραξία) and of physical pain. There is at least prima facie tension between the claim that friendship is intrinsically choiceworthy and the claim that everything is choiceworthy for the sake of pleasure alone, since to say something is intrinsically choiceworthy is standardly to say that it is choiceworthy without regard to anything else." Eric Brown, "Epicurus on the Value of Friendship (Sententia Vaticana XXIII)," *Classical Philology* 97, no. 1 (2002): 69–70.

19. Bernard Collette-Dučić, "Making Friends: The Stoic Conception of Love and its Platonic Background," in Stern-Gillet and Gurtler, *Ancient and Medieval Concepts of Friendship*, 87.

20. Collette-Dučić, "Making Friends," 87.

21. Konstan notes, "Epictetus may reflect a severe strain of Stoic thought in respect to friendship, virtually evacuating the concept of its ordinary content." Konstan, *Friendship in the Classical World*, 114.

22. Konstan, *Friendship in the Classical World*, 114.

23. Anne Banateanu, *La théorie stoïcienne de l'amitié: Essai de reconstruction*, Vestigia 27 (Fribourg, Switzerland: Éditions Universitaires, 2001), 204.

culture and reflection.[24] Though earlier scholars argued that Roman friendship
related mainly to political association devoid of emotional connection, such a
notion has been challenged in recent decades.[25] Contrary to a limited notion
of *amicitia*, Peter Brunt maintains, "The range of *amicitia* is vast. From the
constant intimacy and goodwill of virtuous or at least like-minded men to the
courtesy that etiquette normally enjoined on gentlemen, it covers every degree
of genuinely or overtly amicable relation."[26] Representative Roman thinkers
with regard to friendship include Cicero and to a lesser extent Seneca, both
significantly influenced by Stoicism.[27] An additional consideration within the
discussion of friendship among Romans was the notion of the patron-client
relationship. This intricate social relationship involved wealthy benefactors
(patrons) supporting individuals with financial or political need (clients), who
then in turn support their patron through various acts of service.[28]

FRIENDSHIP IN THE *POLIS*

A proper understanding of the nature of the *polis* is necessary when assessing
friendship in antiquity, particularly in the writings of Aristotle.[29] The *polis*, or
"city-state," was the fullest expression of civilization wherein human flourishing could be sought and obtained. The conglomeration of citizens within the
polis set the context for cooperation toward the good life. It was in this setting
that friendship with others could be pursued. John T. Fitzgerald notes, "[The]
emergence of the *polis* had important implications for the ethics of guest-friendship."[30] This practice of "guest-friendship," or *xenia*, was important for understanding political friendship, particularly hospitality, in ancient tradition.

---

24. Konstan, *Friendship in the Classical World*, 122.

25. For a summary of scholarly and recent reflection on friendship in Roman perspective,
see Verboven, "Friendship among the Romans," 404–21.

26. P. A. Brunt, *The Fall of the Roman Republic and Related Essays* (Oxford: Oxford University
Press, 1988), 381.

27. Seneca did not write a specific treatise on friendship, but in his philosophical works and
especially his letters his understanding of friendship emerges. For understanding friendship in
Seneca's letters, see Catharine Edwards, "Absent Presence in Seneca's Epistles: Philosophy and
Friendship," in *The Cambridge Companion to Seneca*, ed. Shadi Bartsch and Alessandro Shiesaro
(Cambridge: Cambridge University Press, 2015), 41–53.

28. For an overview of social relationships, including the patron-client relationship in
ancient Rome, see J. E. Lendon, "Roman Honor," in Peachin, *Oxford Handbook of Social Relations
in the Roman World*, 377–466.

29. Fitzgerald, "Friendship in the Greek World," 27.

30. Fitzgerald, "Friendship in the Greek World," 27.

Since the *polis* emerged as a significant place of friendship formation, political motivations form a fundamental facet of friendship. The political nature of friendship did not delegitimize its practice. Political friendship, despite modern connotations, did not necessitate insincerity in ancient perspective. For Greek city-states, political friendships were important for the proper functioning of society, and as such, had the potential to be quite intimate even if serving an expedient purpose. In fact, in Roman perspective, some have posited discussions of friendship were merely political, lacking little to no element of personal closeness.[31] Recent studies have challenged this narrow view of friendship within Roman ethical and political thinking, positing that "complex personal relationships could cut across political discords."[32]

The moral and relational aspects of the *polis* was nowhere more explicit than in the political thought of Aristotle. The Aristotelian *polis* represented the quest for virtue; in fact, the discussion of politics was synonymous with discussions of moral theory.[33] C. C. W. Taylor notes that for Aristotle, "The reason is that the ethical treatises are practical enquiries directed toward the achievement of the good life, an aim which, given the social nature of human beings, cannot be achieved except in the context of a political society."[34] Human interaction, therefore, was fundamental for the *polis*. According to Aristotle, the communal life is intimately related to the good life. Having introduced friendship in ancient perspective, I now turn to specific ancient traditions and their specific contribution to the conversation regarding friendship.

FRIENDSHIP IN THE PLATONIC PERSPECTIVE

As previously mentioned, Plato discussed friendship primarily in his philosophical treatise *Lysis*, though some reflections upon friendship can be found in various other dialogues.[35] The *Lysis*, an early dialogue of Plato, explored the tension between individual and common good by providing an extensive

---

31. Lily Ross Taylor states, "[*Amicitia*] was the good old word for party relationship." Lily Ross Taylor, *Party Politics in the Age of Caesar* (Berkeley: University of California Press, 1949), 8.

32. Brunt, *Fall of the Roman Republic*, 367. For another perspective on the complexity of Roman friendship, specifically as seen in Roman theatre, see P. J. Burton, "Amicitia in Plautus: A Study of Roman Friendship Processes," *American Journal of Philology* 125, no. 2 (2004): 209–43.

33. C. C. W. Taylor, "Politics," in *The Cambridge Companion to Aristotle*, ed. Jonathan Barnes (New York: Cambridge University Press, 1995), 233.

34. Taylor, "Politics," 233.

35. For the purposes of this chapter, I will focus primarily upon Plato's *Lysis* for platonic reflection on friendship. For more on the relationship between friendship and *eros*, see C. D. C. Reeve, "Plato on Eros and Friendship," in *A Companion to Plato*, ed. Hugh H. Benson (Malden,

discussion of friendship. This tension, according to Mary P. Nichols, was first introduced in the *Republic*.[36] In this dialogue, Socrates recounted his conversation with a group of young men. Among this group was the jaded lover Hippothales who was pining over Lysis, a younger male.[37] Socrates was soon introduced to Lysis and his friend, Menexenus. This prompted Socrates to enquire as to the nature of friendship. The problem created in seeking to balance the individual and common good is that true friendship appears, on the surface, to be of a more personal nature, which can in turn neglect the needs of the larger community.

David Bolotin has argued that Plato's *Lysis* conceived of true friendship as problematic at best and an illusion at worst.[38] James Haden also provides a helpful analysis of reflection on *Lysis* within twentieth-century scholarship. He notes that while some have concluded that *Lysis* represents a failed attempt at ascertaining friendship, the conventional opinion is that Plato does offer important reflection, though his conclusions may be obscure or open to question.[39] While there does appear to be a hurdle regarding the place of friendship within public life, Nichols successfully argues that Plato gives friendship a positive status within a larger framework of the community.[40] By relating the act of friendship to the pursuit of philosophy, Plato thus conceived of friendship as providing for both personal and community benefits.

Socrates began by demonstrating that Lysis and Menexenus were not as truly free as they thought. They have guardians and parents over them asserting Lysis's need for wisdom and demonstrating his ignorance in the matter

---

MA: Wiley-Blackwell, 2009), 294–307; for reflection on friendship in other dialogues, see El Murr, "*Philia* in Plato," 3–27.

36. Mary P. Nichols, "Friendship and Community in Plato's *Lysis*," *Review of Politics* 68, no. 1 (2006): 1.

37. The relationship between Hippothales and Lysis likely entails the common ancient Greek practice of pederasty, where an older male pursues a sexual relationship with a younger male, supposedly for the purpose of teaching virtue. This accepted Greek homosexual pursuit was based on the notion of beauty being found within certain ideal males and the belief that such a relationship would instill virtue in the younger participant. For a thorough treatment on pederasty, see William Armstrong Percy III, *Pederasty and Pedagogy in Archaic Greece* (Urbana: University of Illinois Press, 1996). For a broader perspective on homosexuality in ancient Greece, see K. J. Dover, *Greek Homosexuality* (Cambridge, MA: Harvard University Press, 1989).

38. David Bolotin, *Plato's Dialogue on Friendship: An Interpretation of the Lysis, with a New Translation* (Ithaca, NY: Cornell University Press, 1977), 211.

39. Haden, "Friendship in Plato's *Lysis*," 330–35.

40. See Nichols, "Friendship and Community in Plato's *Lysis*," 17–19.

of friendship. Through his conversation with Lysis, walking him through the necessity for wisdom in order to be an independent person capable of ruling, Socrates presents wisdom as the necessary and sufficient circumstance for ownership and profiting from things. Only the truly wise shall be rulers over people and things. Such a ruler therefore would be the beneficiary of many friends based on his qualities of being useful and good.

Socrates approached his discussion on friendship as one who appreciated the merits of friendship and desired to know others more deeply as friends. In seeking to help Lysis and Menexenus understand the nature of friendship, Socrates led them along a journey of questions. These questions elicit a series of responses that allow his audience to see the essence of friendship as loving one as another self. One question that arose in Socrates's discussion was the notion of one who is truly good and their need for friendship. If one is good, they have all they need in themselves, and therefore friendship is superfluous.[41] Likewise, it is impossible, according to Socrates, for the bad to befriend one who is good.[42] From here Socrates attempted to convince his listeners that a friend was one who was neither good nor bad, but as such, desired to attach himself to the good by means of friendship.

By the end of this Platonic dialogue, Socrates concluded that defining friendship was a difficult task. This has led some to conclude that Plato saw such a discussion as a lost cause.[43] The course of the dialogue, however, focused on attributes of particular friends, rather than arriving at a guiding and universal norm of friendship. After discussion Socrates admits, "Don't we have to arrive at some first principle which will no longer bring us back to another friend, something that goes back to the first friend, something for the sake of which all the rest are friends too?"[44] The dialogue reveals the puzzling, and almost inexplicable, nature of friendship. As Socrates's dialogue with the young Lysis and Menexenus demonstrates, *philia* is both reasonable and mysterious.

---

41. Plato, *Lysis*, 215b, in *Other Selves: Philosophers on Friendship*, ed. Michael Pakaluk (Indianapolis: Hackett Pub., 1991). Unless otherwise noted, quotations from *Lysis* will be from Pakaluk's edition.

42. Plato, *Lysis*, 218a.

43. W. K. C. Guthrie, *Plato: The Man and His Dialogues; Earlier Period*, vol. 4 of *A History of Greek Philosophy* (Cambridge: Cambridge University Press, 1975), 143–44.

44. Plato, *Lysis*, 219d.

Socrates admitted at the conclusion of their discussion that they had yet to discover the nature of a friend.[45] Such an admonition was not a sign of defeat but rather ratification. Friendship, being multifaceted and seemingly out of reach except perhaps for the truly wise, was an unsolved problem. It exists, yet it cannot be defined solely based on the sum of its parts. As the dialogue ended, it leaves the reader to begin discerning for themselves, based on the discussion, the nature of a friend and friendship; the dialogue also opened the door toward understanding friendship, inviting the reader to enter and begin exploring for themselves.

FRIENDSHIP IN THE ARISTOTELIAN PERSPECTIVE

Michael Pakaluk observes, "Much of the subsequent work on friendship in the Western tradition can be understood either as building upon and supplementing Aristotle's views or as reacting against them."[46] Upon relating the importance of understanding friendship, Aristotle observed:

> Friendship—its nature and qualities, what constitutes a friend, and whether the term friendship has one or several meanings, and if several, how many, and also what is our duty towards a friend and what are the just claims of friendship—is a matter that calls for investigation no less than any of the things that are fine and desirable in men's characters.[47]

Building upon Plato, Aristotle provides the most comprehensive commentary on friendship. Though the *Nicomachean Ethics* begins with a discussion of the *polis*, it ends with a treatment of friendship in antiquity. The moral life, and friendship in particular, is at the center of social relations among the *polis* comprised of free citizens. These social relationships contribute to the flourishing of society, including the pursuit of the happy life. As Paul Wadell notes, "The moral life is a function of the polis, for it represents not the individual's, but the community's pursuit of the good, the community's commitment to

---

45. Plato, *Lysis*, 223b7–8.

46. Pakaluk, *Other Selves*, 28.

47. Aristotle, *Eudemian Ethics* 7.1234b, in *Athenian Constitution, Eudemian Ethics, Virtues and Vices*, trans. H. Rackham, Loeb Classical Library 285 (Cambridge, MA: Harvard University Press, 1935), 358–59.

discover, embody, and sustain the virtues."[48] Thus, when Aristotle discussed friendship as part of a broader project on ethics, he presented something which was "present in his account of the moral life all along."[49]

In Aristotle's account, those who experience the fullest extent of friendship are those who love each other because of their virtue, rather than their incidental characteristics. Regarding friendship in Aristotle, Paula Gottlieb notes, "Friendship requires reciprocated goodwill, and awareness of that goodwill. Since only good people know what is really good and are able to wish that for their friends for the friends' own sake, the friendship of good people is the best type of friendship."[50] Thus, while Aristotle described different types of friendship, there is a significant difference between the ideal of friendship based solely on virtue and its lesser expressions.

Aristotle addressed the topic of friendship primarily in certain books of the *Nicomachean* and *Eudemian Ethics*, though an exploration of *philia* can also be found in the *Magna Moralia*, a work of collected sayings and notes likely compiled after his death.[51] For the present discussion I will focus primarily upon his reflections found in the *Nicomachean* and *Eudemian Ethics*. As in Plato, *philia* is a wide term to describe numerous relational connections. One could describe *philia* between kin, friends, citizens, or other similar relationships. Thus, when discussing the nature of *philia*, Aristotle did not solely prioritize friendship. Since *philia* covered such a wide range of relationships for Aristotle, some have observed that Aristotle did not provide any reflection on friendship comparable to a modern concept.[52] While this

---

48. Wadell, *Friendship and the Moral Life*, 46.

49. Wadell, *Friendship and the Moral Life*, 47.

50. Paula Gottlieb, "Aristotle's Ethics," in *The Oxford Handbook of the History of Ethics*, ed. Roger Crisp (Oxford: Oxford University Press, 2013), 60.

51. For an exploration of the *Magna Moralia* as it relates to Aristotle's moral philosophy, see John M. Cooper, "The Magna Moralia and Aristotle's Moral Philosophy," *American Journal of Philology* 94, no. 4 (1973): 327–49. The Aristotelian content of this text is contested, though Cooper argues that the ideas represented in the text cohere too closely with Aristotle for him not to be the originator. Cooper notes, "[The] Magna Moralia is a very important document for scholars and philosophers interested in understanding Aristotle's moral philosophy" (329).

52. Recent research has challenged standard models of Aristotelian friendship by positing that friendship for Aristotle is only discussed in terms of potentiality, not actuality. According to this view, friendship's "possibility" does not necessarily diminish Aristotle's useful reflection; it simply categorizes it toward a singular understanding (friendship is only ever possible, but not fully actualized). For more on this reassessment of Aristotelian friendship, see Bradley Bryan, "Approaching Others: Aristotle on Friendship's Possibility," *Political Theory*, 37, no. 6 (2009): 754–79.

may be the case, it is not true that Aristotle neglected affectionate relationships between certain individuals.[53] Such relationships, however, must be
accounted for in the social environment of the Greek *polis*. As F. M. Schroeder
notes, "An understanding of Aristotelian friendship must pay attention to
its social setting. ... All friendship finds its situation in the communal life of
the classical polis. Thus, the larger network of social obligation frames all
of Aristotle's discussion of friendship."[54]

In books 8 and 9 of the *Nicomachean Ethics*, Aristotle established a relationship between acts of virtue and friendship itself. Friendship is "most
necessary for our life."[55] Whether poor, rich, young, or old, friends are necessary for caring for and building one another. Even the rich, who seem to
have all they need, require friendships in order to provide an "outlet for benef-
icence."[56] In these two books, Aristotle presented a taxonomy of friendship
which includes friendship as utility, pleasure, or virtue.[57] The most genuine
friend is one who loves another person for the sake of that person. In developing his taxonomy, he concluded that it was only in friendship based on
character and virtue, the highest form of friendship, that one desires the
good and benefit of other for their own sake. This would seem to rule out
friendships based on utility or pleasure as true friendships. Aristotle contended, "But complete friendship is the friendship of good people similar in
virtue; for they wish goods in the same way to each other in so far as they
are good, and they are good in themselves."[58]

Aristotle did not preclude lesser forms of friendship, choosing to maintain
the more common and looser term of "friend." That said, Aristotle considered

---

53. Konstan addresses this objection and notes, "[One] type of *philia* corresponds closely
to friendship, namely, the affection that obtains between *philoi* or friends. ... In particular, he
reserves the noun *philos* for the category of friends, in accord with ordinary Greek usage; when
he speaks of other kinds of *philia*, for example that between parents and children, he does not
mention *philoi*." Konstan, *Friendship in the Classical World*, 68.

54. F. M. Schroeder, "Friendship in Aristotle and Some Peripatetic Philosophers," in
Fitzgerald, *Greco-Roman Perspectives on Friendship*, 36.

55. Aristotle, *Nicomachean Ethics*, 8.1155a1-2.

56. Aristotle, *Nicomachean Ethics*, 8.1.1

57. Many commentators have posited this traditional threefold view of Aristotelian friendship. A representative reflection on this view includes John M. Cooper, "Aristotle on Friendship,"
in *Essays on Aristotle's Ethics*, ed. Amélie Oksenberg Rorty (Berkeley: University of California
Press, 1980), 301-40.

58. Aristotle, *Nicomachean Ethics* 8.1156b9-11.

the amount of people able to maintain the ideal form of friendship to be small in number. He asserted, "[It is] impossible to be many people's friend for their virtue and for themselves. We have reason to be satisfied if we can find even a few such friends."[59] Goodwill also plays a factor in establishing friendship based on virtue. Aristotle stated,

> Goodwill would seem to be a feature of friendship, but still it is not friendship. ... Hence we might transfer [the name "friendship"], and say that goodwill is inactive friendship, and that when it lasts some time and they grow accustomed to each other, it becomes friendship. It does not, however, become friendship for utility of pleasure, since these aims do not produce goodwill either.[60]

As A. W. Price notes, "It is goodness alone, in both friends, that can ground loving the other not coincidently, but for himself."[61]

Finally, Aristotle discussed the relationship between friendship and self-love. Knowledge of ourselves can only come in relationship to others. Aristotle observed, "The defining features of friendship that are found in friendships to one's neighbors would seem to be derived from features of friendship toward oneself."[62] There is a reciprocal nature to friendship—as a person grows in knowledge of his or her friend, he or she grows in knowledge of himself or herself. Thus, self-love is concomitant with friendship.[63] The friend is another self and contains the sort of features that one sees in themselves.[64] Suzanne

---

59. Aristotle, *Nicomachean Ethics* 9.10.1171a19–20

60. Aristotle, *Nicomachean Ethics* 9.5.1166b30, 9.5.1167a10–15.

61. A. W. Price, *Love and Friendship in Plato and Aristotle* (Oxford: Clarendon, 1989), 104.

62. Aristotle, *Nicomachean Ethics* 9.4.1166a1–2.

63. For a helpful analysis of self-love in relation to friendship in Aristotle, see Lorraine Smith Pangle, *Aristotle and the Philosophy of Friendship* (Cambridge: Cambridge University Press, 2008), 169–82. Pangle observes, "The love of self and the love of another are not different in kind, one basely seeking to acquire the good and the other nobly indifferent to it. Both aim at the good and take their bearings by what promotes human happiness. If it is good to seek the good of another, how can it be bad to seek the good of oneself? If it is right to love the benefactor that one has in another, how is it wrong to love the even greater benefactor that one has in oneself? Aristotle argues that it is not merely natural but good and just that one should do so, and wholly in accord with his contention that we should love not just anything but what is good, and good for us. By these criteria, the very best man, being his own greatest benefactor and most truly lovable for his own sake, should have not the least but the greatest love for himself." Pangle, *Aristotle and the Philosophy of Friendship*, 170.

64. Aristotle, *Nicomachean Ethics* 9.4.1166a30–32.

Stern-Gillet concludes that for Aristotle, the truly virtuous self-lover will be free to give their love to the friend, able to attend to their needs as they have been set free from "the sway of their appetites and false conceptions."[65]

FRIENDSHIP IN THE EPICUREAN PERSPECTIVE

Epicureanism is "refreshingly unlike" any dominant philosophical school in antiquity.[66] Epicurus (341–270 BCE) was a citizen of Athens and showed an interest in philosophy from an early age, becoming a student of the Platonist philosopher Pamphilus. It was in Colophon, following the migration of his family after the death of Alexander the Great, that Epicurus began his philosophical movement. His three brothers were among his first adherents. For Epicurus, the good is related to pleasure and the absence of pain. Recognizing pleasure as good, and therefore seeking this good, places one in a state of blessedness. The maxim of Epicurus that states "the happy and eternal being is itself free from trouble" undergirds the epicurean understanding of friendship."[67] Safety, living an undisturbed life, is also key toward understanding friendship for Epicurus. Peace and wisdom, living in a blessed state, is the ongoing experience of the gods, who in their state of blessedness share the experience of friendship. Accordingly, to share in friendship is to have a god-like experience. As such, friendship for the noble one is a good which is immortal according to Epicurus.[68]

In Epicurean perspective, *philia* was the more reasonable contrast to *erōs*. Epicurean notions of friendship were built upon complete mutual dependence. Friendship was a lifelong commitment to the other and thus led to the possibility of laying one's life down for the friend. This sort of friendship relates to the basic aim of pleasure in Epicurean philosophy, including its concomitant pursuit of freedom from anxiety (*ataraxia*). Thus, Epicurus emphasized friendship in achieving blessedness.[69] The possession of friends helps to avoid bodily pain and mental anguish. Thus, a fully trustworthy friend is vital for a pleasurable life. Friendship aids in the pursuit

---

65. Suzanne Stern-Gillet, *Aristotle's Philosophy of Friendship* (Albany: State University of New York Press, 1995), 101.

66. James Warren, introduction to *The Cambridge Companion to Epicureanism*, ed. James Warren (Cambridge: Cambridge University Press, 2009), 4.

67. Epicurus, *Principal Doctrines*, 1.

68. Epicurus, *Vatican Sayings*, 78.

69. Tim O'Keefe, *Epicureanism* (Berkeley: University of California Press, 2009), 4.

of blessedness because it refers to helping those in need at their greatest moment of neediness.

This trustworthiness is obtained only if one is able to give it, and therefore the mutual establishment of friendship based on fidelity to the other is the foundation for the Epicurean concept of friendship, so that one feels tortured when a friend is undergoing torture.[70] Epicurus appealed to confidence or trust in others in order to reduce the uncertain fate of individual vulnerability.[71] An Epicurean friend is one who is completely trustworthy, even to the very point of death if necessary. This sort of friendship seems counterintuitive to the pursuit of pleasure, but actually it is the logical conclusion in the Epicurean perspective on friendship. As Lesser explains,

> For, even if [giving one's life] is required, and it may be, the peace of mind one enjoys up to this point, the way one can rely on help from one's friends, and the pleasure one gets from their company easily outweigh the pain endured at the end of one's life: hence the commitment is not a gamble, according to Epicurean values, because even if the sacrifice is required, it is a good price to pay for the previous gains.[72]

For Epicureans, friendship was cultivated in community, referring to philosophical adherents as *philoi*. It was also communal, focusing less on "one-on-one interaction between friends" and more on a "network for friends who look out for one another."[73] Epicurean community was different, however, from the community of friends represented in the traditional Greek *polis*.[74] The communal experience of friendship also included the commemoration of past friends. Epicurus notes, "Let us show feeling for our friends not by lamenting but by reflecting."[75] The passing of friends was not to be lamented, but an occasion for reflecting on their faithfulness and their contribution to the community.

The question of friendship as utility also arises when considering Epicureanism. *Philia* serves as a security and mutual aid. Friendship brings

70. Epicurus, *Vatican Sayings*, 56.

71. Konstan, *Friendship in the Classical World*, 109.

72. Lesser, "Erōs and Philia in Epicurean Philosophy," 126.

73. O'Keefe, *Epicureanism*, 148.

74. Eric Brown, "Politics and Society," in Warren, *Cambridge Companion to Epicureanism*, 182.

75. Epicurus, *Vatican Sayings*, 66.

protection from the evils of this life, ensuring that nothing dreadful is "eternal or long-lasting."[76] Additionally, the wise or noble person supposedly is "most concerned with wisdom and friendship."[77] *Philia* has a more lasting quality, above the supposed practical benefits of friendship.[78] John Rist observes, "[It] is from needs that friendships arise."[79] Friends, therefore, seem to be more for the purpose of immediate usefulness. This distinction is often explained in terms of Epicurean anthropology. Humans, originally self-sufficient and solitary, developed the need for affection and friendship based on the need for mutual aid. Humanity, as Lucretius reports, was "not easily capable of being harmed by heat or cold or unusual food or any damage to the body."[80] It was sex that later softened mankind and "sapped their strength, and children by their charm easily broke their parents' stern demeanour," which in turn lead to the formation of friendships for the purpose of protection and assistance.[81]

Eric Brown notes that there "is no evidence that Epicurus finds friendship or friends to be valuable for their own sake."[82] Thus, the dictum that friendship exists for one's own pleasure seems to be the final understanding of friendship for Epicurus. The summation of our feelings for friends is ultimately our own pleasure. One's pleasure is the final word, even if one's actions appear to prioritize the other person. Thus for Epicurus, we should seek the pleasure of our friends as much as we seek our own.[83]

FRIENDSHIP IN THE STOIC PERSPECTIVE

Stoic philosophy posited that only the truly wise (the sage) was capable of attaining true friendship. The philosopher Seneca (c. BCE 4-65 CE) remarked, "Natural promptings, and not [the sage's] own selfish needs, draw

---

76. Epicurus, *Principal Doctrines*, 28.

77. Epicurus, *Vatican Sayings,* 78.

78. Konstan, *Friendship in the Classical World*, 110.

79. Rist, "Epicurus on Friendship," 122.

80. Lucretius 5.929-30, in A. A. Long and D. N. Sedley, , vol. 1, *Translations of the Principal Sources, with Philosophical Commentary*, vol. 1 of *The Hellenistic Philosophers* (Cambridge: Cambridge University Press, 1987). Unless otherwise noted, citations from Lucretius come from Long and Sedley's edition.

81. Lucretius 5.958.

82. Brown, "Politics and Society," 189.

83. Brown, "Politics and Society," 189.

him into friendship."[84] This sort of moral autonomy pervaded Stoic thought. Friendship was a product of wisdom in Stoic conception. There is nothing lacking in the sage that prompts the need for friendship; rather, friendship arises out of moral commitment and certitude.[85] What we understand as the Stoic conception of friendship comes mostly from Seneca's moral letters to his disciple Lucius. Founded three centuries prior to Seneca by the philosopher Zeno of Citium (c. BCE 334–c. 262), early Stoic reflection on friendship is sparse.[86] That said, there is some fragmentary evidence of Zeno's conception of friendship.

The Stoic conception for friendship as belonging only to the truly good can be discerned in the earliest writings of Zeno. The historian Diogenes Laertius (fl. fourth century CE) summarized Zeno's estimation of friendship as belonging only to the good.[87] Diogenes provides further reflection upon Stoic friendship as arising out of their definition of love (*erōs*). Collette-Dučić concludes, "In order to understand Stoic friendship we need first to study how it is produced, and hence its cause: love."[88] Whereas friendship exists only among sages, love takes place within both sages and non-sages. There is a measure of indifference with love, occurring neither as a good nor bad quality. Such love is a knowledge or virtue specifically exercised by the sage, particularly toward the young, for the purpose of instilling virtue. Joannes Strobaeus (fl. fifth century CE), recording the various ideas and sayings of classical philosophers, noted how Stoics understood and engaged in love:

> They understand virtue exercised at a symposium as similar to virtue in erotic matters, the one being knowledge which is concerned with what is appropriate at a symposium ... and the other is knowledge of how to hunt for young boys that are naturally predisposed, which encourages them to virtuous knowledge; and in general, knowledge of nobly loving. ... [They] say that the man with good sense (that is,

---

84. Seneca, *Ad Lucilium epistulae morales* 9.17.

85. Konstan, *Friendship in the Classical World*, 113.

86. This absence is most likely due to the loss of Zeno's writings except in fragmentary quotations by later writers.

87. *Lives of Eminent Philosophers* 7.1, in *Diogenes Laertius: Lives of Eminent Philosophers*, vol. 2, trans. R. D. Hicks (Cambridge, MA: Harvard University Press, 1925), 235.

88. Collette-Dučić, "Making Friends," 88.

the sage) will be in love. … But love is not desire nor is it directed at any worthless thing, but is an effort to make friends from the appearance of beauty.[89]

Thus, the aim of Stoic love as a virtue practiced by the sage was to make and acquire new friends.

FRIENDSHIP IN THE WRITINGS OF CICERO

Cicero (106–43 BCE) presented a theoretical treatment of friendship that drew upon various philosophical traditions. His theory of friendship is mostly contained in his *On Friendship*. This treatise, written in 44 BCE, offers not only a theoretical foundation, but contains practical views relating to political relationships. In his political life, Cicero demonstrated a concern for his own political stability and promotion. Thus, we see in Cicero both the lofty ideals of friendship, as well as its the utilitarian import. Along with *On Friendship*, his letters and his treatise *On Duties* also offer helpful insight into his outlook on friendship.[90]

For Cicero, friendship arose out of *benevolentia* and *caritas*, which indicates that he saw friendship as more than a wise and reasoned relationship (such as the Stoics) or as something arising out of nature (as the Epicureans would affirm). Cicero declared, "For friendship is nothing else than an accord in all things, human and divine, conjoined with mutual goodwill and affection, and I am inclined to think that, with the exception of wisdom, no better thing has been given to man by the immortal gods."[91] Other virtues associated with friendship include *constantia*, *fides*, and *veritas*. These virtues characterize true friendship, as opposed to mere flattery, the antithesis of friendship. True friendship based on the aforementioned virtues, therefore, outlives any other sort of friendship based on utility. Friendship in Cicero's

---

89. As quoted in Collette-Dučić, "Making Friends," 89. Responding to modern interpreters, Collett-Dučić argues that *erōs* is indeed a virtue in Stoic conception which builds a bridge to friendship.

90. For the purposes of this summary view, I will focus primarily on *On Friendship* as it presents more of Cicero's theory of friendship. For a more comprehensive look at Cicero's act of letter writing, including its historical and social milieu, see Peter White, *Cicero in Letters: Epistolary Relations of the Late Republic* (New York: Oxford University Press, 2012).

91. *On Friendship* 6.20, in *Cicero: On Old Age, On Friendship, On Divination*, trans. W. A. Falconer, Loeb Classical Library 154 (Cambridge, MA: Harvard University Press, 1923), 131.

perspective actually results in "greater advantages" for the other since they "vie with him in a rivalry of virtue."[92]

Pursuing the life of friendship, according to Cicero, required great care and diligence. Friends suffer pain together, share in the joys of the other's fortune, and bear the weight of the other's disgrace. True friendship shares mutual love and joy. Cicero recognized that such true friendship is difficult to attain. Through *On Friendship* he remarks, "True friendships are very hard to find among those whose time is spent in office or in business of any kind. For where can you find a man so high-minded as to prefer his friend's advancement to his own?"[93] One of the greatest threats to true friendship, therefore, is self-interest manifested in the form of attaining glory or the use of friends for political advancement.

FRIENDSHIP IN THE LATIN WEST AFTER CICERO

Writers in the Latin West continued to display notions of *amicitia* following Cicero up to the time of Augustine. Particularly, Latin Christian epistolary literature demonstrated adherence to friendship conventions within a Christian theological frame of reference. During this period "Christians used *caritas* and *dilectio* to identify an ideal that they perceived as higher and more universal than that of *amicitia* as celebrated by ancient philosophers."[94] Those who preceded Augustine, such as Cyprian of Carthage (c. 200-258 CE) and Ambrose of Milan (337-397 CE), all provide ample evidence of a Roman inheritance of friendship-language, particularly within their epistolary literature.

Cyprian's letters, many written during times of persecution, provide readers with instances of affectionate language demonstrating epistolary *amicitia* with added layers of Christian *caritas*. In his Letter 2 to Eucratius, Bishop of Thena, Cyprian describes his recipient as *frater carissime* ("dearly beloved brother") who shares in a mutual *dilectione* with Cyprian.[95] In numer-

---

92. Cicero, *On Friendship* 9.32.

93. Cicero, *On Friendship* 17.64.

94. Constant J. Mews and Neville Chiavaroli, "The Latin West," in *Friendship: A History* ed. Barbara Caine, Critical Histories of Subjectivity and Culture (London: Routledge, 2014), 79.

95. Cyprian of Carthage, *Epistulae* 2.1 in *Saint Cyprian: Letters (1–81)*, trans. Sister Rose Bernard Donna, Fathers of the Church (Washington, DC: Catholic University of America Press, 1964), 5. For the Latin text of *Epistula* 2, see CSEL 3.2:467–69..

ous letters, *frater carissime* was the standard description given to many of Cyprian's recipients.

One hundred years after Cyprian, Ambrose of Milan provided additional reflection upon friendship within his letters but especially in his work *On the Duties of the Clergy*, which was greatly influenced by Cicero's work *On Duties*.[96] In an increasingly Christianized world post-Constantine, Christian leaders such as Ambrose were able to spend more time reflecting on biblical and theological themes, yet Ambrose represents a figure most interested in showing the compatibility of classical learning with Christian theology. Thus, Carolinne White conjectures whether or not Ambrose represents a more Ciceronian or Christian example of friendship. She notes that Ambrose "retained the influence of Classical literary and philosophical forms and ideas ... particularly in his thought about friendship."[97] Hence his reflection on friendship did not undergo the sort of transformation that we see in the thought of Augustine.

White notes that friendship for Ambrose remained an "ethical question rather than being transformed into a theological one."[98] In Book 3 of his *On the Duties of the Clergy*, Ambrose considers the nature and duties of friendship and provides an optimistic evaluation:

> Preserve, my sons, that friendship which you have begun with your brother; for nothing in the world is more beautiful than that. It is indeed a comfort in this life to have someone to whom you can open your heart, with whom you can share confidences and to whom you can entrust the secrets of your heart. It is a comfort to have someone trustworthy beside you who will share your happiness, sympathise with your troubles and encourage you in persecution.[99]

---

96. The extent of Cicero's influence upon Ambrose's work has been debated. For a representation of the views pertaining to Ambrose's use of Cicero, see Alcuin F. Coyle, "Cicero's De Officiis and the De Officiis Ministrorum of St. Ambrose," *Franciscan Studies* 15, no. 3 (1955): 224–56. See also Goulven Madec, *Saint Ambroise et la philosophie* (Paris: Études augustiniennes, 1974).

97. White, *Christian Friendship in the Fourth Century*, 111.

98. White, *Christian Friendship in the Fourth Century*, 115.

99. Ambrose, *Off.* 3.22.131 in Ambrose, *Selected Works and Letters*, trans. H. De Romestin, Nicene and Post-Nicene Fathers, series 2, vol. 10 (Peabody, MA: Hendrickson, 1996).

This positive outlook, however, was often understood in terms of duties and obligations meant to be "repaid with interest by friends … [with] these human obligations coming into conflict with man's duty to God."[100] Hence, Ambrose provides readers with a significant witness to friendship in Christian perspective within the Latin West, though it would be Augustine less than a generation later who would transform classical notions of friendship into a deeply theological and spiritual relationship.

SUMMARIZING CLASSICAL FRIENDSHIP

David Konstan notes, "That there exists in the classical languages a vocabulary for friendship is an important index of its social role, but the concept does not depend exclusively on one locution."[101] It is important in understanding classical friendship that there is no ubiquitous definition. While there is similarity in reflection across the great thinkers of antiquity, there are contextual and philosophical nuances which make classical friendship worthy of deeper consideration. Ancient thinkers tended to focus less on individual traits and more so on traits that reside within the realm of the good. Individuality was graded against the philosophical notion of the good (variously defined), and excellence was of a kind. As noted, the good often related to the community, or *polis*, and therefore friendship often found its place within this context. Likewise, to be absent from the company of friends was perceived as a form of suffering.

Friendship was widely recognized as a necessary relationship for the purpose of mutual care and support. Friends existed for the sake of the other, which involved both sympathy and action.[102] In this way it demonstrated a certain level of intimacy, an idea of the friend being trustworthy.[103]

Friendship also served as a binding force of those in mutual activity. This facet receives little discussion in the classical literature as it is assumed as

100. White, *Christian Friendship in the Fourth Century*, 115

101. Konstan, *Friendship in the Classical World*, 19.

102. Bennett Helm, "Friendship," *Stanford Encyclopedia of Philosophy*, ed. Edward N. Zalta, https://plato.stanford.edu/archives/fall2017/entries/friendship.

103. For a helpful assessment on "trustworthiness" in classical notions of friendship, see Mark Alfano, "Friendship and the Structure of Trust," in *From Personality to Virtue: Essays on the Philosophy of Character*, ed. Alberto Masala and Jonathan Webber (Oxford: Oxford University Press, 2016), 186–206.

a fundamental of friendship.[104] This might best be understood as a "plural agent" understanding of friendship, wherein friendships emerge when a group of people demonstrate similar care for a specific activity or concern.[105]

Friendship in the classical tradition was focused primarily on the temporal life, whether conceived in a political realm like the *polis* or in a community of friends such as what Stoics practiced. While Aristotle conceived of friendship in terms of virtue, he tended to focus more on the excellent character already present within a friend rather than the goal of encouraging and increasing virtue.

Friendship for some, such as the Epicureans, was self-focused as such a relationship was meant to ultimately bring pleasure to an individual even if one was dedicated to serving and caring for the other. Though friendship in classical traditions included such aspects as mutual caring, relational intimacy, shared activity, and valuing the other, an eternal aspect is absent from classical renderings. Even in the Ciceronian definition of agreeing on things human and divine, such agreement ultimately had a temporal lifespan.

Classical friendship was also devoid of any emphasis on a specific deity which informed friendship and gave it its shape. Latin Christian writers before Augustine, especially Ambrose of Milan, would reflect upon friendship but primarily in classical terms.

As will become clear, the eternal nature of friendship, as well as the explicit desire to see mutual growth in virtue focused on Christ, informed and gave shape to Augustine's notion of spiritual friendship. Augustine's idea of friendship certainly had temporal qualities and shared many facets with the classical tradition prior to him, but his was a radically different understanding of the purpose and practice of friendship.

CONCLUSION

In this chapter I have summarized the classical tradition of friendship from Plato to Cicero and the Latin West prior to Augustine. While there are others who have contributed to reflection on friendship, these main philosophical schools and thinkers provide the foundation for classical reflection upon

---

104. Helm, "Friendship."
105. Bennet Helm, "Plural Agents," *Noûs* 42, no. 1 (2008): 17–49.

which later generations would stand. While there are many themes which, on the surface, could be influential to Augustine's concept of friendship, the missing element of divine love establishes Augustine as unique within the tradition. His intimate portrayal of friendship, though similar to earlier philosophical schools, involved a deeper spiritual element than any previous tradition would allow. Understanding the classical tradition helps readers grasp the contribution of classical thinking on friendship, yet even more that that allows us to see the significant differences between classical renderings of friendship and what will emerge in Augustine's practice of spiritual friendship specifically within his letters. As we turn now to Augustine's epistolary content, we will see how his paradigm of promoting divine love for the purpose of building Christlike virtue in the friendship relationship truly set him apart from previous thinkers and practitioners.

4

—

"WOUNDS FROM A FRIEND"

Jerome and Spiritual Friendship as Correction and Christian Love

Would that we deserved your embraces and that by conversation with each other we either learned something or taught something!

—Jerome to Augustine[1]

INTRODUCTION

Augustine's relationship with Jerome (c. 347-420 CE) has been well explored in scholarly literature. Some scholars have provided in-depth analysis of the exegetical issues at hand in their debate,[2] while others have attempted to analyze the tone and tenor of the exchange in order to address Augustine's epistolarity.[3] Yet others have provided a helpful overview of the correspondence between Augustine and Jerome, in order to better understand

---

1. Augustine, *Letters 1-99*, ed. John E. Rotelle, trans. Roland Teske, *Works of Saint Augustine* II/1 (Hyde Park, NY: New City Press, 2001), 261.

2. The seminal work in this area is Ralph Hennings, *Der Briefwechsel zwischen Augustinus und Hieronymus und ihr Streit um den Kanon des Alten Testaments und die Auslegung von Gal. 2, 11-14* (Leiden, Netherlands: Brill, 1994). For a recent analysis as it relates to Augustine's view of Paul and the Law, see J. A. Myers, "Law, Lies, and Letter Writing: An Analysis of Jerome and Augustine on the Antioch Incident (Galatians 2:11-14)," *Scottish Journal of Theology* 66, no. 2 (2013): 127-39.

3. See Alfons Fürst, *Augustins Briefwechsel mit Hieronymous*, Jahrbuch für Antike und Christentum. Ergänzungsband 29 (Münster, Germany: Aschendorffsche Verlagsbuchhandlung, 1999). See also Ebbeler, *Disciplining Christians*, 101-50.

Christian friendship broadly in late antiquity.[4] J. N. D. Kelly, in his biography of Jerome, addresses the nature of their relationship in brief.[5] While these studies provide helpful insight into this complicated and, at times, precarious relationship, more can be said regarding the exact nature and mechanics of their relationship.[6] Jerome, as Augustine perceived, was a friend equipped and capable to enter into scholarly debate regarding various exegetical and theological questions. Jennifer Ebbeler has done well to note the nature of corrective correspondence in Augustine, and here one can see this practice begin to blossom.[7] This corrective correspondence, however, was based on Augustine's vision of Christian friendship and spiritual growth. Correction is a natural extension of true Christian friendship. Thus, rather than seeing the expression of correction as being antithetical to Christian love, Augustine viewed such expressions as its natural consequent. Christian love demands correction. As will be seen in the exchange with Jerome, such an idea was not immediately reciprocated throughout the epistolary dialogue, yet love for one another remained a core topic of discussion. Christian love was the glue that bound these two men together even in the midst of relational tension and uncertainties.

Kelly has noted, "[In] these letters, so different in literary style and controversial tactics, both men spring startlingly to life, and the lineaments of each, his personal traits and foibles, his greatnesses and weaknesses, become more sharply etched by comparison with the other."[8] It is important to note that the meeting of these two great minds took place solely through written letters. Augustine expresses the angst he feels in not having Jerome close by for conversation:

---

4. Carolinne White, *The Correspondence (394–419) between Jerome and Augustine of Hippo* (Lewiston, NY: Edwin Mellen, 1991). See also White, *Christian Friendship in the Fourth Century*, 132–33.

5. J. N. D. Kelly, *Jerome: His Life, Writings, and Controversies* (Peabody, MA: Hendrickson, 1998), 263–72.

6. For an overview of the quarrelling nature of their relationship, see Robert J. O'Connell, "When Saintly Fathers Feuded: The Correspondence between Augustine and Jerome," *Thought: Fordham University Quarterly* 54, no. 4 (1979): 344–64. O'Connell notes that Augustine, despite Jerome's caustic character, found him "oddly irresistible" (364).

7. Ebbeler, *Disciplining Christians*, 75. This letter, according to Ebbeler, falls within the "experimental stage" of Augustine's epistolary corrective agenda.

8. Kelly, *Jerome*, 272.

Oh, if I were only permitted, even if not living in the same house, at least nearby, frequently to enjoy in the Lord a pleasant conversation with you. But since God has not granted this, I ask that you strive to preserve, increase, and make perfect our being together in the Lord as much as we can be and not disdain to reply, however rarely.[9]

Here, Augustine provides a glimpse into his desire for Jerome as a friend. His spiritual vitality is of utmost importance, and since a face-to-face encounter is not likely, the two friends must trust that the Lord will provide the spiritual sustenance that might otherwise be aided by physical interaction as friends. Despite the physical separation, Augustine chose to engage Jerome as a dear friend, speaking plainly to him as if in the flesh.[10] His desire was to engage Jerome as a friend and participate in a mutual exchange of Christian correction for the purpose of growing in Christlike virtue and a better apprehension of biblical truth, even if Jerome did not see their relationship in the same way. In Augustine's mind, this was a friendship of equals, yet with much to offer the other in terms of spiritual growth and insight.

There are numerous topics of discussion which arise in their exchange. Augustine's first letter to Jerome was supposedly lost in transit, only to be published in Italy apart from Augustine's knowledge and against his wishes.[11] Jerome's reaction, believing such an action to be a deliberate censure, drove Augustine to provide a clarifying response, further extending the hand of friendship. Their interaction famously stems from a question regarding an interpretative issue in Galatians and Jerome's Latin Bible translation project.[12]

LETTERS 28, 39, 40, 67:
ESTABLISHING THE RELATIONSHIP

Ebbeler notes the unique nature and content of Letter 28, the first letter between Jerome and Augustine, which should be analyzed on its own terms.[13] While this is true, it is helpful to see these three letters as a grouping, with

---

9. *Epistula* 67.3.

10. Since Augustine and Jerome never met in person, they often relied on their respective letter couriers to recount their physical appearance to one another.

11. *Epistula* 67.2, 2.

12. For a helpful overview on Jerome's translation of the Vulgate, see Dennis Brown, "Jerome and the Vulgate," in *The Ancient Period*, vol. 1 of *A History of Biblical Interpretation*, ed. Alan J. Hauser and Duane F. Watson (Grand Rapids: Eerdmans, 2008), 355–79.

13. Ebbeler, *Disciplining Christians*, 75.

Letter 40 and Letter 67 serving as an extension of Letter 28. In Letter 28, Augustine established the framework, yet Letters 40 and 67 buttress Letter 28 as subsequent appeals to address the topics of discussion raised in the initial letter. The latter two letters express Augustine's sorrow at not receiving a reply from someone with whom he was seeking to establish and maintain a friendship based on mutual Christian love.

LETTER 28

Letter 28 begins the correspondence between Augustine and Jerome, though this letter arrived seven years after it was first penned around 395.[14] The letter spent a considerable time circulating around Rome and other regions before finally landing with its intended recipient.[15] Based on its circulation before reaching him, Jerome had come to believe that the much younger bishop of Hippo had actually composed this as a treatise against him. This letter, filled with cordial language meant to extend the hand of fellowship and friendship, begins with Augustine praising the life and work of Jerome, whom he had never met nor would meet. The lack of physical presence, notes Augustine, is supplemented by the excellent biblical and theological work of Jerome. Augustine relates how the only impression he has of Jerome was given to him by Alypius so that Augustine, in a sense, saw Jerome "with his eyes."[16]

This friendship, asserted Augustine, was one wrought in the Spirit for unity. Augustine wishes to establish the spiritual character of their friendship from the outset.[17] Additionally, Augustine affirms the mutual endeavor

---

14. For dating of these letters, I rely upon Teske's notes in *Letters 1–99*.

15. The deliverer of *Epistula* 28, Profuturus, never made it to Bethlehem to give Augustine's letter to Jerome because he was consecrated bishop of Cirta in Numidia. This led to the circulation of *Epistula* 28 in Rome and other places before coming to Jerome. Ebbeler notes, "Neither Profuturus nor Augustine made arrangements for the letter to be carried to Jerome in Bethlehem by another messenger. ... [Augustine] had probably retained a copy of *Epistula* 28, since he forwarded it to Jerome as an attachment to a subsequent letter (*Epistula* 71). It is almost as if after drafting the letter, Augustine lost his nerve and decided not to send it." Ebbeler, *Disciplining Christians*, 80.

16. *Epistula* 28.1.1. Alypius was Augustine's long-time friend and colleague, eventually becoming the bishop of Thagaste around 395. Chap. 5 discusses more on his friendship with Augustine. Alypius and Augustine often worked together against Pelagius and his followers, as well as working to repair the Donatist schism in North Africa. The nature and extent of Alypius and Jerome's relationship is unknown, though it is clear from Augustine's description that they had met.

17. *Epistula* 28.1.1.

toward understanding Jesus Christ.[18] By affirming this mutual pursuit, Augustine was able to introduce the goal of his letter, which was to encourage Jerome in his translation project. This project could have either beneficial or deleterious effects on the congregation over which Augustine was shepherd, and indeed the "whole of zealous society of African churches."[19] Augustine was seeking assurances that Jerome's Latin translation would have the sort of interpretive consistency Augustine's congregation had grown to expect in the Septuagint.[20] This accepted Greek translation of the Old Testament had been attested by centuries of use, whereas Jerome's contemporary work had not. Therefore, Augustine sought Jerome's confidence that both in translation procedure and content, this new work was sound.

Additionally, Augustine saw fit to confront Jerome on a matter of interpretation with regard to Galatians 2. Jerome, apparently in an effort to protect the authority and sanctity of the apostle Peter, presented an interpretation of Paul wherein Paul effectively lies in regard to Peter's action. Such a notion utterly destroys the authority of Scripture and hence can lead anyone to reject whatever teaching they wish. To Augustine, it is a serious matter for both the doctrine and morality of the church. Paul's use of lying was supposedly meant to elicit a greater good, according to Jerome. The idea that deception is advocated within Scripture must be avoided at all costs, for it is an idea that will lead along a pathway of spiritual ruin, Augustine avers. Even the introduction of a useful lie discredits and irrevocably damages the veracity of Scripture and the ability to talk authoritatively from the holy books.[21]

While Augustine was adamant on this point, he remained open to rebuke and correction. In this, Augustine points to the distinction between a friend and a flatterer, citing Psalm 141:5.[22] Reproach leading to healing demonstrates love for a person, whereas a flatterer allows one to proceed unchecked. Augustine submitted himself to the judgment of Jerome as part of their progressive dialogue, seeking to remain humble though he retained the

---

18. *Epistula* 28.1.1.

19. *Epistula* 28.2.2.

20. In this exchange, Augustine demonstrates his preference for the LXX. Though his preference for the LXX remained constant, his views of the Hebrew Bible did evolve throughout his lifetime. For more on Augustine and his views of the LXX and the Hebrew Bible, see Edmon L. Gallagher, "Augustine on the Hebrew Bible," *Journal of Theological Studies* 67 (2016): 97–114.

21. *Epistula* 28.4.6.

22. *Epistula* 28.4.6.

convictions mentioned in the letter. Though this letter is unique within the exchange of Augustine and Jerome, it represents the key terms and points of their growing—though often strained—friendship. In this letter, Augustine engaged as one wishing to develop a friendship for the purpose of mutual growth, opening a corrective dialogue which might persuade Jerome to reconsider his exegetical position for the good of God's people and the defense of biblical truth. A love for God and a love for the other, for Augustine, would be one of the driving factors for this exchange.

LETTERS 39 AND 40

Jerome, not having received Letter 28, wrote a short letter, Letter 39, to Augustine around 397. He mentioned a previous letter, which is no longer extant, noting that he believed it had been received by Augustine.[23] Jerome saw this letter as a "duty" (*officium*) in order to return the greetings for Augustine's previous letter, likely as a courtesy in connection with their blossoming relationship.[24] In it, Jerome commended the deacon Praesidius to Augustine in order that he might form "friendships with good men" and receive "the greatest benefit in forming such friendships."[25] Jerome here demonstrated the importance of making such friendly connections with Augustine, revealing how he viewed Augustine and the potential for friendship. Jerome also mentioned the tribulations of monastic life and requested Augustine's prayers in order to help him and his fellow monks in Bethlehem "endure the troubles of our earthly pilgrimage."[26] This short letter was received by Augustine at the end of 397. It would have been confusing to Augustine, as it did not address the questions posed to him in his Letter 28.

Though he thanked Jerome for the courtesy of his reply in Letter 39, Augustine penned Letter 40 to make up for the supposed loss of Letter 28. He also decided to take this opportunity to expand and further explain his position, hoping that perhaps Jerome had changed his views in the meantime.[27]

---

23. *Epistula* 39.1.1.

24. *Epistula* 39.1.1.

25. *Epistula* 39.1.1. Praesidius served as letter bearer of *Epistula* 39 and was "very close" to Jerome, though nothing else is known of his background and relationship to either Jerome or Augustine.

26. *Epistula* 39.2.2.

27. *Epistula* 40.5.8.

As he began Letter 40, he acknowledged the Spirit-wrought oneness between him and Jerome: "Hence, enter into this conversation by letter with us so that we do not allow bodily absence to do much to keep us apart, though we are united in the Lord by oneness of the Spirit, even if we rest our pen and are silent."[28] Jerome's books were able to substitute, albeit not completely, for his presence with Augustine.[29] In this Augustine offered high praise for Jerome's work, which, in essence, was high praise to Jerome himself.

Augustine soon addressed the matter at hand regarding the dispute between Peter and Paul in Galatians 2:11-14. The idea that Paul was telling a "useful lie" created a significant moral problem in the mind of Augustine. If one grants that Paul knowingly lied or acted inconsistently with his apostolic charge, then many "great and inexplicable evils" follow.[30] Though Augustine lays out the argument for Jerome, he affirms that Jerome is more than capable of understanding the issue. The "few coins" of Augustine could never add to the "fine mind ... [of] solid gold" that Jerome possesses.[31] Jerome likewise was best suited with his skills of translation to address the issue. After addressing his concern, Augustine asked that Jerome correct and recant his error for the sake of the beauty of the gospel, which is "more beautiful than the Helen of the Greeks."[32] Augustine's request to sing a palinode (παλινῳδία), a recantation song, is not because he believed Jerome had lost his vision of the truth but so that he may "turn back those healthy and watchful eyes" that had been temporarily blinded to the consequences of his exegetical ideas.[33]

Toward the end of the letter, Augustine acknowledged the delivery mishap of Letter 28. With this in mind, he took the occasion to express his desire to be humble were his view to be different from the truth. He was willing to be wrong on this point, but nevertheless was adamant that he was in the right adding, "[If] your view is different and better, you should readily pardon my fear."[34] Augustine concluded the letter with an enquiry regarding Jerome's *De viris illustribus*. Augustine believed that Jerome should be more

28. *Epistula* 40.1.1.
29. *Epistula* 40.1.1.
30. *Epistula* 40.4.5.
31. *Epistula* 40.3.3.
32. *Epistula* 40.4.7.
33. *Epistula* 40.4.7.
34. *Epistula* 40.5.8.

explicit about those men who held heretical beliefs. Though he singled out
Origen of Alexandria (184–253 CE), he had others in mind as well. He rec-
ommended that Jerome publish a short book of heretics and their teachings who have "tried to spoil the rectitude of the Christian faith either by
impudence or by stubbornness."[35] This he mentioned as a request of brotherly love from his "lowly self."[36] In this regard, he did not feel the need to
ask incessantly as he counts on Jerome's love in return.[37] Augustine, citing
the mutual cause of love, was confident that Jerome would reciprocate and
respond accordingly.

LETTER 67

Letter 67, written sometime around 403, was a short letter from Augustine
that he wrote upon hearing of Jerome's reception of his previous letters.
This short letter expressed Augustine's sorrow in awaiting a reply from
Jerome. Though sorrowful, he was not bitter, recognizing that there "had
undoubtedly been some obstacle."[38] Augustine addressed the issue of the
much-delayed original letter—Letter 28—and the controversy it had caused.
He asserted that his intentions were pure and that he never set out to write
a book against Jerome and distribute it behind his back. Any of Augustine's
writings that were contrary to Jerome's ideas should not be taken as an intentional attack, but were simply Augustine's thoughts on the matter. Augustine
invited correction if it was necessary; otherwise he asked Jerome to believe
and trust that he meant no harm. Augustine stated, "For I will rejoice either
over my correction or your good will."[39]

In this short letter, Augustine expressed an affectionate tone toward
Jerome and a desire to continue their relationship in person. Augustine
yearned for personal conversation with Jerome and wished that they could
live, even if not in the same house, "at least nearby" in order to enjoy their
relationship in the Lord.[40] Recognizing this was not the case, Augustine
was determined all the more to solidify and continue his friendship with

---

35. *Epistula* 40.6.9.
36. *Epistula* 40.6.9.
37. *Epistula* 40.6.9.
38. *Epistula* 67.1.1.
39. *Epistula* 67.2.2.
40. *Epistula* 67.2.3.

Jerome and, in his words, "make perfect our being together in the Lord as much as we can."[41]

LETTERS 68, 71, 72, 73, 75:
UNSETTLING THE RELATIONSHIP

This next group of letters represents the bulk of the corrective dialogue between the two friends. In Letter 68, Jerome seemed uncertain as to Augustine's intention regarding Letter 28. Not wishing to reply rashly out of malice as well as attending to the sickness of Paula of Rome (347–404 CE), a wealthy Roman who founded a monastery in Bethlehem, kept Jerome from initially replying.[42] Beginning with Letter 68, and in his subsequent replies to Augustine's queries, Jerome continued to demonstrate a desire for friendship, yet as one who was troubled by the one whom he considered a "youth in the field of scripture."[43] In the heat of the exchange, both men continued to confess a love for one another based on their shared Christian convictions, even if Jerome did not entirely appreciate Augustine's desire for corrective engagement.

Letter 68

This letter, written in 402, represents Jerome's first reply to Augustine's inquiries regarding his exegetical conclusions. In it, Jerome clearly recognized the corrective position that Augustine had taken toward him. Jerome did not assume any ill-intent and withheld his reply to avoid a hasty response. Nevertheless, Jerome proceeded to take a defensive position, stating that he himself would not dare "tamper with anything in the books" of Augustine.[44] Jerome took the opportunity to quote a host of classical authors so as to depict Augustine as a brazen youth looking for nothing but recognition. It is important to note that Augustine had invited Jerome to be critical of him.[45] Augustine would have received any such criticism in the spirit of

---

41. *Epistula* 67.2.3.

42. In 404, Jerome composed a lengthy epitaph to commemorate Paula, who was his long-time patroness and monastic associate. For an assessment of Jerome's commemoration of Paula, see Andrew Cain, "Jerome's Epitaphium Paulae: Hagiography, Pilgrimage, and the Cult of Saint Paula," *Journal of Early Christian Studies* 18, no. 1 (2010): 105–39.

43. *Epistula* 68.2.

44. *Epistula* 68.2.

45. Ebbeler argues that Augustine portrayed himself as "immune to friendly epistolary correction." Ebbeler, *Disciplining Christians*, 13.

friendship, even if he perceived it as somewhat severe. Despite his blunt characterization of Augustine, Jerome continued to affirm a measure of love for the North African theologian who was, compared to himself, a "youth in the field of scripture."[46] Jerome noted that "a real reason for reproach among friends" would be if one were to fixate on the other's "knapsack" while neglecting their own "satchel."[47]

Jerome writes with the tone of a worn-out old man who did not wish to engage in what he considered to be the youthful diversions of his correspondent. Yet despite this vexation, he warned that he was prepared to engage in dialogical combat if necessary.[48] Jerome admitted that his preference would be to have a friendly conversation in person: "Would that we deserved your embraces and that by conversation with each other we either learned something or taught something!"[49] In the end, Jerome expressed his love, though somewhat sardonically, by consciously choosing not to reply to what he perceived as Augustine's provocations.

Letter 71

Augustine wrote this letter in 403 partly to enquire as to Jerome's lack of response to his previous letters. He also wished to continue a dialogue on various issues. First, Augustine expressed concern at Jerome's word choice when translating Jonah 4:6 from the Hebrew to Latin.[50] Next, he inquired from Jerome, asking him to elaborate on passages in the Septuagint that differed from their Hebrew equivalent.

---

46. *Epistula* 68.2.

47. *Epistula* 68.2.

48. *Epistula* 68.2. Jerome refers here to the instance in Virgil's *Aeneid* 5.368–484, wherein the older Entellus pummels the younger Dares before the fight is broken up by Aeneas.

49. *Epistula* 68.2.

50. This issue had caused quite a stir in the church of a "certain brother bishop" in North Africa. Having translated the Hebrew word קִיקָיוֹן (*qîqayôn*) meaning "shade plant," Jerome's Latin word choice (*hedera*) differed from the old Latin translation (*cucurbita*) based on the Septuagint (κολοκύνθη). When the bishop used Jerome's new translation, the people noticed the difference and "so great an uproar" ensued (*Epistula* 71.3.5). For a history of translation of the Hebrew word *qîqayôn* including Jerome's translation, see Bernard P. Robinson, "Jonah's Qiqayon Plant," *Zeitschrift für die Alttestamentliche Wissenschaft* 97, no. 3 (1985): 390–403. For an overview of Augustine and Jerome's exchange on Jonah 4:6, see Anne Fraïsse-Bétoulières, "Comment traduire la Bible? Un échange entre Augustin et Jérôme au sujet de la 'citrouille' de Jonas 4,6," *Études Théologiques et Religieuses* 85, no. 2 (2010): 145–65.

Augustine was concerned by Jerome's lack of response, given that he desired to engage in friendly debate and dialogue. This clearly demonstrated Augustine's continued desire to connect with Jerome on a personal level. Augustine lamented that his Letter 28, originally carried by Profuturus, had not yet reached its destination and had had such a tumultuous journey. Augustine asserted how much he desired to converse with Jerome: "[How] much I suffer because the senses of your body are so far distant from me by which my mind might have access to your mind."[51] Although Jerome received Letter 28, it was clear to Augustine that he still harbored bitterness toward him regarding the entire ordeal.

LETTER 72

Jerome began his response to Augustine by addressing the fiasco of Letter 28. He expressed concern regarding the unauthorized circulation of the letter in Rome and raised doubts regarding Augustine's explanation. Jerome thus articulated a maxim of friendship: "all suspicion should be removed" in order that "one should speak with a friend just as with another self."[52] It was because of this that Jerome had delayed his response, noting that he considered the letter not original to Augustine, or else "it was a sword coated with honey."[53] He also claimed that his desire was to avoid any presumptuous reply to a bishop, as he himself was a presbyter, and does not want to spark a war of criticism.[54]

Augustine's Letter 71 had not yet arrived in Jerome's hands, as he indicated by requesting the original Letter 28 with Augustine's signature.[55] Augustine left the door open to debate and conversation, yet Jerome wished him to "stop pestering an old man hiding in his cell" if Augustine was only concerned to display his intellectual prowess.[56] After all, there were many in Rome who would be happy to "do battle ... and hold their own with a bishop in a discussion of the holy scriptures."[57] Toward the end of his response, Jerome con-

---

51. *Epistula* 71.1.2.
52. *Epistula* 72.1.1.
53. *Epistula* 72.1.2.
54. *Epistula* 72.1.2.
55. *Epistula* 72.2.3.
56. *Epistula* 72.2.3.
57. *Epistula* 72.2.3.

tinued to question the sincerity of Augustine's intentions. He demanded an
affirmation that Augustine did not write a public critique of him, and he also
questioned why Augustine would invite him to take aim at his own writings.
In this, Jerome believed that Augustine was seeking to "provoke an old man ...
[and] goad a silent one ... [and] boast of your learning."[58] The corrective perspective of Augustine, which he believed derived from love and a Christian
understanding of friendship, was obviously not entirely shared by Jerome.[59]

Jerome directly confronted Augustine's corrective agenda, noting its
destructive nature to the "laws of our relationship."[60] Augustine's corrective
request to recant his views on Galatians 2:11–14 were causing injury to their
friendship, according to Jerome. As such it could easily lead to doing battle "in
a childish manner."[61] Even though he offered a warning, Jerome also admitted
that he had a love for Augustine, which had blossomed before they began to
know one another. This, according to Jerome, was the guard which kept him
from engaging in overly destructive dialogue. Jerome's affection for Augustine
previously led him to rejoice "as he rose up after [him] in the learning of the
scriptures."[62] Even in the midst of agitation and questioning the motives of
Augustine, Jerome had not lost faith in their friendship and counted Augustine
as an honored friend. Though his "son in terms of age," he considered him to
be his "father in terms of dignity."[63] This honorific language was perhaps a
way to encourage the younger Augustine toward propriety in future discourse,
especially since Jerome encouraged him to ensure that any future writing came

---

58. *Epistula* 72.2.4.

59. As Ebbeler has noted, it was clear that Jerome did not take kindly to Augustine's corrective correspondence. Though he still considered Augustine a friend, the resistance to corrective
conversation reveals a difference from Augustine in how Jerome viewed friendship. For a helpful
overview of Jerome's view of friendship, see White, *Christian Friendship in the Fourth Century*,
129–45. White notes, "Throughout his life, it would seem, Jerome was able to engage in close relationships only with people who were willing to show him due respect and would not contradict
him. Woe betide anyone who criticized Jerome or refused to fit in with his way of thinking" (129).
For a study on Jerome and friendship with women, see Edward Cletus Sellner, "An Inclination
of the Heart: Jerome and His Female Friendships," *Spiritual Life* 47, no. 3 (2001): 161–77.

60. *Epistula* 72.2.4. Though Jerome used this terminology of "father" and "son," in reality
he was less than ten years older than Augustine.

61. *Epistula* 72.2.4.

62. *Epistula* 72.2.4.

63. *Epistula* 72.3.5.

directly to him first.[64] Regardless of any additional intentions, the extension of affection would be received as genuine by the younger Augustine.

LETTER 73

In his reply to Jerome written in 404, Augustine lamented that his previous letters had been met by such consternation. But he also expressed his own offense at Jerome's vitriolic reply. Augustine found it curious that Jerome sought to offend him when he was still uncertain that Augustine had actually written a diatribe against him. If there was uncertainty as to the original intent, why would Jerome proceed to go on the offensive? Rather than continuing to spar, Augustine requested Jerome's forgiveness for the original offense and asked that he not "repay evil with evil by offending [him] in turn."[65] Augustine affirmed that he was not above correction, but only wished that such correction was based on truth, rather on a baseless desire to defame. Augustine desired correction "given out of great friendship" and "fatherly love."[66] This further revealed Augustine's notion of correction as integral to the act of friendship. With this in mind, Augustine chose to see Jerome's rebuke as a sort of healing, though there was still some hurt in the midst of it. Referencing Cicero's *On Friendship*, Augustine affirmed that a rebuke from enemies was more beneficial than friends who were afraid to admonish the other. Friends who do not wish to spoil the "sweetness of friendship" do a disservice to their friend and "manifest less freedom" when it comes to rightly judging the other's actions.[67] Friendship without rebuke was not true friendship. To this end, Augustine invited any additional correction and criticism should it be necessary, imploring Jerome to "put your foot down on me with more force" and affirming that he desired the "chaff of [his] fault" to be crushed.[68]

Augustine praised Jerome's "great knowledge of the Scriptures," lamenting that he was unable to dwell on the details, as his congregation would likely not allow such scholarly rabbit trails.[69] Augustine was obligated to put his scriptural knowledge to use for the people, whereas Jerome was able

---

64. *Epistula* 72.3.5.
65. *Epistula* 73.2.3.
66. *Epistula* 73.2.3.
67. *Epistula* 73.2.4.
68. *Epistula* 73.2.4.
69. *Epistula* 73.2.5.

to spend time writing, reflecting, and deeply engaging with the Scriptures, both in personal study and in conversation with others. This reveals part of Augustine's motivation for engaging Jerome. Though perhaps his initial manner was unorthodox, his desire seems to have been to garner a friend with whom mature scriptural dialogue could take place. In this regard, there could be no better friend for this purpose than the learned biblical scholar Jerome. This desire for deep engagement was evident not only in the initial criticism regarding Jerome's interpretation of Galatians 2:11-14, but was woven throughout the entire exchange. It was also evident in Augustine's insistence in receiving correction from Jerome. Augustine continued to emphasize his desire for correction throughout the letter, noting that if such actions could not be done free from "suspicion of hatred and an injury to [their] friendship," then he desired that they cease from engaging one another so as not to impede any spiritual progress.[70]

In this letter, Augustine mentioned another of Jerome's friendships—that with Rufinus of Aquileia (345-411 CE).[71] This friendship had broken up over their conflicting interpretation of Origen. As Mark Vessey notes, Rufinus had used Jerome's translation of Origen "as a warrant for his own version of that writer's treatise *On First Principles*."[72] Augustine laments this and began to deconstruct what happened. In doing so, he alludes to his own relationship with Jerome and what could easily happen to them if they were not to pursue love for one another. He referred to that possibility when he stated, "What friend should not be feared as a future enemy if there could arise between Jerome and Rufinus this hostility we deplore?"[73] While one may know him-

---

70. *Epistula* 73.3.9.

71. Rufinus was born into a wealthy and noble family and completed his education in Rome, where he met and befriended Jerome. Upon his return to Aquileia around 370, he was baptized and joined an ascetic community. He was greatly inspired by the monastic life, even making a pilgrimage to Egypt in 372 or 373. He translated and added to the *Historia Ecclesiastica* of Eusebius of Caesarea (c. 260-340 CE). For a modern translation of Rufinus's *Church History*, see Rufinus of Aquileia, *History of the Church*, trans. Phillip R. Amidon (Washington, DC: Catholic University of America Press, 2016). For a definitive biography of Rufinus, see Francis X. Murphy, *Rufinus of Aquileia (345-411): His Life and Works* (Washington, DC: Catholic University of America Press, 1945).

72. Mark Vessey, "Jerome and Rufinus," in *The Cambridge History of Early Christian Literature*, ed. Frances Young, Lewis Ayres, and Andrew Louth (Cambridge: Cambridge University Press, 2007), 323.

73. *Epistula* 73.3.6.

self now, Augustine observed, "he does not know what he will be afterward."[74]
This was an occasion for Augustine to further engage Jerome in theological
enquiry, asking his opinion on the angelic foreknowledge of Satan. Such
a conversation, typically shared among like minds in theological dialogue,
was yet another reason Augustine lamented their distance from one another.
In bemoaning their physical separation, Augustine emphatically said, "If I
were this letter of mine that you are reading, you would already have told
me what I asked for."[75] In this sentiment he affirmed Jerome's previous words
from Letter 68, "'Would that we deserved your embraces and that by conversation with each other we either learned something or taught something,'
if it were in any way possible that I should teach you."[76] These words have
become Augustine's as well as Jerome's, expressing a mutual desire though
it would never be realized. This further caused Augustine to recoil in pain
at the reality of Jerome and Rufinus's broken friendship, perhaps feeling the
sting of what such a break in friendship would mean for him. This friendship
seemed to be similar to his and Augustine's, discussing biblical interpretation so that together they might "savor together the honey of the scriptures."[77]

Augustine feared that a broken friendship could happen with him and
Jerome, especially upon receiving the "indications of [Jerome's] indignation."[78]
His goal was for discussion to take place free from bitterness or hostility.
Augustine wished to avoid the pursuit of knowledge at the expense of building up love, noting that is far from the ideal of one who does not offend with
his words, citing James 3:2. With this, Augustine continued to ask for Jerome's
pardon and mercy. Distance should not preclude forgiveness, according to
Augustine. He then took a moment to discuss the value of other friends that
they both possessed. Here, Augustine revealed an intimate detail about his
view of friendship. He admitted,

> I admit that I find it easy to abandon my whole self to the love of
> them. ... I find rest in that love without any worry. I, of course, feel
> that God is in that person to whom I abandon myself with security

---

74. *Epistula* 73.3.6.
75. *Epistula* 73.3.7.
76. *Epistula* 73.3.7.
77. *Epistula* 73.3.8.
78. *Epistula* 73.3.9.

and in whom I find rest in security. ... For, when I perceive that a man is aflame with Christian love and has become my loyal friend with that love, whatever of my plans and thoughts I entrust to him I do not entrust to a human being, but to him in whom he remains so that he is such a person.[79]

Augustine affirmed the love he had for Jerome and reminded his friend of the love that he was certain Jerome possessed for him.

This letter sought to rectify any previous harm done by Augustine to his and Jerome's friendship. That said, he was not afraid to be forthright regarding his feelings at Jerome's response and the attitude he perceived between him and Rufinus. His desire was to see unification take place between these two estranged friends, as well as salvage his own friendship with the revered biblical scholar. The reality of the broken friendship was a "great and sad source of wonder" and Augustine desired that the "original oneness of heart" be restored. He also wanted to maintain a oneness of heart with Jerome.[80] Did he hope that by analyzing another broken relationship it might help Jerome understand Augustine's feelings toward their own friendship? It seemed as if Augustine was speaking of himself when he said of Rufinus, "[Who] among the wise would not see how you ought to bear with patience and with the consolation of a good conscience the present incredible hostility of someone who was once a very close and intimate friend?"[81]

LETTER 75

Jerome's Letter 75 was composed around 404, many years after Augustine's initiating letter had been penned.[82] This letter represented a "veritable short treatise" which was described by Jerome as a haphazard construction, yet in truth was a magnificent work of style, likely planned "with an eye to

---

79. *Epistula* 73.3.10.

80. *Epistula* 73.3.10.

81. *Epistula* 73.3.10.

82. While Jerome never states exactly what kept him from writing, Kelly suggests that so many had been excited by the exchange that "a formal response ... could no longer be deferred without loss of face." Kelly, *Jerome*, 269. Additionally, Fürst suggests that Jerome finally penned his response to defend his translation and inform Augustine of translation practices in general. Fürst, *Augustins Briefwechsel mit Hieronymous*, 140–45. Ebbeler also suggests that Jerome wished to avoid any undue criticism for defending Origen, who had received numerous posthumous condemnations. Jennifer Ebbeler, "Pendants in the Apparel of Heroes? Cultures of Latin Letter-Writing from Cicero to Ennodius" (PhD diss, University of Pennsylvania, 2001), 176–217.

wider publication."[83] This rather lengthy reply to Augustine's various questions raised in Letters 28, 40, and 71 demonstrated that he was suspicious of Augustine's praise and desire to carry on a humble dialogue of common correction. In fact, Jerome interpreted Augustine's kind words as a blandishment, stating, "I am silent about the flattery by which you strive to soften your criticism of me."[84] From here, Jerome began to address each issue raised by Augustine. One of the most significant issues was Augustine's disagreement regarding Jerome's interpretation of Galatians 2:11–14. He began his defense by citing his own commentary which stated that his view on the matter was affirmed by Origen and a small sampling of Greek authors, including John Chrysostom (c. 349–407 CE). It was up to Augustine to determine if they were wrong in order that Jerome might correct his own view. Jerome again cited his own commentary that challenged readers to demonstrate how Paul could criticize Peter when Paul himself was guilty of the same error, according to Jerome. Jerome's goal was to present the view from the Greek authors, not as definitive, but in such a way that the reader would decide "whether those ideas should receive approval or disapproval."[85] If Jerome was in error, therefore, he was in error with other prominent men, and Augustine was thus challenged "to produce at least one supporter" of his claim, which Jerome considered novel and unsubstantiated.[86]

Based on this, Jerome accused Augustine of arguing that Jews were required to keep the law after belief in Christ. He also could not see how Augustine could overlook the supposed wealth of evidence regarding Paul's hypocrisy of accusing Peter for something which he himself seems to have done. From here he launched into a review of various instances throughout the book of Acts where Paul subjected himself and others to the Jewish law. It was actually Peter in Acts 15 who declared that the gospel was both for Jews and Gentiles and that God has "made no distinction between us and them" (Acts 15:9). Peter in this instance was a champion for inclusion, a fact about which Paul would not have been ignorant. Jerome continued to provide numerous texts demonstrating how Paul acted in certain ways for fear of other Jews, so as not to offend them.

---

83. Kelly, *Jerome*, 269.
84. *Epistula* 75.1.2.
85. *Epistula* 75.3.4.
86. *Epistula* 75.3.6.

Jerome asserted that Peter and Paul "on account of fear of the Jews ... both equally pretended to observe the commandments of the law."[87] Jerome declared rather sardonically, "You will surely say something better since you have found fault with the view of the earlier writers."[88] The view that Augustine wished to defend, according to Jerome, was actually on par with those of Cerinthus or Ebion![89] Jerome's supposed crime was simply to introduce readers to different views on a passage, whereas Augustine sought "to reintroduce into the Church a most criminal heresy."[90] Jerome took a position against Augustine's argument and declared that any who observe Jewish traditions as Christians "[have] descended into the pit of the devil."[91]

Jerome continued to force Augustine and his arguments into a corner, asserting that Augustine's line of reasoning amounted to upholding the law and rejecting the new era of grace under Christ. Jerome was puzzled that Augustine would assert that Jewish ceremonies were to be observed, though they were not necessary for salvation. Jerome could not see how observance could be seen as "something indifferent" rather than implicit approval.[92] In the end, Jerome found that Augustine's argument worked in his favor, stating that Paul's desire to imitate both Jews and Gentiles demonstrated that he was simply putting himself in a position to draw others to the faith and doing so by whatever means, which would favor Jerome's interpretation of Paul's actions in Galatians 2:11–14. Jerome offered a final admonition to his

---

87. *Epistula* 75.3.11.

88. *Epistula* 75.3.11.

89. Both Cerinthus and Ebion were early heretics. Cerinthus was a late first- and early second-century opponent of Christianity. He lived in Asia Minor and was deemed heretical by early church fathers (e.g., Irenaeus, *Against the Heresies* 1.26.1; Hippolytus of Rome, *The Refutation of All Heresies* 7.21; Eusebius, *Church History of Eusebius* 3.28–35, 7.25.3). According to these sources, Cerinthus denied the virgin birth and taught that Jesus was a normal human who was exceedingly wise and that he was empowered by the Christ-spirit upon his baptism. He appeared to affirm many facets of a gnostic cosmology wherein the world was made by a lesser being and claimed that Jesus spoke of a previously unknown supreme god and that the Jewish law was created by the lesser being.

The Ebionites, whose leader was identified as Ebion by various early heresiologists and early historians (e.g., Irenaeus, *Adversus Haereses* 1.26.1–2, 5.1.3; Eusebius, *Ecclesiastical History*, 3.27.2), were a type of Jewish sect in the late first and early second centuries. They maintained the authority of the Hebrew Bible, and thus held to the necessity of observing the Mosaic law. They argued that God adopted Jesus at his baptism, thus rejecting his preexistence and virginal conception. In this way they shared the Christological views of Cerinthus.

90. *Epistula* 75.4.13.

91. *Epistula* 73.4.13.

92. *Epistula* 75.4.16.

epistolary companion: "Do not stir up against me a crowd of the ignorant who reverence you as bishop and welcome you with the honor due to the priesthood as you preach in the church, but who look down on me as someone at the end of his years and almost decrepit."[93] While seeking to stave off Augustine's criticism, he once again remarked that any subsequent letter, referring to the original delay of Letter 28, should be sent to him directly, "before Italy and Rome receives it."[94]

Though spending the majority of his time discussing the interpretative disagreement on Galatians 2, Jerome obliged Augustine by also addressing various other translation questions. He took a moment to explain why various markings were present in Jerome's newest translations. He also addressed why a new word could be introduced into the Scriptures, namely, that his new translation was not composed of any words that he had invented, but translated from "the words of God ... in the Hebrew."[95] The issue of translation was addressed in his commentary on Jonah, so Jerome spent little time addressing his choice of the alternate word in Jonah 4 besides saying that it fit better with the context and was more true to the original and was in accordance with other translators. This was all that Jerome wished to say on the matter, noting that any Jew who said otherwise "either [does] not know the Hebrew language or [wants] to lie in order to mock the gourd-lovers."[96]

Jerome engaged Augustine with the forcefulness of a great debater, at times taking on the role of an adversary. This was most evident in his accusations of Augustine's tacit promotion of heresy, though he stopped short of actually declaring Augustine to be a heretic. In all this, he continued to affirm a level of friendship, yet remained assertive in his discussion. This exchange, however, should have been welcomed by Jerome, since Jerome had extended an invitation to his commentary readers to challenge his views. Augustine took Jerome up on his offer, presenting a different view of how Paul could participate in Jewish ceremonies and activities and yet challenge Peter for doing the same; however, Jerome did not accept this criticism. Biblical evidence, particularly from Acts, as well as a tradition stemming from Origen, were on his side. It was a closed case according to Jerome

---

93. *Epistula* 75.4.18.
94. *Epistula* 75.4.18.
95. *Epistula* 75.6.20.
96. *Epistula* 75.7.22.

and he was evidently tired of dealing with the issue any further. He implored the younger Augustine, "I beg you not to force an old man now at rest ... to risk his life. You, who are a young man and have been raised to the height of the episcopacy, go, teach the people, and enrich the houses of Rome with the new harvest from Africa."[97]

LETTERS 81 AND 82:
MENDING THE RELATIONSHIP

After this debate, though Augustine and Jerome maintained a basic commitment to Christian love, relational mending needed to take place between them. Letter 81 represents Jerome's attempt to smooth over the rough edges he perceived in his responses to Augustine. In Letter 82, Augustine sought to clear the air and affirm his desire for friendship based on Christian love, which in turn would provide an opportunity to discuss important matters of faith, including the responsibility to mutually admonish the other for the sake of growth. Love for the other continued to be affirmed though they both recognized that certain wounds had been inflicted.

LETTER 81

This letter, written after Letter 75 and around 404–405, is a sort of apology from Jerome. Taking advantage of a mutual friend, Firmus, who was traveling back to Africa, Jerome took the opportunity to soften the blow of his previous letter. Jerome, it seemed, wanted to move past their various disagreements. He insisted, "Let such complaints be banished from here; let there be between us sincere brotherhood, and from now on let us send each other letters filled, not with questions but with love."[98] This short letter sought to encourage Augustine and soothe their disagreement, as well as dissuade him from taking further issue with translation choices. Jerome closed his letter with an invitation to "playfully exercise on the field of the scriptures

---

97. *Epistula* 75.7.22. Ebbeler notes, "Jerome imagined that he and Augustine were competing for the patronage of Roman Christians. By this point in the difficult correspondence, Jerome could not be dislodged from his view that Augustine had challenged him to defend his scholarly practices in order to humiliate him in the very city that formerly had witnessed his disgraceful departure." Ebbeler, *Disciplining Christians*, 138–39.

98. *Epistula* 81.1.1.

without causing injury to each other."[99] This invitation, innocent as it may seem, would be cause for Augustine to reflect critically on the purpose of their ongoing discussion. Augustine's response was not a playful one, but a serious rebuttal of the scholar-monk's supposedly casual view toward scriptural debate and dialogue.

Letter 82

This letter, written around 404–405 and soon after Letter 81, was a lengthy reply to Jerome—specifically a reply to his Letters 72, 75, and 81. Though Jerome had previously requested to playfully engage one another in the "field of the scriptures," Augustine does not wish to take such a playful approach. Augustine's desire was to approach Jerome based on his "learned and leisured wisdom" and his "long, studious, and gifted application."[100] At this point, Augustine saw his task not as one playing in a field, "but like someone gasping for air in the mountains."[101] Augustine did not want to find fault with Jerome's intention, but rather desired to remind Jerome of the seriousness of their discussion. Augustine viewed their debate as involving nothing less than the veracity of Scripture. Augustine admitted,

> I learned to show this reverence and respect only to those books of the scripture that are now called canonical so that I most firmly believe that none of their authors erred in writing anything. [If] I come upon something in those writings that seems contrary to the truth, I have no doubt that either the manuscript is defective or the translator did not follow what was said or that I did not understand it.[102]

This same line of thinking did not apply to non-biblical authors, according to Augustine. He granted that Jerome felt the same way as well, and that Jerome would not desire people to read his own writings as if they were free from error. From here Augustine sought to bring their discussion back to that of Paul and Peter. If Jerome was able to assure Augustine of his sincerity in desiring his embrace and conversation, how much more should one

---

99. *Epistula* 81.1.1.
100. *Epistula* 82.1.2.
101. *Epistula* 82.1.2.
102. *Epistula* 82.1.3.

trust Paul and his sincerity as an apostle of Christ? Augustine's defense of Scripture was premised upon the reality that men, no matter how praiseworthy otherwise, need to be "corrected or condemned."[103] The authority of God's word was more precious than protecting the reputation of any person. To claim an error in the Scripture would give heretical groups an opportunity to manipulate the situation. The Scriptures, commonly accepted as the "canonical peak of authority," must be defended as "true and indubitable in every respect."[104]

For Augustine, if Paul said it, he believed it and that was the crux of the issue.[105] An apostle could not lie when writing Scripture, but an apostle could have need of correction due to a temporary lapse in judgment. It did not help to defend the erring apostle by denying the inerrant Word. From here, Augustine demonstrated how Paul could participate in the ceremonies and signs of the old covenant without denying the reality of their fulfillment in Christ. Their efficacy was now void, but they were not in themselves evil since they were created and instituted by God. Furthermore, for Paul to practice them in a period of transition at the dawning of the gospel age was not to say he denied the grace of Christ. He only wished to demonstrate that such practices were not under condemnation. Christ came to fulfill the law, not erase it.

Addressing Jerome's concerns, Augustine stated that one must be careful when considering whether practicing Jewish ceremonies were either good or bad. This dichotomy was unhelpful and forced either an obligation to practice these ceremonies or declare them utterly worthless, even though they were decreed by God for a specific purpose. It was only by the slow and steady preaching of Christ that these ceremonies, which foreshadowed the coming of Christ, were ultimately seen as unnecessary even for traditional adherence. Here Augustine commended Jerome on his warning regarding Ebionite or Nazarean tendencies. Neither Paul nor Peter fell into

---

103. *Epistula* 82.2.5.

104. *Epistula* 82.2.7.

105. For Augustine this issue relates to biblical authority and the inerrancy of Scripture. He affirmed that Jerome too would be concerned with this but might not see how his views could undermine Scripture's authority. For more on Augustine's view of Scripture, particularly in his letters, see Coleman M. Ford, "'He Who Consoles Us Should Console You': The Spirituality of the Word in Select Letters of Augustine of Hippo," *Evangelical Quarterly* 89, no. 3 (2018): 240–57.

this heretical trap, though Peter fell into "a pretense of agreement with it."[106]
Paul's life of preaching clearly indicated that he did not "force anyone to practice them as if they were necessary."[107] The practice of Jewish ceremonies by
Paul in the early years of the fledgling faith was like carrying the bodies of
dead parents, with respect and honor for what they once were. To practice
them now, however, would be like "disturbing ashes at rest" and "wickedly
violating its burial."[108] Paul condemned those who believed that Jewish sacrifices, ceremonies, and customs brought salvation. He did not condemn those
who understood they were a "foreshadow [of] the truth and how long they
ought to last."[109] In all this, Augustine continued to warn against the slippery
slope of admitting that Paul had lied, even for some sort of just purpose. Any
hint of error would open the floodgates of attack and allow detractors to
unduly criticize the Scriptures. Augustine, addressing a work by Porphyry,
no longer extant, entitled *Against the Christians*, asserted, "In Paul we praise
righteous freedom and in Peter holy humility, and in my limited judgement
we need to defend such praise against the slanders of Porphyry, rather than
to give him greater opportunity for his abusive talk."[110]

As Augustine continued to press Jerome on his interpretation, he com-
mented upon Jerome's reliance upon other commentators. Some of these
had left the church, or had significant error in other ways, and some were
simply not known to the wider church. This was a precarious position for
Jerome, according to Augustine. Augustine, on the other hand, claimed the
recognizable authority of Ambrose of Milan (c. 337–397 CE) and Cyprian of
Carthage (c. 200–258 CE) in regard to his interpretation. Though he asserted
their authority in alignment with his position, he nevertheless maintained
the final authority of Scripture as most pertinent to the debate. He asserted,
"And yet, as I said a little before, I owe this complete obedience only to the
canonical scriptures, and by it I follow them alone in such a way that I have
no doubt that their authors erred in them in absolutely no way and wrote
nothing in them in order to deceive."[111] Though he could have found more to

106. *Epistula* 82.2.15.
107. *Epistula* 82.2.15.
108. *Epistula* 82.2.16.
109. *Epistula* 82.2.19.
110. *Epistula* 82.2.22.
111. *Epistula* 82.3.24.

support his view, it would be unnecessary to do so for, "instead of all these, in fact above all these, the apostle Paul, nonetheless, comes to my rescue."[112] Augustine's focus was on upholding the veracity of Paul and his words, "rather than anyone, however learned, who argues about someone else's letter."[113]

Having provided his multiple points of defense, Augustine returned to the relational dynamic shared between him and Jerome. The concern and love for one another was obvious, and Augustine called upon this confessed love from Jerome as a further salve for their debate. In addition to this affirmation, Augustine used their love for one another as an example of the love that Paul had for his epistolary recipients "whom he begot in the gospel and whom he labored to bring to birth."[114] Augustine, drawing on the apostolic comparison, commended Jerome for attempting to provide correction for Augustine's supposed error, stating, "I am grateful for your mind so kindly disposed toward me, and I at the same time ask that you not be angry to me because I have made known to you my concern when some things in your works disturbed me."[115] The corrective position of Augustine was meant to bolster, not detract from, their friendship. His hope was to establish a firm Christian friendship based on love and mutual admonishment for the sake of the truth. In addressing this Christianized form of friendship, Augustine combats the notion put forth by Terence (c. 195–159 BCE), a Roman playwright, by providing a more biblical emphasis regarding friendship dynamics. He observed, "For I do not know whether friendships should be considered Christian in which the common saying, 'Flattery begets friends, but truth gives birth to hatred,' is more valid than the proverb of the Church, *Wounds from a friend are more trustworthy than the spontaneous kisses of an enemy*."[116] Friends, according to Augustine, should challenge each other's words yet retain love as long as it was focused on truth, "which is owed to friendship."[117] Sincerity of heart and absence of duplicity should be natural among friends, even if one of them may be in error.

---

112. *Epistula* 82.3.24.
113. *Epistula* 82.3.25.
114. *Epistula* 82.4.30.
115. *Epistula* 82.4.30.
116. *Epistula* 82.4.31. Augustine here refers to Prov 27:6, emphasis original.
117. *Epistula* 82.4.32.

As Augustine closed the letter he reiterated his desire for mutual correction and an ongoing friendship based in love. Augustine, though a bishop, refused to place himself over Jerome stating that though "the episcopacy is greater than the priesthood, Augustine is less than Jerome in many ways."[118] Augustine requested that beyond mutual love, they might enjoy true "freedom of friendship" in their exchange. This would ensure that both Augustine and Jerome would not pass over their mutual disagreements.[119] Augustine's desire was that friendship be based on the mutual desire to bring about deeper spiritual insights and increase their love for one another and love for God.

CHRISTIAN LOVE AS CHRISTIAN CORRECTION

This exchange was not the end of their relationship. After a long gap, their epistolary activity reignited around the Pelagian controversy in 415. In this later exchange, Jerome led the charge in addressing Augustine and imploring his aid in defending against the Pelagian error.[120] As such, Augustine took upon himself the posture of student with Jerome as the wise teacher.[121] Ebbeler notes that this subsequent exchange reflected a more traditionally "polite, superficially friendly, [and] highly conventional letter exchange."[122] Though this might be the case, such an exchange would have likely been less affectionate or effective had there not been a relational foundation established decades earlier. A foundation of friendship, based on a corrective posture fueled by Christian love, served to bolster later interaction and provided the background for becoming theological allies.

Carolinne White notes the "dramatic and radical" differences between traditional views of friendship and Augustine's perspective.[123] Though he reflected much of the classical tradition, the notion of Christian love was the

---

118. *Epistula* 82.4.33.

119. *Epistula* 82.5.36.

120. For an overview of Pelagius and his teaching, including Jerome and Augustine's work against him, see Eugene TeSelle, "Pelagius, Pelagianism," in *Augustine through the Ages: An Encyclopedia*, ed. Allan D. Fitzgerald (Grand Rapids: Eerdmans, 1999).

121. *Epistula* 166.1.

122. Ebbeler, *Disciplining Christians*, 149.

123. White, *Christian Friendship in the Fourth Century*, 195.

guiding axis on which Augustine's personal engagement turned.[124] The notion
of frankness in friendship played a large role in this exchange. The desire
to see growth in Christlike virtue was present even in the midst of heated
debate, and even if the desire was one-sided from Augustine. Augustine
assumed that Jerome was a spiritual equal, meeting him in the letter as a
spiritual friend requesting guidance and spiritual insight from a fellow
exegete and spiritual leader. The lengthy exchange discussed above demonstrated that love could be maintained in the midst of admonition. This
admonition, for Augustine, was meant to extend in both directions. Peter
Brown notes that Augustine was unwilling to benefit from criticism, but
this does not seem to be the case upon closer inspection.[125] Augustine conceded to Jerome's point on Hebrew translation and demonstrated restraint
upon receiving a scathing reply from Jerome. Augustine's display of humility seemed less than an "elaborate display" and more a desire to perpetuate
genuine friendship based on Christian love.[126] Correction, in order to further encourage Christian humility, was not in conflict with friendship.[127] It
is the "frankness" of the other which indicates that one is in fact a friend.[128]
Frankness, far from being an isolated trait, flows from the heart of love
for the other. This form of love matched the sort of love that Paul demonstrated to Peter in the incident at Antioch, though Jerome did not seem to

---

124. White, *Christian Friendship in the Fourth Century*, 195–96. White notes Augustine's admis-
sion in *Conf.* 4.4.7 where he stated, "[True friendship is that] which can only really exist when
you cement it between those who hold fast to you by means of the love that is shed abroad in
our hearts by the Holy Spirit, which has been given to us."

125. Brown, *Augustine of Hippo*, 271–72.

126. Brown characterizes their exchange as a "studied courtesy," "rancorous," and displaying
"elaborate gestures of humility." Brown, *Augustine of Hippo*, 271.

127. Konstan, *Friendship in the Classical World*, 159–62. Konstan notes how correction was seen,
in the mind of ancient philosophers, as a natural component to friendship. Augustine's version
of correction was based not on ancient philosophical notions, but on Christian love for the other.

128. Anne P. Carriker helpfully highlights the notion of "frankness" in Augustine, stating,
"It is in this way that friends instruct each other, for disagreement, it seems, is closely related to
mutual instruction. Yet in order to progress from disagreement to agreement, one friend must
correct the other—he must be frank with his friend. True Christian friendship, indeed, requires
frankness." For more on Jerome and Augustine's exchange and the dynamic of "frankness," see
Anne P. Carriker, "Augustine's Frankness in His Dispute with Jerome over the Interpretation of
Galatians 2:11–14," in *Nova Doctrina Vetusque: Essays on Early Christianity in Honor of Frederic W.
Schlatter, S. J.*, ed. Douglas Kries and Catherine Brown Tkacz, American University Studies 207
(New York: Peter Lang, 1999), 121–38.

interpret it as such initially.[129] Augustine's desire to engage Jerome came through his desire to discuss biblical and theological topics of great importance. This led to a frank observation of how Jerome might have taken a misdirected path. Augustine viewed correction in friendship was a natural outflow of Christian love as it provided an opportunity to draw the other closer and bring about greater harmony with the other person. Correction in his relationship with Jerome was loving in that it was intended to bring both of them into a closer relationship with God. Without correction, there was no opportunity for growth.

Notable in this exchange was both Augustine and Jerome's commitment to love even in the midst of heated debate and disagreement. Thus, even if the posture of correction was unexpected or unwanted, this did not seem to extinguish mutual love for one another. Indeed, though one may contradict "the words of another," this should not lead to love being diminished and as they are mutually seeking the truth, such disagreement should "not give birth to hatred."[130] For Augustine, mutual love breeds healthy discussion and disagreement, so long as the focus was "fraternal love with a spirit that is not displeasing in the eyes of God."[131]

---

129. Carriker, "Augustine's Frankness in His Dispute with Jerome," 131.
130. *Epistula* 82.4.32.
131. *Epistula* 82.5.36.

5

—

CONVERSING ON HEAVENLY THINGS

Spiritual Friendship as Mutual Encouragement in the Spiritual Life

I feasted on the spiritual delights of your letter.

—Paulinus to Augustine[1]

INTRODUCTION

In Augustine's letters to monastics, he provided support along the course of temporal life, while consistently directing their gaze toward the beatific vision. He desired the same support from his friends in return. Thus, spiritual friendship included mutual encouragement among friends in their pursuit of the spiritual life by grounding their calling in Christlike humility and relying upon the grace of God. Perhaps the most natural relationship to seek mutual growth in Christlike virtue was with those of the monastic vocation. This is because Augustine deeply identified with those of the monastic vocation, yet his pastoral calling kept him from the monastic contemplation he often desired.[2] Though serving as bishop, Augustine remained committed to the monastic ideal.[3] Based on this, he supported the calling of monastics

---

1. Augustine, *Epistula* 94.1.1.

2. For a recent treatment on Augustine and contemplation, see John Peter Kenney, *Contemplation and Classical Christianity: A Study in Augustine* (Oxford: Oxford University Press, 2013). Though Kenney focuses much of his attention on Augustine's earlier works in light of the Platonist tradition which preceded him, he also provides a helpful look of his post-baptismal and post-ordination view of contemplation.

3. George Lawless notes, "Although Augustine ... exalts the active life of the minister as the best ... he personally preferred, consistently through all the years, a life of contemplation." George Lawless, *Augustine of Hippo and His Monastic Rule* (Oxford: Clarendon, 1990), 41.

and encouraged these friends in their pursuit of a life of rigorous spiritual exercise. Goffredo Mariani thus described Augustine as a "spiritual guide" in these letter exchanges.[4] That said, "spiritual guide" does not adequately encapsulate Augustine's practice of spiritual friendship based on its assumption of hierarchy. Additionally, as some have argued, the notion of Augustine as a "Christian sage" misses the nuances of his desire for mutual encouragement.[5] Thus, for Augustine mutual encouragement was vital for spiritual friendship. This facet of friendship as mutual support in the spiritual life is most evident in his exchange with his monastic friends.

FRIENDSHIP WITH PAULINUS AND THERASIA

Paulinus of Nola (c. 335–441 CE) was born into an aristocratic family in Aquitaine in Gaul. In 381, he served as governor of Campania and married the wealthy Therasia. Their only child, Celsus, lived for only ten days. As governor he visited the shrine of St. Felix in Nola, which perhaps sparked his initial commitment to the Christian life.[6] By 386, he had come into contact with Ambrose of Milan (c. 337–397 CE) and Martin of Tours (c. 316–397 CE) in Vienne. Paulinus was baptized in 389 and four years later, he and Therasia began to part with their wealth in preparation for entering a monastic life.[7] He was ordained as priest in 394, and after Easter of 395 the couple moved to Nola. While in Nola, Paulinus established various monastic communities for both men and women. He was ordained bishop of Nola after 408, the same period in which Therasia died. Of all his writings, fifty-one letters and thirty poems remain extant. His letters were addressed to numerous individuals, including a good friend Sulpicius Severus, a monk

---

4. Goffredo Mariani, *Sant'Agostino Guida Spirituale: Lettere del Vescovo di Ippona a Proba, Giuliana E Demetriade* (Rome: Rogate, 1982).

5. Christine McCann, "'You Know Better than I Do': The Dynamics of Transformative Knowledge in the Relationship of Augustine of Hippo and Paulinus of Nola," Studia Patristica, 43 (2006):191.

6. Joseph T. Lienhard, "Paulinus of Nola" in *Augustine through the Ages: An Encyclopedia*, ed. Allan D. Fitzgerald (Grand Rapids: Eerdmans, 1999), s.v. "Paulinus of Nola."

7. For more on Paulinus and the renouncing of wealth among Christians in late antiquity, see Peter Brown, *Through the Eye of a Needle: Wealth, the Fall of Rome, and the Making of Christianity in the West, 350–550 AD* (Princeton, NJ: Princeton University Press, 2012), 208–23. For a thorough perspective on Paulinus's renunciation as described in his own writings, see Dennis E. Trout, *Paulinus of Nola: Life, Letters, and Poems* (Berkeley: University of California Press, 1999), 79–103.

and writer from Aquitaine who composed a church history as well as a biography of Martin of Tours.[8]

Through his letters, Paulinus also carried on a thriving friendship with Augustine for twenty-five years, though they never met in person. As previously mentioned, some have argued that Paulinus initiated this relationship looking to Augustine not so much as a friend, but as a "Christian sage."[9] While this may have been part of the reason, Paulinus's desire for wisdom from Augustine was not contrary to friendship but rather enhanced by it. As Augustine corresponded with the couple and their friendship blossomed, he sought mutual encouragement between himself and his correspondents in the pursuit of the heavenly life. In this way, the divine love that was central to spiritual friendship according to Augustine was the mutually-cherished nourishment needed for each one to experience deeper levels of heavenly intimacy.

LETTER 24

The beginning of their relationship is represented by Letter 24, a short letter from Paulinus to Alypius, Augustine's close friend. This letter, written in 394, expressed Paulinus and Therasia's gratitude and acknowledged receipt of five books from Augustine against the Manichees.[10] The tenor of their writing suggests that they viewed Augustine with high admiration. In this letter, Paulinus and Therasia indicated a certain desire to come under the tutelage of Augustine, recognizing his authority on spiritual matters.

LETTER 25

Having heard of and read works from Augustine, Paulinus and Therasia were compelled to write to Augustine around the year 394. Paulinus described the intimacy with which he knew Augustine based simply on his writings.[11] Paulinus

---

8. For an introduction to Sulpicius Severus, including a recent translation of his works, see *Sulpicius Severus: The Complete Works*, trans. Richard J. Goodrich, Ancient Christian Writers 70 (New York: Paulist, 2015).

9. McCann, "'You Know Better than I Do,'" 191.

10. These books are likely *On True Religion, On Genesis Against the Manichaeans in Two Books, On the Morals of the Catholic Church*, and *On the Morals of the Manichaeans*. For an overview, see Trout, *Paulinus of Nola*, 203n36.

11. *Epistula* 25.2.

appreciated the five books against Manichaeism, which he had received from Augustine, and requested even more writings in defense of the Catholic faith. Relaying the schemes of the enemy against the faithful, Paulinus asked to be further equipped from Augustine's "armory."[12] Paulinus described himself as a "creeping infant" in need of a spiritual guide to bring him to maturity and help him walk.[13] He was looking to be nourished by Augustine's words as if he were a "suckling child." The imagery of a child or infant was used repeatedly to demonstrate Paulinus's desire to learn from Augustine, who though younger in age, was considered a father in the faith.[14] Paulinus continued to praise Augustine's spiritual leadership and wisdom by comparing him to a "harbor of salvation" in the midst of spiritual storms.[15] Augustine was viewed as not only a man of rich spiritual wisdom, well-versed in Scripture, but as one who has Paulinus viewed as having a combination of wisdom, faith, and love and to whom Paulinus felt himself drawn. Though they share the same ecclesial rank of priest, Paulinus did not count himself spiritually worthy to be ranked as such. Paulinus noted that Alypius, a common friend, had also served as a spiritual father through his writings. The letter ended with an affectionate reminder of their brotherhood, illustrated by a loaf of bread that had been given to demonstrate oneness with Augustine.

LETTER 27

Augustine responded to Paulinus in 396 with spiritual encouragement, noting the impatience of his mind in not being able to see Paulinus physically. A single thought about Paulinus was excruciating for his soul.[16] His impatience revealed a holy dissatisfaction with the current situation, and thereby revealed the depth of friendship between Paulinus and Augustine. His grief was a comfort, for it confirmed the longing for the heavenly Jerusalem.[17] Augustine compared this predicament to having a friend in the same city, yet not knowing where he lived. He mourned, for though he had come to know Paulinus's mind through his writing, he was unable to

---

12. *Epistula* 25.2.
13. *Epistula* 25.3.
14. *Epistula* 25.3.
15. *Epistula* 25.3.
16. *Epistula* 27.1.
17. *Epistula* 27.1.

see the "home" or dwelling-place of that mind.[18] Augustine extoled the level of piety present within Paulinus's writing. His letter exhaled the "sweet smell of Christ."[19] This made it all the more difficult for Augustine to endure the absence of Paulinus though he possessed a small piece of him in his letter.[20] In his letter to Augustine, "Christ is awakened in order that he might graciously calm the winds and the seas for you as you move toward his solid ground."[21]

From here, Augustine sought to encourage Paulinus who had lamented a certain lack of spiritual discernment. Augustine assured Paulinus that Christ was able to calm the storms in his heart and direct his path. Based on his decision to deny the world and its temporary comforts, Paulinus need not worry about lacking any sort of spiritual vitality. In his pursuit of Christian purity, Paulinus had scorned earthly glory in order to gain true glory, and gave up the temporary world in order to gain the better world.[22] He continued to encourage Paulinus, noting how great a "holy love" and "sincere heart" were communicated in his letter to Augustine.[23] Augustine was thus convinced, based on his "letter of pure love," that Paulinus was already practicing the very thing he for which he was searching.[24] In this search, Augustine emphasized he was not the sort of expert that Paulinus portrayed him to be. This admonition sought to deflect the praise away from Augustine and onto God who was the true source of wisdom. Augustine implored Paulinus to pray for those things which he lacked and not presume that he had already obtained them.[25]

Augustine thus demonstrated how to accept praise without allowing it to go to one's head. Though Paulinus recognized his spiritual authority, Augustine was conscious that in this world no one ever truly arrives at the place of spiritual maturity where further growth is not necessary. Augustine was cognizant of the fact that, though the Lord had used him to speak truth,

---

18. *Epistula* 27.1.
19. *Epistula* 27.2.
20. *Epistula* 27.2.
21. *Epistula* 27.2.
22. *Epistula* 27.2.
23. *Epistula* 27.3.
24. *Epistula* 27.3.
25. *Epistula* 27.3.

he was still a weak vessel and capable of error. It was possible for friendship to cloud one's judgment; therefore, all praise was due to God.[26]

Augustine spent the rest of the letter commending both Alypius, their common friend, Romanian, the letter bearer, and Licentius, Romanian's son.[27] These various commendations not only provided a connecting point between Augustine and Paulinus, but also served as a way to further encourage Paulinus regarding his own ability to be a spiritual example. Though the exact situation is now unclear, Augustine conveyed concern regarding Licentius, who was living among the "weeds" and unaware of the spiritual danger he was posing to himself in his life decisions.[28] Augustine was certain that through Paulinus, the wayward Licentius would be "consoled, exhorted and instructed," and that Paulinus would set a strong spiritual example.[29] Augustine concluded the letter by imploring Paulinus to correct and reprove whatever might be displeasing. Augustine sent Paulinus greetings from all the African Christians and extended the invitation to visit if freedom from ecclesiastical duties allowed.

LETTER 30

This letter was written in late 394 before Paulinus had received Augustine's response (Letter 27) to his previous letter. It was written as a reminder, or even an extension of the first letter, so that Augustine would know Paulinus's urgent desire to receive a response. Paulinus stressed that it was through Augustine's writings, and the witness of their common friends Aurelius and Alypius, that his brotherly affection for Augustine continued to burn brightly. To Paulinus, this affection was much more than a new friendship; it was like an old love that "was implanted in us to so that it does not seem that we are beginning a new friendship with you, but resuming an old one, as it were."[30] Paulinus connected the affection they had to the indwelling Spirit, which is shared by all of Christ's body. Employing such "oneness" imagery was central to the mutual connections upon which their affection

---

26. *Epistula* 27.4.

27. Licentius was a common friend who appears in Augustine's early dialogues at Cassiciacum, including his *Against the Academics*, *On the Good Life*, and *On Order*.

28. *Epistula* 27.6.

29. *Epistula* 27.6.

30. *Epistula* 30.2.

was based. The one body of Christ enjoys the common grace and union of faith.[31] Friendship and affection were thus grounded in this oneness of faith shared through Christ and distributed by the Spirit. It was this spiritual nearness that made the physical distance bearable. So strong was this spiritual connection that Paulinus noted that they would be destroyed if they fell away from the common faith that they shared.[32] Paulinus was wrestling with letting go of his desire to see Augustine in the flesh. He affirmed that the resurrection guaranteed their presence with one another in the future, yet Paulinus continued to believe that Augustine's physical presence could have the benefit of encouraging his spiritual life. Were they to spend time face to face, it would undoubtedly enhance Paulinus's spirituality and his "poverty would be enriched by [Augustine's] abundance."[33]

LETTER 31

This letter, written in late 396 or early 397, was Augustine's reply to Paulinus and Therasia's second letter. Augustine had not had a chance to reply to Letter 25 before Letter 30 arrived. Thus, he saw the delay of his first letter as the Lord's kindness, providing another opportunity to write to his friends which was "more conducive to [his] happiness."[34] Augustine went on to highlight the letter-bearers' testimony about Paulinus which provided a sense of Paulinus's presence. This living letter provided Augustine and his community the opportunity to "transcribe in our own hearts what was written in theirs."[35] There was a certain sweetness which came from Paulinus's letter which gave Augustine cause to desire "more avidly" to see Paulinus in person.[36] Their relationship, carried on exclusively through epistolary exchange, was enhanced by the description of their spiritual character and physicality by each letter-bearer.[37]

---

31. *Epistula* 30.2.
32. *Epistula* 30.2.
33. *Epistula* 30.3.
34. *Epistula* 31.1.
35. *Epistula* 31.2.
36. *Epistula* 31.2.
37. For more on the role of the letter-bearer in perpetuating relationships, see Pauline Allen, "Prolegomena to a Study of the Letter-Bearer in Christian Antiquity," *Studia Patristica*, 62 (2013):481–91.

Augustine continued to encourage Paulinus and Therasia by calling attention to their mutual union in Christ's body. This union was expressed in the
love (*dilectio*) they shared with each other, a love by which they were "kept
alive by one Spirit."[38] Thus, love was at the center of this friendship and
was maintained by the Spirit's power. This Spirit-wrought love equipped
Paulinus and Therasia with the ability to persevere in the face of hardship.
Augustine likewise needed the Spirit's power to stand firm in the midst of his
own hardships, particularly those of the episcopate which he shared during
this time with Valerius.[39] In speaking of his burdens, Augustine employed
two images that graphically described his situation: pastoral ministry was
a grinding "chain" capable of harm and a "load" that overtook him in his
"recalcitrance and weakness."[40]

The spiritual union of Augustine with his two correspondents, and his
desire to strengthen their monastic pursuit, led the North African bishop
to focus upon Paulinus and Therasia's renunciation of wealth. Their act of
renouncing earthly goods was undoubtedly sincere, but renouncing one's
wealth was not enough. Those wishing to live a true life of renunciation
ought to give up "not only as much as he was able to have, but also as much
as he wanted to have."[41] Peter Brown reminds his readers, "Paulinus's decision should not be taken for granted. Many options existed in the minds of
fourth-century Christians when they thought of the way their wealth could
be used for pious purposes."[42] Augustine knew these options all too well. Thus,
he implored Paulinus and Therasia to ensure that their renunciation reached
into their hearts as well as their pockets. He prompted them to consider it a
joy to tear away any remaining attachment to worldly goods since "God's eyes
are witnesses of one's desires."[43] Even more so, they must guard themselves

---

38. *Epistula* 31.3 (CSEL 34:3).

39. *Epistula* 31.4. Augustine mentions Valerius as one who likewise longed for Paulinus and
Therasia's presence. Augustine was coadjutor bishop with Valerius from his ordination in 391
until his death in 396 or 397. Edward Smither notes, "Valerius was [Augustine's] most signifi-
cant mentor." Edward L. Smither, *Augustine as Mentor: A Model for Preparing Spiritual Leaders*
(Nashville: B & H Academic, 2009), 112. For more on the influence of Valerius upon Augustine, see
Smither, "Unrecognized and Unlikely Influence? The Impact of Valerius of Hippo on Augustine,"
Irish Theological Quarterly 72, no. 3 (2007): 251–64.

40. *Epistula* 31.4.

41. *Epistula* 31.5.

42. Brown, *Through the Eye of a Needle*, 226.

43. *Epistula* 31.5.

against pride in their renunciation, for renunciation with humility gives glory to God and leads to the "hope of perfection."[44] Augustine encouraged them to make known the deeper nature of their spiritual renunciation, presumably for the benefit of onlookers in need of a worthy example to imitate.[45]

In sum, Augustine sought not only to encourage Paulinus and Therasia, but he also wished to be encouraged by them. This further demonstrated the mutual pursuit of Christlike virtue perpetuated by their friendship. Even though Paulinus and Therasia lauded his spirituality, Augustine was still conscious of his own need for growth and spiritual support. He requested a writing from Paulinus entitled *Against the Pagans* in order to be enlightened by such an "oracle of the Lord."[46] This demonstrates that Augustine's posture was also one of a learner, even though Paulinus and Therasia considered themselves pupils of Augustine. Augustine's encouragement to make their renunciation more visible was a testimony to their spiritual vitality, and he knew it would serve to encourage the greater church. In the end, their spiritual life would require the ongoing protection and grace of God, who was the one who made them truly excellent.[47]

LETTER 94

Paulinus and Therasia wrote again to Augustine in May of 408. Paulinus hoped to have Augustine instruct him further on the spiritual life, as well as to answer various questions that had arisen from his reading of Scripture. He recounted how Augustine's previous letter had been spiritual food for his

---

44. *Epistula* 31.6.

45. *Epistula* 31.6. Smither notes, "Aside from his own example, Augustine believed that imitating holy examples resulted in spiritual growth." Smither, *Augustine as Mentor*, 230. The encouragement to make their example known was yet another way in which Augustine sought to coach Paulinus and Therasia in their monastic journey. Such examples were important for discipleship in the church, as they continue to be today. Thus, Augustine saw the need for spiritual examples in order to encourage the faithful and convert the lost. Athanasius's *Life of Antony* was one such example which provided impetus for Augustine's eventual conversion. Biographies of the era were also written in such a way as to provide a spiritual example to readers. In this tradition, Augustine likely wished for Paulinus and Therasia's example to be made known for the spiritual encouragement of other believers.

46. *Epistula* 31.8. This work is now lost. Analyzing the historical context around Paulinus's renunciation and subsequent loss of face among Roman pagan elite, Trout suggests, "Paulinus's imminent composition of a now lost work 'against the pagans (*adversus paganos*)' may rather signal his desire to distance himself from such old friends and acquaintances." Trout, *Paulinus of Nola*, 113.

47. *Epistula* 31.9.

soul that he had devoured. In Paulinus's words, "[It] was for me most sweet on my lips and in my heart. ... I feasted on the spiritual delights of your letter."[48] Paulinus then took the occasion to highlight the family of Melania the Elder, including her son Publicola, who had recently died.[49] His direct connection to Melania and her family is unclear, though he mentioned elsewhere that a connection by blood existed.[50] Paulinus admired her as a supreme example of Christian virtue, comparing Augustine to her as "a spirit closer to hers or more equal to her soul."[51] Her courage was commendable at the loss of her son, Publicola. This recent circumstance, and Melania's reaction, provide a segue into a deeper spiritual conversation regarding the resurrection and how to properly view one's temporal circumstances.

Paulinus understood that love for Christ is the supreme source of one's desire and ability to "die to the elements of this world."[52] Christ provided the "stability" which enabled believers to wait for future glory and persevere in virtue in this life.[53] The future hope of the resurrection, with Christ being "a mirror for the contemplation of all," leads to a host of questions and reflections from Paulinus to Augustine. Especially important to Paulinus was understanding the nature of the spiritual body given to the saints at the resurrection. This in turn raised the question of angels and their heavenly existence as spiritual beings. Paul's reference to the "tongues of angels" (1 Cor 13:1) caused Paulinus to inquire of Augustine what he thinks this could look or sound like. For one seeking the spiritual life, this was of utmost concern. Was the "tongues of angels" something that could be experienced now, or was this something to look forward to in the life to come? These

---

48. *Epistula* 94.1.

49. For an overview of the life and contribution of Melania the Elder, see Francis X. Murphy, "Melania the Elder: A Biographical Note," *Traditio* 5 (1947): 59–77. The fact that Paulinus was connected to this important figure is noteworthy, especially in light of his own pursuit of monastic spirituality. Murphy notes, "[Melania the Elder] is of particular importance in tracing the history of late-fourth-century asceticism and monasticism. ... [She] was an extremely interesting, well-travelled, and forceful figure coming at the apex of the western patristic period" (59). For more recent perspectives on Melania the Elder, including the contribution of her entire family to doctrine and practice in the early church, see Catherine M. Chin and Caroline T. Schroeder, eds., *Melania: Early Christianity Through the Life of One Family* (Berkeley: University of California Press, 2016).

50. Trout, *Paulinus of Nola*, 26.

51. *Epistula* 94.3.

52. *Epistula* 94.5.

53. *Epistula* 94.5.

tongues, Paulinus concluded, were likely attributed to "glorified flesh" and something to be experienced among "those heavenly and angelic ones" and perhaps as a future reward.[54] Paulinus earnestly desired Augustine to guide him on this particular matter of the spiritual life. As a "needy and poor fellow," Paulinus looked to Augustine as "someone truly wise" and "enlightened with the spirit of revelation."[55]

LETTER 95

At the outset of this letter, composed in late 408 or early 409—on the heels of Letter 94—Augustine expressed love toward Paulinus and Therasia. He longed to see them so much that theoretically he was willing "to cross the sea for the sole purpose of enjoying [their] presence."[56] What prevented Augustine were the "chains" of pastoral ministry which bound him.[57] Augustine then began to address questions posed by Paulinus and Therasia in the previous letter. Their epistolary dialogue centered on the nature of eternal life, as well as how to live one's earthly life fully surrendered to the gospel. Augustine emphasized, "[We] ought to live in this mortal life so that we in a sense prepare ourselves for immortal life."[58]

This affirmation led Augustine to acknowledge a dilemma: how does one live such a life among those who were not yet committed to live in such a way? It was inconceivable to Augustine how one could live and work among such people without having to, at least in a small measure "adapt ourselves to them," in order be an aid in their salvation.[59] The danger, in Augustine's mind, was that such spiritual negotiating would lead to finding delight in lesser things and "weigh down our souls with certain loves that are not merely dusty, but even muddy (*ita pulvereis quibusdam, vel etiam luteis affectibus nostras animas aggravantes*)."[60] Thus, Augustine corrected and coached Paulinus and Therasia toward loves which contribute to building up their souls. Augustine was certain that the correction received in this life directly affected the view and path

---

54. *Epistula* 94.6.
55. *Epistula* 94.7.
56. *Epistula* 95.1.
57. *Epistula* 95.1.
58. *Epistula* 95.2.
59. *Epistula* 95.2.
60. *Epistula* 95.2 (CSEL 34.2:507).

of one's eternal life. He turned to Scripture which contains a considerable number of passages where Christians are called to "judge," "rebuke," or "reprehend" those who are wayward.[61] Scripture also warns Christians not to do so prematurely. He invited Paulinus and Therasia to reflect on this dilemma with him. Augustine recognized that correcting and rebuking could easily lead to hatred "even between very dear and very close friends."[62] Though one could easily judge another's actions prematurely, taking time to reflect and consider was "much better than rashness in making assertions."[63]

Therefore, Augustine wished to avoid any hasty judgment by encouraging and correcting his fellow Christians with a sober mind. In this way, Augustine affirmed Paulinus's desire to reflect critically on their temporal state of life, yet asserted that the "course" was more important than the "state."[64] Their mutual reflection on this matter, according to Augustine, should focus upon the heavenly destination of this earthly life. By keeping this perspective, "the desires of the flesh [will] be reined in, that we should grant to the delights of the bodily senses only as much as is enough for sustaining and living such a life."[65] By viewing their lives in eternal perspective, temporal troubles could be better understood and dealt with, and their concern for their neighbor could increase "with all the zeal of love in order that he may correctly live this life for the sake of eternal life."[66] In the pursuit of the spiritual life, as opposed to the carnal life, one can only succeed by the grace of God; yet how God's grace helps some and not others remained a mystery to Augustine.[67] "I do, however," Augustine confessed, "know that God does this with the highest justice, which is known to him."[68]

Augustine's main concern was to understand how to best live with human beings who may be less inclined to pursue the spiritual life. He begs Paulinus and Therasia to share any wisdom they may have on the matter.[69] Briefly

---

61. *Epistula* 95.3.
62. *Epistula* 95.4.
63. *Epistula* 95.4.
64. *Epistula* 95.5.
65. *Epistula* 95.6.
66. *Epistula* 95.4.
67. *Epistula* 95.6.
68. *Epistula* 95.6.
69. *Epistula* 95.6.

addressing the state of the believer's resurrected body, Augustine could only affirm what had been spoken in Scripture. He took a moment to work through the biblical evidence for the resurrected state, demonstrating all the abilities that will be present, yet affirming a final lack of knowledge on how "the character of a spiritual body, unknown as it is to us, can be either comprehended or taught."[70] This discussion lent itself to reflection on angelic bodies in comparison, though once again, discussion was limited to the occasional biblical evidence. Augustine concluded that "in that divine society" there would be a harmonious praise of God expressed "not only by the spirit, but also by the spiritual body."[71]

In sum, Augustine's correspondence with Paulinus and Therasia reveals a deep and abiding friendship based on a mutual desire to converse on heavenly things. A deep and mutual love existed and grew between these friends as they encouraged one another toward Christlike virtue and reflection upon various matters pertaining to the spiritual life. Though Paulinus and Therasia looked to Augustine as a teacher and guide in all things spiritual, Augustine demonstrated a heartfelt desire not only to instruct, but to know these friends more deeply and personally and to be mutually encouraged by them. While this relationship may have seemed hierarchical, Augustine's being a mentor did not hurt the friendship; rather, it gave it shape and allowed it to flourish.[72]

LETTERS 130, 131, 150:
PROBA AND A LIFE OF PRAYER

Moving to another example, Augustine sought to bring spiritual encouragement to the wealthy Roman widow Proba who wrote to Augustine requesting how she ought to pray. Proba, experiencing the fall of Rome under the Gothic invasion led by Alaric, had come to Africa along with her daughter Juliana, also a widow, and her grand-niece Demetrias.[73] In his response,

---

70. *Epistula* 95.7.

71. *Epistula* 95.8.

72. McCann notes how such discipleship relationships have a hierarchical structure. McCann, "'You Know Better than I Do,'" 192.

73. The fall of Rome in 410–411 under Alaric had driven many wealthy citizens to North Africa for refuge. Augustine dealt variously with the fall of Rome throughout his ministry. For a helpful look at the effects of barbarian invasions of Rome, see Lucien Musset, *The Germanic Invasions: The Making of Europe, AD 400–600*, trans. Edward James and Columba James (University Park: Pennsylvania State University Press, 1975).

Augustine provided a thorough biblical theology of prayer. For Augustine, prayer does not reveal our needs to God, but rather operates on our desires so that our hearts are enlarged to humbly receive whatever God chooses to give us. As George Demacopoulos has noted, "[What] is most interesting is that although Augustine's letters to women lacked a sensitive touch they actually offered more practical advice than those he addressed to his many male correspondents."[74] As will be shown below, not only did Augustine offer practical advice, but his supposed lack of "sensitive touch" was reflective of his desire to encourage and admonish as necessary. Spiritual encouragement, more than sensitivity, was needed for Proba and her desire to live according to monastic ideals. Additionally, as Joseph Clair has noted, Augustine's goal was to present the "better goods" toward obtaining the happy life.[75]

LETTER 130

Letter 130, written around 411, came at Proba's request imploring Augustine to inform her on how to best pray to God. Having been delayed, Augustine undertook the task "in the love of Christ."[76] His response is best described as a "thorough and sophisticated treatise on petitionary prayer," communicating his "most mature and sympathetic statements on his ideal of the Christian life."[77] Augustine began by assessing his recipient's situation. Proba, being a widow of means, did not seem to match the description of being "desolate" given by Paul in 1 Timothy 5:5 (KJV). Though not desolate, Proba nevertheless had persisted in her desire to live a prayerful life. Her call therefore was to regard herself "as desolate in this world" by following

Augustine's response to the fall of Rome is notable in *De civitate Dei* (*The City of God*) though this work morphed into a full-fledged Christian philosophy of history and theodicy. For additional perspectives on Augustine and the fall of Rome, see R. Arbesmann, "The Idea of Rome in the Sermons of St. Augustine," *Augustiniana* 4 (1954): 305–24; T. E. Mommsen, "St. Augustine and the Christian Idea of Progress: The Background of *The City of God*," *Journal of the History of Ideas* 12 (1951): 346–74.

74. George E. Demacopoulos, *Five Models of Spiritual Direction in the Early Church* (Notre Dame, IN: University of Notre Dame Press, 2006), 93.

75. Clair, *Discerning the Good*, 52–65.

76. *Epistula* 130.1.1.

77. Joanna McWilliam, "Augustine's Letters to Women," in *Feminist Interpretations of Augustine*, ed. Judith Chelius Stark (University Park: Pennsylvania State University Press, 2007), 196; Brown, *Augustine of Hippo*, 345.

the apostolic declaration to not place her hope in the riches of this world, but rather to be rich in good works and share her wealth for the purpose of attaining true life.[78] Her situation in life had afforded her much consolation; however, such comforts were ridden with "the fear of their loss" and the reality that mankind does not "become good because of such goods."[79] Happiness was not to be found in this life, however pleasant it could be, but was to be found in love for that "true life" which is found in God alone.[80] The path toward true life, and hence happiness, comes from seeking and finding joy "from what makes one good."[81]

There are those who are able to provide consolation through the trials of this life because God "by his Spirit makes them good [and] does all this in them and through them."[82] Though fearful things will always happen in life, a dear friend is vital to enjoy anything pertaining to humanity.[83] That said, no one can have absolute certainty regarding the stability of one's friend. Where then was the true consolation that Proba should seek? In this life of darkness, Augustine recommends turning to the light of "the divine and holy scriptures, as if to a lamp set in a dark place, until the day dawns and the morning star rises in our hearts."[84] The "ineffable source" of this lamp can only be perceived by the eyes of faith, and it is this source that offers stimulus for prayer.[85] Augustine thus directed Proba's gaze toward the Scriptures as the best place to encounter God and find rest and encouragement. His desire was for Proba to be shaped by the light of Scripture for the purpose of

---

78. *Epistula* 130.2.3.

79. *Epistula* 130.2.3.

80. *Epistula* 130.2.3.

81. *Epistula* 130.2.3. Clair places the discussion of "goods" and "the good" in perspective of *oikeiosis*, the traditional Stoic understanding of ordering the good and one's inclination toward them. He notes the tension of either casting aside goods, or transforming lower-level goods for the purpose of obtaining higher-level goods. Clair notes, "Augustine presents the double-commandment of love to Proba as higher-level *oikeiosis*. In obeying the commands, one's impulse for self-preservation—extending into family life—and one's duty to God and neighbor merge into affective harmony." Clair, *Discerning the Good*, 53.

82. *Epistula* 130.2.4.

83. *Epistula* 130.2.4.

84. *Epistula* 130.2.5.

85. *Epistula* 130.2.5.

prayer.[86] While Scripture is primary, there is the coming day when our prayer will be obsolete as "there will be no temptation. ... [and] no expectation of the good that was promised, but the contemplation of the good that has been received."[87] In Scripture, Proba would find a true description of the future life and the promises of good things to come, which are a motivation, including a life of prayer. Even if this temporal life were not as desolate and uncertain, in comparison, the happiness to come is much greater.[88]

Prayer, therefore, acts as a preparation for eternity, recognizing the desolations of this life and eagerly seeking the consolation of the life to come. Since the consolation of eternity has yet to come, one must persist in prayer. Though Proba wrote to ask him about the nature of prayer, Augustine encouraged her to set her eyes on the greater reality of the heavenly city that in turn informs the practice of prayer in this life. He hoped Proba would feel the desolation of a life of wealth, and citing Paul, he exhorted her to be vigilant that she not live for pleasure.[89] Supporting her spiritual life included Augustine helping her see the utter despondency that would result from placing her hope in this life—the life to come would be much sweeter. Augustine exhorted Proba stating, "If pleasures abound, do not set your heart upon them. ... Disdain and scorn these things utterly in yourself so that you do not seek anything in them but full well-being of the body."[90]

Noting her status as a wealthy widow with a family, Augustine was hesitant to encourage her to divest herself of her wealth for the sake of the poor. Though "many holy men and women" had distributed their riches "as if [they] were the mothers of these pleasures," Proba had previously indicated a desire to retain her wealth for the sake of caring for her family.[91] Though her cause appeared justified, Augustine still warned her of the danger that

---

86. Rebecca Weaver notes, "Augustine insisted that entrusting oneself to the language of Scripture not only teaches one what to desire but actually produces the desire in the one who is taught. Wholehearted engagement with the words molds the consciousness of the one who uses them. In this manner Scripture, rather than the individual, sets the agenda for prayer." Rebecca Weaver, "Prayer," in Fitzgerald, *Augustine through the Ages*, s.v. "Prayer."

87. *Epistula* 130.2.5.

88. *Epistula* 130.2.5.

89. *Epistula* 130.3.7. Referencing 1 Tim 5:6, Augustine observed, "For a person lives amid the things which he loves, which he desires as important, by which he thinks he is happy."

90. *Epistula* 130.3.7.

91. *Epistula* 130.3.8.

riches could have on one's affections. In order to properly pray, and pursue the happy life, Proba needed to ensure that she did not weigh down her heart with temporal pleasures.

With this in mind, Augustine encouraged her to pray for the happy life. The discussion of the happy life, no little topic among philosophers, was readily accessible to Proba since its source was God. The happy life was something all people desired, but only those who truly sought God could attain. Augustine himself had reflected on the happy life early on in his Christian life, amongst friends, including his mother Monica, at Cassiciacum.[92] In the epistolary exchange with Proba, he invited her into this discussion, sharing with Proba his deep philosophical reflection for the purpose of directing her gaze to the proper source of happiness. This topic was not only for the elite few amongst philosophical schools, but it was accessible to any who claimed the name of Christ. Happiness, according to Augustine, related to the desire for the right amount of temporal goods for the right purpose. This included those things necessary for health as well as friendship. Happiness involved showing love to all, which Augustine related to friendship, though he provided some nuance. As he stated,

> Friendship should not be bounded by narrow limits, for it embraces all to whom we owe affection and love, though it is inclined more eagerly toward some and more hesitantly toward others. It, however, extends even to enemies, for whom we are also commanded to pray. Thus there is no one in the human race to whom we do not owe love, even if not out of mutual love, at least on account of our sharing in a common nature.[93]

---

92. Augustine previously stated, "The man who is happy possesses God. ... Whoever comes to the Supreme Measure through Truth is happy. This is the soul's possession and fruition of God." *De vita beata* 4.34; quoted from Eugene TeSelle, *Augustine the Theologian* (New York: Herder & Herder, 1970; reprint, Eugene, OR: Wipf & Stock, 202), 65. Reflecting on Augustine and happiness, TeSelle notes, "Like the movement away from God, the movement back toward God is a change not of place but of affection. ... In part this is a matter of having the right ultimate aims, for happiness can only be found in the possession of something which truly makes man happy and which cannot perish or be taken away; the love of God is therefore the only reasonable and feasible kind of love, the only one that can gain what it seeks." TeSelle, *Augustine*, 111. On relating Augustine and happiness to other— particularly Stoic—notions of happiness, see James Wetzel, *Augustine and the Limits of Virtue* (Cambridge: Cambridge University Press, 1992). For a helpful discussion on the internal and external nature of happiness, see Clair, *Discerning the Good*, 17–26.

93. *Epistula* 130.6.13.

Thus our prayer life should include praying for the acquisition or retention of these basic goods for the purpose of sharing with and loving others.

While affirming the acquisition of basic goods pertaining to bodily and personal health, Augustine warned of the danger to one's soul in preferring temporal things to eternal ones.[94] Augustine implored Proba to remain steadfast in prayer and in the pursuit of love for God and love for others. Since Proba had yet to reach perfection in her ability to love, as he would admit for himself, prayer was therefore vital; otherwise they might suppose "that we are already situated in the happy life itself."[95] Augustine recognized that the world often brought distraction, capable of unsettling one's prayer life. This is why Augustine encouraged Proba to look to the example of the Lord's Prayer in order to reorient her heart back to the happy life.[96] The prayer life of a saint was meant to be simple; yet due to temporal goods clouding one's vision, it was often difficult to see the simplicity of prayer.

In exhorting Proba to the simple prayer life based on the example of Christ, Augustine sought to comfort her by affirming that prayer was not a disclosure of the person's will to God, which he already knows, but a preparation of our desires "by which we can receive what he prepares to give, to be exercised in prayers."[97] This is why prayer should be continually filled with the Christian virtues of faith, hope, and love. This should be the normal posture of prayer for Proba and all who sought to pray in a way that honored God. The words used in prayers should serve to "admonish ourselves [and we will] realize how much we have advanced in this desire, and arouse ourselves more intensely to increase it."[98] Augustine asserted that prayer did not reveal to God what he does not already know, yet was a way in which we become more fully known to ourselves before God. Hence praying for long periods was appropriate, not as an exercise in word proliferation, but as spiritual discipline of being in the presence of the Lord. Christ himself set this example in order to demonstrate "a lasting love" for God.[99]

---

94. *Epistula* 130.7.14.

95. *Epistula* 130.7.14. This demonstrates that Augustine did not perceive that the happy life was fully obtainable in this life.

96. *Epistula* 130.8.15.

97. *Epistula* 130.8.17.

98. *Epistula* 130.9.18.

99. *Epistula* 130.10.19.

Thus prayer was less about words and more about posture according to Augustine. Persistence and fervor were the key traits of a successful prayer life. Sighs rather than words and weeping rather than speaking was the true language of prayer.[100] The words of one's prayers are not for God as if he does not already know, but for the person praying in order that they may be reminded of who God is and the promises that he has made. Specifically, Augustine worked through the Lord's Prayer with Proba to show her the essence of prayer. The Lord's Prayer for Augustine aids the Christian in his or her journey toward God as the singular focus of the believer's desire.[101] Regarding the prayer's line, "deliver us from evil," Augustine explained how such a petition covers a wide range of needs. He noted, "And this petition that is placed last in the Lord's Prayer is, of course, so widely applicable that, in whatever tribulation Christians may find themselves, they utter their groans in it, pour forth their tears in it, begun with it, linger over it, and bring their prayers to an end with it. For it was necessary that the truth itself be committed to our memory by these words."[102] It is helpful to note that Augustine viewed the Lord's Prayer from the perspective of a pilgrim.[103] The instructions he gave to Proba on prayer from the Lord's Prayer provide a helpful reflection for prayer in the Augustinian perspective, as Augustine never produced an individual treatise on prayer or on the Lord's Prayer specifically. This is of particular interest given that he stands in the shadow of previous North African fathers' reflection on the Lord's Prayer.[104]

Augustine prompted Proba to remember her pilgrimage through this world and how it informed her entire life of prayer. All other prayers, though using other words "[are] contained in that prayer of the Lord if we pray correctly and properly."[105] Anything outside these boundaries is a "carnal"

---

100. *Epistula* 130.10.20.

101. Weaver, "Prayer," 672.

102. *Epistula* 130.11.22.

103. Weaver notes, "Augustine's interpretation of the Lord's Prayer coincided with his notion of pilgrimage. ... Those who make these petitions are joined in pilgrimage toward the God who would be the sole object of their desire. ... According to Augustine, in the first three petitions of the Lord's Prayer the pilgrim asks to be made acceptable to God through a process that would begin in this life but be completed only in eternity." Weaver, "Prayer," 672.

104. For more on early Christian interpretations in North Africa, see Michael Joseph Brown, *The Lord's Prayer Through North African Eyes: A Window into Early Christianity* (New York: T & T Clark, 2004).

105. *Epistula* 130.12.22.

prayer.[106] Those who are abiding in the Christian virtues of faith, hope, and love will be certain that their prayers will accord with Christ's pattern.[107] This pattern of prayerful contemplation leads one along the journey toward the "one true and only happy life," which is the eternal delight of contemplating the Lord for eternity, "immortal and incorruptible in body and in spirit."[108] Thus, as Jonathan Teubner has observed, verbal petition is necessary, yet it extends as "a discipline of the affections."[109] The expectations of this life inform one's prayer life: "we must thirst in prayer ... in order that we may be inebriated by the richness of his house and may drink of the torrent of his pleasure."[110] Augustine encouraged his recipient to desire eternity in order to place temporal trials in the proper perspective—our desires will never be satisfied in this life. Even when we struggle to pray as we ought, as Paul intimated in Romans 8:26, such ignorance is a "certain learned ignorance" in order that we would more fully rely on the Holy Spirit in anticipation of "so great a still unknown reality."[111]

Augustine presented Proba with further reflection upon different circumstances that should lead one to pray. Reflecting on Romans 8:26, Augustine maintains that such a confession is not opposed to the knowledge that one should pray the Lord's Prayer. Paul's primary concern was how to pray during times of trial and affliction, according to Augustine. When difficult seasons arise, Proba should identify with Paul in 2 Corinthians 12:9, where Christ's supply of grace proved to be sufficient.[112] Scripture provided ample warning regarding those who petition the Lord impatiently or for selfish gain. Scripture, in this sense, provides the reader with a catalog of impious

---

106. *Epistula* 130.12.22.

107. *Epistula* 130.13.24.

108. *Epistula* 130.13.27. On Augustine and contemplation, John Peter Kenney notes, "Contemplation is a mirror in which we glimpse the shining of our souls in the light of eternity. ... Through its practice were resolved the uncertainties of his earlier life and a spiritual God more real than the material cosmos revealed. His soul was arrested by the certainty of contemplation and, on his account, made newly aware of the poverty of its fallen state. Contemplation thus cleared the way for the action of grace within his soul." Kenney, *Contemplation and Classical Christianity*, 163.

109. Jonathan D. Teubner, *Prayer after Augustine: A Study in the Development of the Latin Tradition* (Oxford: Oxford University Press, 2018), 90.

110. *Epistula* 130.3.27.

111. *Epistula* 130.14.28.

112. *Epistula* 130.14.25. Augustine provides an alternate translation for 12:9, stating that "virtue is made perfect in weakness (*virtus in infirmitate perficitur*)."

petitions so that the Christian may approach the Lord humbly and without pretense. Augustine maintained,

> These events are included in scripture so that no one should think himself great if his prayers are heard when he impatiently asks for something that it would benefit him more not to obtain, or so that one is downcast and despairing about God's mercy toward him if his prayer is not heard when he is perhaps asking for something by which he would be afflicted more terribly if he received it or be corrupted by prosperity and completely ruined.[113]

In this exchange Augustine encouraged Proba to see Scripture as the language of prayer—Scripture "sets the agenda for prayer."[114] Using Scripture to encourage and challenge Proba, he ultimately invited her to step into the world of Scripture as if it is the world of prayer. Thus, Scripture was integral on the journey to align one's desires to the desires of God through prayer. Focusing on Scripture should illumine places in Proba's heart which find consolation in temporal goods rather than the eternal Good, which is God. Only a heart centered on Scripture as the impetus for prayer will be able to progress in this pilgrimage of growing in desire for God above any earthly comforts.

Augustine concluded with this final exhortation for Proba: prayer was a perpetual "struggle to conquer this world" through faith, hope, and love with persistence and patience.[115] Additionally, the calling upon Proba's life was to pray as a widow, for "more diligent concern for prayer is ... to be enjoined specially upon widows."[116] This was God's chosen station for Proba. Only when Proba fully understood this calling would she be able to commend herself to the Lord for his protection. Her widowhood was in Christ, and therefore she could be secured under the "protection of his wings."[117] In this, Proba would be an example to both her daughter-in-law Juliana and the other widows and virgins under her care. In her prayer life, she was to help others come along in the journey of prayer, regardless of their ability. Proba's charge was to encourage those in her household to do what they could. The demand of

---

113. *Epistula* 130.13.26.
114. Weaver, "Prayer," 672.
115. *Epistula* 130.4.29.
116. *Epistula* 130.4.29.
117. *Epistula* 130.3.27.

love for another required as much, yet she was ultimately responsible for her conscience before God.[118] In all his support and motivation, Augustine exhorted Proba herself to become an encourager to others. Thus, his encouragement was to be the foundation for Proba to do the same for others. In this way, Augustine demonstrated how the love of a Christian friend was to be replicated in the life of Proba.

LETTERS 131 AND 150

The subsequent letters—Letter 131 and Letter 150, written between the years 412 to 414—further show how Augustine supported and encouraged Proba in her spirituality. Proba continued to implore Augustine regarding questions of the spiritual life, namely, how to understand the relationship of the body and soul. Such a concern was directly related to a life of prayer, for the soul was "held in the grip of a certain earthly disease" because of its relationship to a fallen and corruptible body.[119] As Brown notes, "In man's fallen state, the body must still be disciplined. It remained for Augustine, a source of unrelieved disquiet."[120] Because of this, and because the desires of this life were deceptive, the soul in prayer centered on Christ is bound to "seek that harbor of true and certain security."[121] Considering the folly of this corruptible life, the rewards of the life to come were to be sought above all else. Augustine requested that Proba even pray for him in this regard, commending himself to the "love and prayer of [those] in whose hearts Christ dwells through faith."[122]

A year or two later, in Letter 150, Augustine commended the consecration of Juliana's daughter Demetrias. Demetrias had chosen the greater path of forgoing earthly marriage to seek a greater happiness by "imitating the life of the angels ... [rather] than by increasing the number of mortals in the flesh."[123] This would hopefully be an example to others who might trade earthly glory for heavenly glory. Under the guidance of Proba and Juliana, Demetrias would flourish in this calling and bring others along with them.

---

118. *Epistula* 130.4.31.

119. *Epistula* 131.

120. Peter Brown, *The Body and Society: Men, Women, and Sexual Renunciation in Early Christianity*, 2nd ed. (New York: Columbia University Press, 2008), 426.

121. *Epistula* 131.

122. *Epistula* 131.

123. *Epistula* 150.

LETTER 188: JULIANA AND DEMETRIAS
AND THE GRACE OF VIRGINITY

This letter, jointly written by Augustine and Alypius, was sent to Juliana as a reply to a letter of hers no longer extant. Juliana was a noble woman of Rome who had fled her home and come to Africa following the fall of Rome under Alaric in 410. Her family appears to have been influenced by the teachings of Pelagius, as her daughter Demetrias had received a letter from him at the request of Juliana, urging her toward a life of consecrated virginity.[124] In this letter, Pelagius extols inner strength and power as the means for pursuing a virginal vocation. This teaching, troubling to Augustine as it appeared to deny the necessity of God's grace, was dangerous and had to be corrected. The ability to fulfill the virginal calling, far from being innate, necessitated the grace of God, as it was a gift from him and thus was like a treasure to be stewarded. This notion combats pride and directs all boasting to the Lord. In this, both Augustine and Alypius supported and encouraged the vocation of virgins, seeking to correct false notions and coaching their correspondents toward a biblical understanding of life as a virgin.

The letter begins with an affirmation of love for Juliana and her daughter Demetrias, the recipient of Pelagius's troubling letter. There had arisen a "storm" of "fashionable, ascetic form of treatises on virginity," which were having deleterious effects on the laity according to Augustine.[125] Juliana and Demetrias had personally ministered to Augustine and Alypius by means of hospitality in their home among their family. It was in this context that the two bishops came to know Demetrias and her saintly manner of life, perceiving in her the desire to seek "the spiritual embrace of that husband … whom virgins marry in order to have a greater fecundity of the spirit."[126] It was only after their departure that they learned that Demetrias had taken vows as a consecrated virgin. In this letter, they sought to inform Demetrias that her calling was primarily a gift of God, yet one "which he plants and

---

124. Alison Bonner argues that this letter and related teachings by Pelagius have been misclassified as teachings separate from the ascetic movement. According to Bonner, Pelagius defended what had been considered accepted teachings on asceticism, and he is seen as one representative within the development of the ascetic movement in the West, especially as it evolved into the medieval monastic movement. For more, see Alison Clare Bonner, "The Scale, Context, and Implications, of the Manuscript Transmission of Pelagius' *Ad Demetriadem*" (PhD diss., University of Cambridge, 2012).

125. Brown, *The Body and Society*, 412.

126. *Epistula* 188.1.1.

waters through his servants."[127] Thus, they sought to warn their readers against the error of Pelagius and those "teachings opposed to the grace of God."[128] In fact, Juliana had welcomed such admonitions in her previous letter, which Augustine and Alypius quoted. Juliana and her family adhered to the Catholic faith, yet they were allowing the deadly error of Pelagius to creep in. This false teaching asserted that "nature and doctrine are by themselves the grace and help of God for living righteously and correctly."[129] The error of merit-based virginity insisted that the capacity for the virginal call came solely from within. Thinking oneself capable apart from God's gift of grace was spiritually detrimental. Augustine cited Paul in Romans 5:5 to demonstrate that the desire to love and follow God can come from him alone, namely by the Holy Spirit.[130] Therefore, the pursuit of godly things must have God as its primary and sustaining force.

To believe the contrary would nullify the grace of God and turn one's focus inward rather than upward. This keeps one from attaining "perfect happiness."[131] If one were to think that such goods existed in oneself, as Pelagius had asserted, the result would be "entirely poisonous."[132] Citing numerous passages from Paul, Augustine and Alypius asserted that the human heart is truly poor and that only the goods of the Bridegroom can adorn the bride.[133] Augustine and Alypius helped their correspondents to see virginity as a gracious gift, which ought to promote gratitude and humility.[134]

These examples highlight Augustine and Alypius's response as a biblical defense of a virgin's calling. They also used 2 Corinthians 11:2–3 to help Juliana and Demetrias understand the true nature of virginity and be wary of contrary arguments. In this text, Paul warned the church against an alternate spirit as opposed to the true gospel of Christ which he proclaimed. Paul's goal

---

127. *Epistula* 188.1.1.

128. *Epistula* 188.1.2.

129. *Epistula* 188.1.3.

130. *Epistula* 188.1.3.

131. *Epistula* 188.2.4.

132. *Epistula* 188.2.5.

133. Regarding their encouragement to Demetrias, Clair notes, "Celibate women marry themselves to Christ on earth, in the here and now, forgoing the temporal good of marriage out of a longing for Christ's spiritual embrace." Clair, *Discerning the Good*, 57.

134. *Epistula* 188.2.6.

was simple: presenting the church as a pure virgin to Christ. Paul desired to present the church to Christ as a pure virgin. In a similar way, Augustine conceived the vocation of virginity as an offering to Christ empowered by Christ. The gift of virginity was conferred by God, imparted by grace, so that they may fulfill the calling of chastity for the sake of the Lord.

Augustine and Alypius continually emphasize the idea of "gift" when it comes to the vocation of virginity. Such a calling "does not belong to her from herself, but is the gift of God, though one bestowed upon someone who believes and is willing."[135] Though this calling is a gift, a willing spirit must accompany the endowment. This bestowal, therefore, is from above and not primarily mustered up from one's will alone. Augustine and Alypius quote James 1:17 in tandem with their argument, noting that "all good gifts come from above." Virginity, therefore, is a vocation which has its original source with God. Augustine and Alypius point out the greater nature of this vocation from that of marriage. They describe the unique nature of this vocation in the following manner:

> This holy virginity, in which you who approve of it, and rejoice in it, have been excelled by your daughter, who, coming after you in birth, has gone before you in conduct; descended from you in lineage, has risen above you in honor; following you in age, has gone beyond you in holiness; in whom also that begins to be yours which could not be in your own person. For she did not contract an earthly marriage, that she might be, not for herself only, but also for you, spiritually enriched, in a higher degree than yourself, since you, even with this addition, are inferior to her, because you contracted the marriage of which she is the offspring. These things are gifts of God, and are yours, indeed, but are not from yourselves; for you have this treasure in earthly bodies, which are still frail as the vessels of the potter, that the excellency of the power may be of God, and not of you.[136]

For everything, even our daily bread, is a gift "so that it may not be thought to come from us."[137]

---

135. *Epistula* 188.2.6.
136. *Epistula* 188.2.6.
137. *Epistula* 188.2.7.

Therefore, Augustine and Alypius's encouragement was to pray without ceasing that this gift and the appreciation of God's bestowal would be perpetuated. They provided further admonition by means of 1 Corinthians 4:7, a passage of Scripture Augustine quoted often in regards to the Pelagian controversy.[138] True virginity, and the ability to abide in the vocation, comes through God's gift alone—for anything one has, as Paul asserts, comes from God. In one's ability to fulfill the virginal life, all boasting should be directed toward God alone. Human will, unaided by the grace of God, would never be able to accept such a vocation. Augustine and Alypius declared, "For, even if they come from her on account of personal choice, without which we do no good work, still they do not come only from her, as this fellow [Pelagius] said. Unless one's own choice is helped by the grace of God, a good will cannot exist in a human being."[139]

Thus, the vocation of virginity was a key battle ground for understanding nature and grace in Augustinian perspective. Praising one's own deeds is antithetical to understanding the work of God's grace. One should glory in the Lord alone. The one who sent Juliana and Demetrias the book commending their merit in virginity (presumably Pelagius) wrote of grace in ambiguous terms to the point where grace was no longer the subject. According to Pelagius, God's grace was best displayed in providing us Christ as an example for holy living. Augustine and Alypius, while affirming Christ as an example, rebuffed the notion that this was the best sign of God's grace. Grace affects the heart so that we act in love and grow in our appreciation of grace and love through learning.[140] Grace works on the will so that man desires to apprehend that which has been presented through knowledge. Christ's example is only useful if one is arrested in their soul by the grace of God.

In their concluding exhortation, Augustine and Alypius exhorted Demetrias to see that the grace of God, which gave justifying faith, was shown

---

138. Gerald Bonner describes a certain "enlightenment" regarding 1 Cor 4:7 that came to Augustine in writing against Pelagian teaching. He notes, "During the Pelagian controversy Augustine was more than once to draw attention to the effect of this illumination upon his thought in convincing him that grace is given by God without regard to merit and that the beginning of faith is itself the gift of God, thereby refuting Pelagian doctrine by anticipation long before the heresy arose." Gerald Bonner, "Anti-Pelagian Works." in Fitzgerald, *Augustine through the Ages*, s.v. "Anti-Pelagian Works."

139. *Epistula* 188.2.7.

140. *Epistula* 188.3.11.

through acts of love. Without interior transformation, knowledge and works will puff up, echoing Paul, rather than flowing from love which fulfills the law. Faith, hope, and love are the effects of grace, and Augustine and Alypius "failed to find any such statements in the writings" of Pelagius.[141] Augustine and Alypius sought to persuade Juliana and Demetrias against Pelagius, who commended a self-focused life of virginity and did not "wish her to boast in the Lord, but to boast as if she had not received them."[142] True virginity did not cohere with such a notion. Since everything was a gift from the Lord, this included one's ability to faithfully pursue virginity for God's glory alone. As Augustine and his friend Alypius came alongside these women, they sought to help them to discern the sweet sounds of grace as opposed to the dissonance of error.

CONCLUSION

In this chapter, I have argued that spiritual friendship, specifically with monastics and virgins, included encouragement and mutual support regarding spiritual matters. Augustine was particularly drawn to those seeking a monastic vocation based on his own innate desires to live a monastic life, which were ultimately thwarted upon his consecration as bishop in Hippo. Augustine's friendship in this perspective sought to provide wisdom and insight, while also seeking mutual encouragement from his friends. Augustine himself identified with his correspondents in their desire for rigorous spiritual exercise. He recognized in his friends the burning love and desire for heavenly things which he too possessed. Though he assumed the posture of guide, Augustine never denied the need for God's grace working through the Holy Spirit in order to persevere in the spiritual life.

Augustine also framed his discussion in light of eternity by affirming that the goal of the spiritual life—happiness—would be incomplete until the coming day of God's heavenly city. This provided impetus for prayer and fervent spiritual practice, knowing that temporal goods and experience were a vehicle for one's spiritual journey. Though his correspondence with Proba and those in her family took a more instructive posture, the spiritual life which Augustine promoted was near and dear to his heart and mirrored

---

141. *Epistula* 188.3.13.
142. *Epistula* 188.3.14.

his own spiritual life and journey. This was especially true in the wake of the Pelagian controversy, in which Demetrias was a potential spiritual casualty. Attaching oneself too greatly to earthly goods and personal merits would greatly impede one's spiritual progress and ultimately cause untold damage upon one's happiness in this life in preparation for the life to come.

6
—

"BE IMITATORS OF THEM, AS THEY ARE OF CHRIST"

Spiritual Friendship with Fellow Clergy

Love increases in us and we acquire it more to the extent that we pay the debt of love to more persons.

—Augustine to Celestine[1]

INTRODUCTION

Augustine sought to extend friendship and enter spiritually enriching relationships not only with those who held a monastic vocation, but also with fellow clergy. The pursuit of Christlike virtue was important for those caught up in the affairs of pastoral ministry, including teaching, overseeing daily business, providing soul care, and leading the church through the various theological controversies of the late fourth and early fifth centuries. Augustine entered pastoral ministry in 391 upon his forced ordination to the prebyterate and eventually became co-adjutor bishop alongside Valerius, a highly unusual move in that day.[2] Valerius insisted upon such a move to secure the bright and formidable Augustine for his congregation and for the ministry in general. It was this sort of situation that had kept Augustine from

---

1. Augustine, *Epistula* 192.1.

2. For a helpful overview of Valerius, including his efforts to keep Augustine from other potential pastorates and his maneuvering within the ordination process to have Augustine made bishop, see Michael Cameron, "Valerius of Hippo: A Profile," *Augustinian Studies* 40, no. 1 (January 2009): 5–26.

visiting any church whose bishop seat was vacant.[3] Yet upon his ordination, he viewed his task with the utmost sobriety, requesting time to adequately study the Scriptures in order to be effective for pastoral ministry.[4]

Augustine viewed ministers as those called into the service of the church who, by virtue of their ecclesiastical office, were called to proclaim God's word. Ministers are therefore authorities in the church. The minister is the "dispenser of the evangelical word and the sacrament."[5] This definition of a minister was affirmed early on in his own pastoral ministry, following his ordination as presbyter in 391.[6] Up to the end of his life he affirmed this basic definition.[7] Ministers were engaged in the "ministry of the word," which was primarily the act of preaching, an action that defined the bulk of Augustine's pastoral life. Though there are instances of presbyters rather than bishops preaching and leading congregations in Augustine's day, the standard was to have the bishop of each local congregation as the main preacher and overseer of the church's ministry.[8] Christopher Beeley summarizes the role of bishop in Augustine's context:

> For many centuries bishops functioned primarily as senior pastors of particular Christian communities, even after they began to exercise wider authority over other clergy in a given region. ... In the early church a "bishop" was first and foremost a pastor, not an administrative official. When we speak here of bishops, we are therefore talking

---

3. Possidius, *Life of St. Augustine* 4, in Pontius and Fathers of the Church, *Early Christian Biographies: Lives of St. Cyprian, St. Ambrose, St. Augustine, St. Anthony, St. Athanasius, St. Paul the First Hermit, St. Jerome, St. Epiphanius, with a Sermon on the Life of St. Honoratus*, ed. Roy J. Deferrari, trans. Roy J. Deferrari et al., Fathers of the Church 15 (Washington, DC: Catholic University of America Press, 1954), 77.

4. *Epistula* 21.4. Augustine asked, "But how am I to exercise this ministry for the salvation of others, *not seeking what is beneficial for me, but for many, that they may be saved* (1 Cor 10:33)?"

5. *Contra litteras Petiliani* 3.55.67; quoted from Joseph T. Lienhard, "Ministry," in *Augustine through the Ages: An Encyclopedia*, ed. Allan D. Fitzgerald (Grand Rapids: Eerdmans, 1999), s.v. "Ministry."

6. Writing soon after his ordination, Augustine remarked, "I learned through actual experience what a man needs who ministers to the people the sacrament and word of God (*homini necessarium qui populo ministrat sacramentum et verbum Dei*)." *Epistula* 21.3 (CSEL 33:51).

7. *Epistula* 228.2, in *Letters 211-270, 1*-29**, trans. Roland Teske, ed. Boniface Ramsey, *Works of Saint Augustine* II/4 (Hyde Park, NY: New City Press, 2005).

8. Lienhard, "Ministry," 569.

about the primary leaders of local churches, and we are reminded
that all types of church leadership are rooted in pastoral ministry.[9]

Early church leaders understood the great responsibility that pastors held
within the Christian community. As Beeley notes, "Simply put, church leaders are capable of doing either enormous good or great harm."[10] Pastors are
to be servants of the church and the people of God, a calling that bears much
weight and a calling few should eagerly accept. The testimony of early church
leaders shows that they were not eager to accept the pastorate because of this
heavy responsibility. This had less to do with a lack of theological acumen
or administrative ability; rather, it was a testimony to their understanding
that the pastorate was not a casual affair.[11] Throughout his letters Augustine
displayed a clear sense of a theology of ordained ministry. His notion of
an ordained ministry was thoroughly Christocentric, particularly focusing on the humility of Christ as the chief characteristic meant to be displayed in the life of the minister. It is this virtue, among other related virtues,
that Augustine continued to focus upon as he interacted with his friends.[12]
Additionally, though theological acumen was important to the pastoral task,
Augustine and his friends sought to mutually encourage each other in the
pursuit of virtue. Hence, the pursuit of Christlike virtue, along with gaining
knowledge of the truth and the practice of wisdom, was encouraged as these
friends dispensed their ministerial duties. Seeing the vocation of ministry as
a sober task, Augustine, as a fellow presbyter and bishop, sought to motivate
these friends toward a more faithful ministry and a more profound theological reflection, hoping they would do the same for him as well.

---

9. Christopher A. Beeley, *Leading God's People: Wisdom from the Early Church for Today* (Grand
Rapids: Eerdmans, 2012), 6.

10. Beeley, *Leading God's People*, 7.

11. For more on views of pastoral ministry in the early church, see Andrew Purves, *Pastoral
Theology in the Classical Tradition* (Louisville, KY: Westminster John Knox, 2001).

12. This notion of ordained ministry in the letters of Augustine is thoroughly explored in
Lee Francis Bacchi, *The Theology of Ordained Ministry in the Letters of Augustine of Hippo* (Lanham,
MD: International Scholars, 1998).

AUGUSTINE AND ALYPIUS

Alypius of Thagaste was a colleague and former Manichaean hearer alongside
Augustine, though he was the younger of the two men. He was also born in
Thagaste, his parents being of a "high rank."[13] A man of high mental dexter-
ity and one who exhibited great integrity, he was considered by Augustine
to be a true soul friend.[14] Alypius's conversion, like Augustine's was fueled
by a reading of Athanasius's *Life of Antony*. This soon prompted a desire
for monastic retreat, and Alypius participated with Augustine and others,
including Augustine's mother Monica, in the dialogues of Cassiciacum in
late 386 and early 387.[15] Alypius entered the baptismal waters in Milan alongside Augustine and Augustine's son Adeodatus, receiving baptism by the
hand of Ambrose on Easter Day in 387. Sometime before March 395, he was
elected bishop in Thagaste, and would continue to collaborate and interact
with Augustine. Their epistolary relationship demonstrates two like-minded
friends who shared the burden of pastoral ministry yet conversed like those
engaged in ongoing monastic reflection. They shared in the effort to combat
the Donatist schism and the Pelagian error. They shared not only in these
endeavors, but generally sought mutual comfort and wisdom, especially in
the trials of pastoral ministry. Their friendship, based on their history but
also their shared pastoral conviction, provides insight about how two men
in the late fourth and early fifth centuries interpreted their circumstances
and shared their burdens together. In the exchange that follows, an intimate
relationship unfolds in which the trials of pastoral ministry are shared and
mutual support is sought so that the pastoral calling may be sustained and so
that growth in Christlike virtue would be further pursued. Thus, friendship
took the shape of pastoral sharpening and mutual burden-sharing over the
course of a decades-long ministry.

---

13. *Conf.* 6.7.11.

14. *Conf.* 9.4.7.

15. For more on the Cassiciacum writings, see Joanne McWilliam, "Cassiciacum Dialogues"
in Fitzgerald, *Augustine through the Ages*, s.v. "Cassiciacum Dialogues." McWilliam notes, "Alypius,
Augustine's steady friend of many years, is given his own part at Cassiciacum. We know a good
deal about Alypius's earlier life from the *Confessions*, and the Cassiciacum silhouette accords
with the portrait painted there."

LETTER 29

Though their relationship had long been established, their epistolary exchange appears to have begun in 395. Augustine began this letter by recollecting how he had preached against the practice of African churches celebrating saints' feast days through drunken banquets. Augustine lamented, "In calling it 'joy', they try in vain to hide the term 'drunkenness.' "[16] Through a series of gospel readings in the worship at Hippo Regius, Augustine was able to address the issue by commenting on Matthew 7:6 and Matthew 21:12–13. Having preached on Jesus's act of clearing the temple, Augustine recounted, "I asked them whom they thought a den of thieves resembled more, those selling necessities or those drinking immoderately."[17]

Augustine delivered biblical text after text dealing with the issue at hand. He implored them to look to Christ as an example. Additionally, Augustine recounted, he preached to the point that "if they scorned all these words that were read and spoken to them, [Christ] would visit them with the rod and scourge, but would not allow them to be condemned along with this world."[18] Augustine's final encouragement was to remind his hearers that judgment belonged to those who practiced evil and disobeyed God's commands. Augustine recounted how a continual exhortation toward holy living, promoted by a reading from 1 Peter, eventually led to church members abandoning their drunkenness. Augustine provided a final encouragement from 1 Corinthians 6:13, comparing the "carnal binge" of heretics to the more pleasing spiritual celebration of those who have "tasted how sweet the Lord is."[19]

LETTER 83

Augustine wrote this letter in 404 or 405 to address a matter regarding the recently-deceased Honoratus, a presbyter from Thiave. He had died in the monastery in Thagaste, where Alypius was bishop. The issue was who should receive the property he had left behind. Alypius suggested that half be given to the Christians of Thiave and the other half be given to Augustine. Augustine took issue with this proposal. Such an idea might lead people

---

16. *Epistula* 29.1.
17. *Epistula* 29.3.
18. *Epistula* 29.7.
19. *Epistula* 29.11.

to view the episcopacy with suspicion. Augustine was certain that "people [would] see quite clearly that our concern has been only financial."[20] It might be the case that the people who had previously held their bishops in "high esteem" would now view them as "tainted with filthy greed."[21] This issue would not have arisen if Honoratus had divested himself of earthly goods upon entering the monastery. Augustine sees this as an opportunity for others to scrutinize ministry leaders for possible wrongdoing. For those in ministry, "even the appearance of wrongdoing" should be avoided for the sake of pastoral virtue, which must be maintained in order to be an example of service and leadership.[22]

LETTER 125

This letter, written about five years after Letter 83, relays an issue regarding an instance of slander on the part of Augustine's congregation toward Alypius. The people of Hippo revealed their greed and selfishness in wishing to retain a wealthy layman, Pinian, whom they wished to see made a presbyter. Alypius, however, was suspected of trying to lure Pinian away. Augustine's encouragement to Alypius was that pastors should be responsible for removing suspicion, rather than focusing on their greed and hence assigning blame. In other words, the pastoral task was to heal suspicions by promoting the truth. Otherwise, the people would be "poisoned by such deadly suspicions."[23] In this, pastors were to offer themselves as "an example of good works."[24]

Augustine used this occasion to discuss the nature of greed and how easy it was for people to view the episcopacy as nothing but a means to greater comfort and power. Augustine observed, "[Hostility] is roused up ... especially against the bishops, whose lordly rule is seen to be excessive and who are thought to use and enjoy the possessions of the Church as their owners and lords."[25] Again, Augustine exhorted his friend to be a good example by

---

20. *Epistula* 83.2.
21. *Epistula* 83.2.
22. *Epistula* 83.4.
23. *Epistula* 125.1.
24. *Epistula* 125.1.
25. *Epistula* 125.2.

ensuring that those who were "weak" would not be harmed.[26] Additionally, Augustine affirmed that Pinian's oath to stay in Hippo was binding from the perspective of a Christian confession. For if even famous pagans can keep their oaths, and they do so without any knowledge or regard for "the sacraments of Christ" or God's warnings, then surely those who understand the revelation of God should not fail to honor their commitments.[27] Augustine used the example of Pinian to demonstrate that pastoral ministry was founded on a minister's promise to abide by his calling. To leave without any intention of returning was contrary to the "conduct and good faith" of one serving in leadership.[28] Augustine encouraged Alypius not only to set a good example, but to follow through on his commitments. The instance of Pinian served as an occasion to encourage a friend toward ongoing pastoral fidelity.

LETTER 9*

This letter, part of the Divjak collection, written between 422 and 429, addressed a serious matter which Alypius was adjudicating. This issue involved a man who had been accused of kidnapping a nun for his own pleasure, and upon being caught, was beaten by a group of clerics. Thus, this letter reveals an aspect of pastoral ministry in late antiquity, namely, the judicial responsibility of bishops. Augustine himself often saw such tasks as a way to gain a friend, instructing both parties "in the truth of the divine law" and reminding them "of the way by which they might obtain eternal life," as his biographer recounts.[29] Augustine lamented the issue at hand, revealing that such things "[tend] to wear us down" because of the lack of punishment for such sin and the thorny relationship between the church and civil laws in prosecuting such crimes.[30] It appeared that the accused one held some sort of position of honor as a government or legal professional, which certainly

---

26. *Epistula* 125.2.

27. *Epistula* 124.3.

28. *Epistula* 125.4.

29. Possidius, *Life of St. Augustine*, 19.

30. *Epistula* 9.2*; For a helpful look at how bishops interacted with imperial law, both in the enforcement of such laws and influencing their legislation, see Maria Victoria Escribano Paño, "Bishops, Judges, and Emperors: CTh 16.2.31/CTh 16.5.46/Sirm. 14 (409)," in *The Role of the Bishop in Late Antiquity: Conflict and Compromise*, ed. Andrew Fear, José Fernández Urbiña, and Mar Marcos Sanchez (London: Bloomsbury Academic, 2013), 105–26. See also Claudia Rapp, *Holy Bishops in Late Antiquity: The Nature of Christian Leadership in an Age of Transition* (Berkeley: University of California Press, 2005), 242–53; Raymond van Dam, "Bishops and Society," in *Constantine to c. 600*, ed. Augustine Casiday and Frederick W. Norris, vol. 2 of *The*

muddied the waters. As bishops, both Augustine and Alypius must give an account to the Lord and therefore must intervene and exert some measure of spiritual authority over these matters.[31]

With this in mind, and to bolster church discipline, Augustine encouraged his friend to help him "seek, find, and establish a regular penalty for these restless and wicked persons."[32] This would ensure consistent punishment for like crimes. Yet in the meantime, a minister should not be punished for seeking to enact justice "in defense of the house of the Lord," which would still be less severe than civil law might allow in order to instill the proper amount of fear of future punishment.[33] Augustine affirmed that the true nature of the crime would come to light in the forthcoming tribunal. He sought to help his friend see the light of justice on the other side, even though the outcome was yet to be determined.

LETTER 10*

This letter, also a part of the Divjak collection, was likely written in 428.[34] Augustine expresses concern regarding various pastoral issues. First, Augustine addressed the writings of Julian of Eclanum (c. 380–454), who was bishop of Eclanum (near modern day Benevento, Italy), and a Pelagian sympathizer. He along with eighteen other bishops, refused to sign Pope Zosimus's *Epistula Tractoria*, which condemned the teachings of Pelagius.[35] These writings were of great interest to Augustine as he engaged with Julian on various points pertaining to the validity of marriage and the concept of

---

Cambridge History of Christianity, ed. Augustine Casiday and Frederick W. Norris (Cambridge: Cambridge University Press, 2007), 343–66.

31. Augustine would have understood the nature of pastoral authority as a necessary function of the spiritual gift and responsibility given by God. Rapp notes, "Spiritual authority indicates that its bearer has received the *pneuma*, the Spirit from God. Spiritual authority has its source outside the individual. It is given by God, as a gift. Spiritual authority has its source outside the individual. It is given by God, as a gift." Rapp, *Holy Bishops in Late Antiquity*, 16. That said, Robert Eno reminds readers, "Augustine frequently downplayed his own authority as a theologian and urged others not to exaggerate the weight of his views. Moreover, as an individual bishop, he does not seem to have an exaggerated opinion of his own authority." Robert B. Eno, "Authority" in Fitzgerald, *Augustine through the Ages*, s.v. "Authority."

32. *Epistula* 9*.3.

33. *Epistula* 9*.3.

34. According to Roland Teske, this letter could have also been written earlier, around 423–424. Augustine, *Letters 211–270, 1*–29*, 262.

35. Mathijs Lamberigts, "Julian of Eclanum," in Fitzgerald, *Augustine through the Ages*, s.v. "Julian of Eclanum."

original sin.[36] Julian's sympathies with Pelagius also brought him into conflict with the older Augustine. Along with the writings of Julian, Augustine also mentions the writings of Caelestius who likewise supported Pelagius and was condemned at the Council of Carthage in 411. The exact writings of Caelestius that Augustine was referring to are unclear in this letter, though Roland Teske suggests that Augustine is speaking of the writings of Julian.[37] In the opening paragraph, Augustine recounted the events of one Turbantius, who at one point went along with Julian in following the teaching of Pelagius, but who had since recounted his error and "was taken back into the Catholic peace by Pope Celestine."[38] Alypius seems to have forgotten this detail, and it was important that Augustine reiterate this fact.

Augustine spent little time discussing the content of these writings or their theological ideas in this letter. After his introduction he moved to discuss a more immediate pastoral issue. Augustine was concerned that an increased number of slave merchants in Africa were unlawfully obtaining slaves to sell overseas.[39] These enslavers were taking advantage of this system and selling such people as permanent slaves. This was causing a "drain ... of [Africa's] human population" as a "multitude of trappers and raiders" had arisen to feed this human trafficking market.[40] Such raiders were often disguised as barbarians or soldiers and would invade small villages to carry off its inhabitants. Augustine heard of this practice through "a certain girl" who was among the many set free from slavery through finances provided by the church.[41] These occurrences were certainly impacting Alypius. Augustine recounted severe laws passed by Emperor Honorius that sought to

---

36. For a summary of Augustine on marriage, including his debates with Julian, see David G. Hunter, "Marriage" in Fitzgerald, *Augustine through the Ages*, s.v "Marriage." See also Elizabeth Clark, ed., *St. Augustine on Marriage and Sexuality* (Washington, DC: Catholic University of America Press, 1996). For a helpful overview of Christian views of marriage and sexuality in the time of Augustine, see David G. Hunter, "Sexuality, Marriage, and the Family," in Casiday and Norris, *Constantine to c. 600*, 585–600.

37. Teske in Augustine, *Letters* 211–270, 1*–29*, 262n1. Teske suggests these writings were Julian's *Ad Turbantium*, or his *Ad Florum*, to both of which Augustine provided responses.

38. *Epistula* 10*.1.

39. For a helpful overview of Roman slavery and slavery practices, see Sandra R. Joshel, *Slavery in the Roman World* (Cambridge: Cambridge University Press, 2010).

40. *Epistula* 10*.2.

41. *Epistula* 10*.3.

discourage the maltreatment of slaves yet did not try to address the unlawful man-stealing that was taking place in Augustine's context.[42]

Augustine believed this law could still prove useful in amending this tragedy, and he implored Alypius to intercede as well. In fact, Augustine hoped to alleviate the traditional punishment for those who helped to free slaves.[43] The traditional punishment, scourging with a leaden whip, often led to death. Augustine was concerned that more free people would be "deported into perpetual servitude" were he and others to "cease out of fear of these punishments."[44] Christian, even human, pity demanded that something be done to protect such individuals. This "infectious disease" not only affected innocent individuals but worked its way into the hearts of men by way of greed.[45] Augustine identified the perpetuators of this disease as a certain group of Galatian merchants.[46] This disease had even affected those within the church, causing a member of the church to sell his wife not because of "any failing on her part but driven only by the heat of this plague."[47] Hence, Augustine saw this issue not only as a human rights violation, but as an important pastoral matter. This disease was infecting the hearts of his flock, something that Alypius would understand as a fellow pastor.

Augustine closed this letter with a final appeal to his friend to consider the scope and severity of this situation imploring, "In charity, I beg that I may not have written this to you in vain."[48] If such cruelty was taking place

---

42. *Epistula* 10*.3. The late Roman Empire of Augustine's day was still very much dependent on slavery for its economic success. For a convincing argument regarding the ubiquitous nature of Roman slavery in the time of Augustine, see Kyle Harper, *Slavery in the Late Roman World, AD 275–425* (Cambridge: Cambridge University Press, 2011). Harper asserts that what Augustine was witnessing were simply normal Roman slave-traders who had previously worked among the "frontiers of imperial power" but were now "folding in upon the Roman Mediterranean." Harper, *Slavery in the Late Roman World*, 93. Hence, this was nothing new according to Harper, simply new to Augustine.

43. *Epistula* 10*.4. Augustine alludes to members of his church who helped to bring back captured slaves, though it is not certain by this letter how this was accomplished. Hence Augustine was making an appeal to his friend to protect his church members against punishment. In *Epistula* 10*.7, Augustine recounted an instance where 120 people were set free from a transport ship by people from his church. The exact details are not given, but this seems to have been a covert operation.

44. *Epistula* 10*.4.

45. *Epistula* 10*.6.

46. *Epistula* 10*.7.

47. *Epistula* 10*.6.

48. *Epistula* 10*.8.

in Hippo Regius, it was likely that it was also taking place "elsewhere on the coast."[49] Augustine hoped to garner his own patrons for this cause, just as these Galatian merchants had gathered their own patrons in order to retrieve slaves the church had freed.[50] Additionally, the church in Hippo Regius was in need of support in order to feed those who had been freed. There was both a physical and spiritual need to rid their area of this disease, and Augustine sought help from his friend Alypius and those within his influence. In this way, Augustine hoped that Alypius would shoulder the pastoral burden alongside him and come to his aid soon.

Letter 227

This short letter was written as both Augustine and Alypius were in their last years of life, sometime between 428 and 429. In it, Augustine recounted the baptism of new converts including the miraculous nature of one conversion in particular, that of Dioscorus, a prominent physician. Dioscorus's daughter had fallen ill and nothing else could be done to help her. He prayed to God and vowed that he would become a Christian if his daughter was healed. She soon recovered, yet Dioscorus reneged on his vow and did not become a Christian. Despite this, "God's hand was still upon him."[51] From there, a series of issues plagued Dioscorus, from blindness to becoming paralyzed and finally losing his ability to speak. This series of events, according to Augustine, was based on his ongoing recalcitrance. Having been admonished in a dream, Dioscorus confessed in writing (for his speech had not returned) why these events were taking place. His stubbornness and refusal to submit to the Lord and memorize the creed prior to baptism had caused this series of afflictions.[52] Dioscorus finally relented and submitted to memorizing the creed and was baptized.

---

49. *Epistula* 10*.8.
50. *Epistula* 10*.8.
51. *Epistula* 227.
52. The recitation of the creed (Lat. *symbolum* or *fides*) was the standard practice prior to baptism. Candidates were given the creed a few weeks prior to their baptism and expected to "give it back" (*redittio symboli*). Dioscorus's baptismal creed of Hippo can be mostly seen in Augustine's. For more on the baptismal creed in Augustine see Joseph T. Lienhard, "Creed, Symbolum" in Fitzgerald, *Augustine through the Ages*, s.v. "Creed, Symbolum." For more on baptismal rites in late antique Christianity, see Robin M. Jensen, "Baptismal Rites and Architecture," in

This short letter and summary was written to encourage Alypius by high-lighting God's work in Dioscorus's life. Augustine indicated that Alypius knew Dioscorus who, despite having a "certain natural goodness," was "highly sac-rilegious" because he "used to insult Christians."[53] Clearly God was the one who had "taken from him all that childish nonsense."[54] Since he had been a man of prominence, this episode in Dioscorus's life would have been hum-bling. For the ministers, the miraculous nature of this conversion would have been gratifying.[55] Thus, Augustine encouraged his friend with an account of God's miraculous work so that they might mutually "sing a hymn to the Lord and exalt him above all forever."[56]

AUGUSTINE AND EVODIUS

Evodius and Augustine were longtime friends, and eventually came to share the episcopal burden together. Evodius (fl. late fourth-early fifth century) was also a native of Thagaste and had set his course toward a secular career. By 387, he had connected with Augustine and his group of friends in Italy, having already been baptized.[57] Augustine engaged Evodius in two early dia-logues, *The Measure of the Soul,* and *On the Free Choice of the Will.* Evodius remained within the part of the "circle of 'monks' at Thagaste" and con-tinued his personal connection with Augustine and his literary activities.[58] Their ordination as bishop occurred relatively at the same time, Evodius taking the episcopal seat at Uzalis near Carthage (modern day El Alia in Tunisia). Though little of his writing survives, readers are given a glimpse at the relationship he shared with Augustine through their correspondence. In this exchange, readers can discern the concerns of one pastor shared with another. More than sharing mutual office and faith, they shared mutual

---

Late Ancient Christianity, ed. Virginia Burrus, A People's History of Christianity 2 (Minneapolis: Fortress, 2005), 117–44.

53. *Epistula 227.*

54. *Epistula 227.*

55. For more on miraculous conversions in the life and ministry of Augustine, see William Harmless, *Augustine and the Catechumenate,* rev. ed. (Collegeville, MN: Liturgical, 2014), 139–45.

56. *Epistula 227.*

57. *Conf.* 9.8.17.

58. James J. O'Donnell, "Evodius of Uzalis" in Fitzgerald, *Augustine through the Ages,* s.v. "Evodius of Uzalis."

affection with one another based on their shared love of Christ. This mutual affection took shape in pastoral encouragement for one another under the recognition of their shared episcopal burden.

LETTER 158

Evodius began this series of correspondence with Augustine to enquire on a number of items. The correspondence of Letters 158–161 took place between 414 and 415. Augustine provided a thorough reply to these questions in his Letter 162, yet this first series of letters demonstrates the crux of their conversation and the various pastoral issues with which Evodius was concerned. Evodius began by requesting a "payment of the debt" which his previous letter required.[59] Evodius continued by describing a young man who had become a "rather close and dear friend" and was faithfully pursuing the Christian life after "God rescued him" through the ministry of Evodius.[60] Having fallen ill, this young man eventually died, yet the memory of him powerfully remained in Evodius's soul and comforted him with "a certain brightness by his presence."[61] Recounting the event, Evodius related that the young man's soul was now free from the defilement of the body, being released from "its house of clay."[62] From here, Evodius moved to an instance regarding the widow Urbica of Figentes who had a dream in which a "certain deacon who had died four years previously" along with various virgins and widows were preparing a place for the young boy. In the dream, she saw his body taken to heaven, and in its place, "branches of virgin roses" sprang up.[63] Evodius did not doubt this unusual episode. In fact, for him, it was a normal consequence of the "journeying of this soul" of the young man.[64] It did, however, raise numerous questions that he then posed to Augustine.

Evodius was chiefly concerned about the state of the soul following death, namely what, if any, body does the soul possess after leaving the earthly body. Though he proposed various ideas, he was ultimately uncertain and

---

59. *Epistula* 158.1.
60. *Epistula* 158.1.
61. *Epistula* 158.2.
62. *Epistula* 158.2.
63. *Epistula* 158.3.
64. *Epistula* 158.4.

wished to learn from Augustine.[65] The soul must be contained in some fashion, argued Evodius, otherwise there would be "one soul for all."[66] Based on the biblical witness, some sort of body is necessary for the soul following one's death.[67] The composition of the soul after death is further compounded by the reality of the resurrection, wherein the soul is joined to the resurrected and renewed body. This would seem to indicate that the soul had previously been without any sort of body in the in-between state.[68] Evodius wished to avoid the affirmation that the soul was completely inactive between bodily death and the resurrection. Such a thought could lead one to affirm that "the soul is dead," as if "it were buried and living in hope, otherwise doing nothing."[69]

Evodius continued to press Augustine regarding visitations from heavenly (or demonic) beings, as well as those who have passed from this life. Evodius recounted a time when he had been visited by certain "holy men of the monastery" who had previously died. What they spoke to him and what they said eventually came to pass.[70] In recounting these and other occurrences, Evodius claimed ignorance regarding how to comprehend such matters. He exclaimed to Augustine, "Who will teach us with great reliability about such hidden causes? The turmoil of my heart is poured out to you in the time of my trouble."[71] Evodius concluded that the soul must possess some sort of body. Wishing to receive Augustine's insights, Evodius implored him for correction and right teaching on these matters.

LETTER 159

To this complex question, Augustine offered a terse yet heartfelt response in Letter 159. Having no recollection of a previous letter, Augustine proceeded to address the question regarding a *post mortem* state of the soul. Augustine, pressed for time and admitting that the question required much deeper reflection, stated simply that he did not think "in any way that the soul leaves

---

65. *Epistula* 158.7.
66. *Epistula* 158.5.
67. *Epistula* 158.5. Here Evodius cited the parable of Lazarus and the rich man in Luke 16:19–22.
68. *Epistula* 158.6.
69. *Epistula* 158.7.
70. *Epistula* 158.9.
71. *Epistula* 158.10.

the body with a body."[72] Augustine did not dismiss the issue, even if he did not address all its intricacies. The mind is a complicated organ, able to provide vivid images, and yet there are also instances of dreams and visions that cannot be dismissed. Augustine briefly recalled a similar instance with a man named Gennadius. After Gennadius had dreamed twice of a young man leading him through a hymn-filled city, the young man affirmed to him the truth of the afterlife. This relieved the man's doubts, something which could only come from "God in his providence and mercy."[73]

LETTERS 160–161

Evodius had moved on from the question of the soul's *post mortem* state. In Letter 160 and Letter 161, written in 414, he turned to questions about the nature of reason as well as inter-trinitarian relations. Evodius began by working through the implications of reason's eternality. Evodius discussed the relationship between reason and God, concluding that God is reason and reason is God.[74] One would not exist without the other. This he relates to the relationship between the Father and the Son, stating that just as reason is eternally related to God, so is the Son eternally related to the Father. The Son reveals the Father just as reason reveals God, and vice versa.

Evodius continued the theological dialogue with Augustine in Letter 161, this time focusing on a slightly different question relating to the virgin birth of Christ. Evodius took issue with Augustine's statement that the virgin birth must be one of a kind to remain unique and awe-inspiring. Evodius, while not denying the uniqueness of the virgin birth, was able to point to other examples in nature where offspring were seemingly produced without any male seed.[75] Evodius believed that God demonstrated that virgin birth was a possibility by placing other examples of such throughout nature. This did not diminish their wonder but served to convince the unbeliever of the nature of Christ's birth. Evodius also broached the question of Christ's ability to "see the substance of God" in his glorified body.[76] Evodius denied this possibility

---

72. *Epistula* 159.1.
73. *Epistula* 159.4.
74. *Epistula* 160.3.
75. *Epistula* 161.2.
76. *Epistula* 161.3.

and intimated that Augustine's reasoning for the virgin birth would lead some to believe that a glorified body could see God in his essence. The tone of his inquisition never reached the point of abrasion, yet a friendly disagreement ensued, necessitating clarification (or perhaps correction) on the part of Augustine.

LETTER 162

In this letter, written in 414, Augustine provided a more detailed reply to Evodius and his questions posed in Letters 158, 160, and 161. Noting that such questions were difficult, Augustine hoped their dialogue would not be used by those who were "less sharp and less well trained" and especially those who had "a hostile intention."[77] Augustine reminded Evodius of his *The Trinity* and *On Genesis Literally Interpreted* which provided answers to many of the questions posed in previous letters. Augustine then turned to the question of experiencing visions and dreams of loved ones and angelic beings. Augustine resorted to brief biblical citations of such visions and visitations, concluding that such things "are disturbing and are sources of wonder because they have a more hidden cause than one human being can see or convey to another."[78] Regarding the question of seeing God with bodily eyes, Augustine simply noted that God is not a bodily mass consisting of parts.[79] Had Augustine more time, he admitted, he would have said more on this issue in the letter. As an occupied and involved minister, time had gotten away from him and hence the letter needed to end.

LETTER 163

Letter 163 from Evodius, written in 414, added one additional question to the discussion. Based on the introduction of this short letter, it appeared that Evodius had yet to receive the answers Augustine provided in Letter 162. His added question pertained to the origin of Christ's soul as well as the nature of his descent into hell, referencing 1 Peter 3:18–19.[80] According to Evodius, the origin of Christ's soul must be in accord with the origin of the human soul. Additionally, Evodius was unsure as to the nature of the spirits

---

77. *Epistula* 162.1.

78. *Epistula* 162.6.

79. *Epistula* 162.8.

80. The exchange of *Epistula* 163 and *Epistula*. 164 represent, as Anne-Marie la Bonnardière observes, "one exceptional episode ... of the history of the Augustinian interpretation of 1 Peter." Anne-Marie La Bonnardière, "Evodius et Augustin (Lettres 163 et 164)," in *Saint Augustin et la Bible* ed. Anne-Marie La Bonnardière, Bible de tout le temps 3 (Paris: Éditions Beauchesne, 1986), 213.

to whom Christ preached the good news in his descent. Does this mean that hell is now empty until the day of judgment? Evidenced in this letter was Evodius's continued desire for theological dialogue with his friend and fellow minister. In this, Evodius continued to demonstrate the posture of a learner with Augustine serving as teacher or master.

LETTER 164

In 414, Augustine mounted a considerable response to Evodius's numerous questions. Addressing the issue of Christ's descent to hell, Augustine noted various issues in the interpretation of 1 Peter 3:18–19. Augustine affirmed, "It is clear enough that the Lord, having been put to death in the flesh, entered into hell."[81] Yet he also admitted to the difficulty of Christ's descent and its arrangement among other passages of Scripture, as well as other images of the afterlife. Augustine dismissed any notion that Christ came to release the patriarchs and prophets.[82] Certainly Christ's descent accomplished what Peter says it did; however, Augustine himself struggled to understand how all the pieces fit together, especially considering his promise to the thief on the cross of entrance into paradise.[83] From here Augustine presented a thorough biblical argument regarding the nature of Christ's descent, the identity of the "prisoners" in hell, and how they all related to Christ's person and work. In the end, Augustine affirmed the plain biblical account of Christ's work, including his crucifixion and resurrection, citing 1 Corinthians 15:3–4.[84] From here Augustine discussed the nature and origin of Christ's soul. He asserted that Christ created his own soul, just as he did with any human soul. His flesh was not true sinful flesh but only in likeness, though he was certainly fully human.[85] In the end, Augustine admitted his loss at the final and firm interpretation of Peter's words: "If anyone can solve those problems by which, as I mentioned, I am disturbed, so that he removes all doubt about them, he should share the solution with me."[86] Even while Augustine implored others to "solve these problems" that disturbed him and freely share the solution,

---

81. *Epistula* 164.2.3.
82. *Epistula* 164.3.6–7.
83. *Epistula* 164.3.8; cf. Luke 23:43.
84. *Epistula* 164.5.14.
85. *Epistula* 164.7.19.
86. *Epistula* 164.7.22.

he encouraged Evodius with the assurance that the interpretation presented in the letter "is not proven false."[87]

LETTER 169

In 415, Augustine wrote Letter 169 in order to address interpretive issues regarding the Trinity. Specifically, Augustine addressed 1 Corinthians 14:38 and the idea that one must be able to fully comprehend God. Augustine assured that this was not the proper understanding of this verse. No person can fully understand the essence of God. Our response is to believe in the Triune God with "solid piety."[88] From here, Augustine further explained the analogy of memory, understanding, and will in humanity as a triune form analogous to the Trinity. Though comparable, this analogy does not "match in every respect."[89] Augustine focused on the inseparable operations of the Trinity in order to best understand God's nature and work. Knowledge of the Trinity informed Augustine's knowledge of Christ and his work. The Word and the man are one person; Christ remained God the Son while adding to himself human flesh.[90] Augustine also spoke to the nature of the Spirit, specifically in the form of the dove as a sign. This was "the bodily form presented to the eyes but did not indicate the nature of a living animal."[91] Augustine explained how some depictions of God in Scripture were signs, such as the voice of the Father or the rock in the desert which symbolized Christ.[92] These did not add to the triune nature of God but served to make it known. In closing, Augustine expressed his hopes that his response would suffice in being "obedient to [Evodius's] love."[93] He realized that his response might not satisfy every theological craving of Evodius, but hoped that if nothing else, it would serve as a sign of their mutual love and affection.

---

87. *Epistula* 164.7.22.
88. *Epistula* 169.2.5.
89. *Epistula* 169.2.6.
90. *Epistula* 169.2.7–8.
91. *Epistula* 169.3.10.
92. *Epistula* 169.2.9; cf. 1 Cor 10:4.
93. *Epistula* 169.4.12.

AUGUSTINE AND OTHER CLERGY

Augustine wrote numerous short letters to priests and various presbyters. Though his friendship with Alypius and Evodius was more established, the way in which Augustine engaged with other clergy demonstrated a certain level of friendship unique to the pastoral task which they all shared. He sought to provide counsel and encouragement in particular pastoral tasks. Though these various letters are occasional and do not represent a sustained conversation, collectively they illustrate how Augustine consistently sought to motivate fellow clergy toward more faithful ministry, Christlike virtue, and wise theological reflection.

LETTER 36 TO CASULANUS

Augustine penned this letter to a minister in Africa named Casulanus sometime in 397. Casulanus had written to Augustine twice before enquiring about Augustine's perspective on fasting, particularly on the Sabbath. Seeing as the original letter was written in the "fraternal and most just law of love" that united Casulanus and Augustine, Augustine sought to return that love in his reply.[94] In doing so, Augustine decided not to refute the views of a certain "man of the city" (*Urbicus*) based on time and attention needed for "more urgent works."[95] This man of the city had upset "the whole Church of Christ" by arguing for fasting on the Sabbath regardless of local tradition.[96] Casulanus had previously sent Augustine a treatise by this man and requested a response, yet Augustine encouraged his younger ministerial colleague to "use that fine mind," which he loved in him "as God's gift," in order to discern the proper way to think about the question at hand.[97]

Augustine spent the majority of the letter recounting the biblical teaching on fasting. He sought to help Casulanus see the absurdity of Urbicus's argument that fasting was required on the Sabbath. In seeking to defend the Roman church, this man was making them out to be "drunks and belly-worshippers."[98] Augustine pointed to numerous biblical texts which disproved this man's faulty reasoning, demonstrating that his view of Scripture was facile

---

94. *Epistula* 36.1.1.
95. *Epistula* 36.2.3.
96. *Epistula* 36.1.2, 36.2.3.
97. *Epistula* 36.2.3.
98. *Epistula* 36.2.3.

and undeveloped. Taking Jesus's words literally in Matthew 5:21, Urbicus concluded that to be more righteous than the Pharisees was to fast more often.[99]
This man believed that more, not less, fasting was required of all Christians.
Augustine's direction to Casulanus was two-fold: look to the long-standing
tradition of the church and its practices of fasting and submit to the practices of one's local church. Doing the former reveals a tradition of fasting on
the fourth and sixth days of the week (Wednesday and Friday), and and doing
the latter was a wise practice Augustine had learned from Ambrose of Milan.[100]
Augustine recounted Ambrose's words, "'And to whatever church you come ...
observe its custom, if you do not want to be scandalized or to give scandal.' "[101]
Augustine closed with the same advice, noting that he had "probably said more
than enough on this topic."[102] Casulanus would do well to follow his bishop on
this matter, just as Augustine had done with Ambrose previously.

LETTER 48 TO EUDOXIUS

In 398, Augustine addressed the abbot and presbyter Eudoxius who was
located on the island of Capraria. This short letter shows Augustine bring-
ing encouragement and guidance to those called to the monastic life. As one
who himself desired to live out the monastic ideal, he was able to give appropriate guidance to this community, primarily through its leader.

Augustine recounted the feeling of love that he found in the thought
of Eudoxius and the monks gathered with him. This love was expressive
of the "one body under one head," which should prompt them to pray for
Augustine and the church.[103] Augustine cautioned this monastic community to not become too enamored with their spiritual leisure and focus their
attention on the needs of the church. He implored them, "Rather, obey God
with a meek heart, submitting yourselves with gentleness to him who rules
you, who guides the meek in justice, who teaches the meek his ways."[104] In
doing so, they would not be quick to neglect praying for the church and

---

99. *Epistula* 36.4.8.
100. *Epistula* 36.13.30, 36.14.32.
101. *Epistula* 36.14.32.
102. *Epistula* 36.14.32.
103. *Epistula* 48.1.
104. *Epistula* 48.2.

serving the church based on a potential "attraction of indolence."[105] Augustine argued that the church was primary as one who birthed and continued to nourish those in the monastic life. Hence, this life required constant spiritual diligence and the neglect of "earthly delight" and the avoidance of Satan's temptations to unduly "love leisure."[106]

In their monastic pursuit, Augustine's main encouragement was to ensure that they performed all actions primarily for God's glory.[107] The monastic ideal, as Augustine perceived it, was to be "fervent in spirit. ... For this is the action of someone on the straight road."[108] Neither diligent work nor contemplative leisure will interfere with this guiding action. Augustine's encouragement came not because he believed that this community was lacking these virtues, but rather, wished to see them increase. Augustine demonstrated an act of friendship by exhorting these men toward greater spiritual maturity, asking that his recipients would consider including him in their prayers, thereby completing the circle of spiritual friendship.

Letter 64 to Quintian

Quintian was a presbyter in Carthage who had been at odds with his bishop and was seeking Augustine's help to adjudicate between them. Augustine wrote to him toward the end of 401 and began by reminding Quintian that Christians' souls are not yet as beautiful as they will be in eternity. Thus, the call of all Christians is to endure temporal trials with hope and patience.[109] Augustine hoped this would encourage his friend in his present circumstances with his bishop Aurelius, since they were not in communion. This disunity affected the unity of Quintian and Augustine, though Augustine chose to act in charity.[110] Augustine asked Quintian to have patience and he also offered for Quintian to stay in Hippo, provided that he was calm and desired "to preserve the discipline of the Church."[111] Augustine, knowing the demands of episcopal ministry, was certain that Aurelius would want to seek

---

105. *Epistula* 48.2.
106. *Epistula* 48.2.
107. *Epistula* 48.3.
108. *Epistula* 48.3.
109. *Epistula* 64.1.
110. *Epistula* 64.2.
111. *Epistula* 64.2.

peace though he was caught up in the work of ministry.[112] Identifying with the episcopal duties of Aurelius, Augustine stated, "We ask you believe the same thing about the demands upon us, because you likewise cannot know them."[113]

In the end, Augustine wished to help but encouraged Quintian to find a bishop closer in proximity to whom to plead his case. That said, Augustine still chose to send a letter to Aurelius to communicate Quintian's innocence, yet refused to write a preemptive letter to a congregation "who had not been entrusted to [his] governance."[114] In this same way, Augustine encouraged his priestly friend to avoid scandal in the church by not reading those things which are not approved by the church. This would include non-canonical writings that "heretics, and especially Manichees, often use ... to throw the minds of the unlearned into confusion."[115] Augustine noted the recent councils of Hippo (393) and Carthage (397), where the matter of the biblical canon was discussed.[116] Thus by pointing to this conciliar authority, Augustine encouraged Quintian toward reconciliation by addressing with his own bishop the issues that were bothering him. In this way, Augustine prompted Quintian toward the virtues of humility and love. Augustine closed with this pastoral encouragement: "Brother, be careful; the devil is very clever, but Christ is the wisdom of God."[117]

LETTER 190 TO OPTATUS

Optatus was serving as bishop of Milevis when Augustine wrote to him sometime in the latter half of 418. The topic of this letter was the origin of souls. At the outset, Augustine admitted his difficulty in understanding the origin of the soul.[118] While the question is important, Augustine asserted that it was not the most central issue to the Christian faith.[119] What was important was

---

112. *Epistula* 64.2.

113. *Epistula* 64.2.

114. *Epistula* 64.2.

115. *Epistula* 64.2.

116. The Council of Hippo was also one step toward building a Catholic theological majority against groups such as the Donatists. For a helpful background on the Council of Hippo, see Jane Merdinger, "On the Eve of the Council of Hippo, 393: The Background to Augustine's Program for Church Reform," *Augustinian Studies* 40, no. 1 (2009): 27–36.

117. *Epistula* 64.4.

118. That said, Teske notes, "From the time of the Cassiciacum dialogues the human soul was a central focus of Augustine's interest." Roland J. Teske, "Soul" in Fitzgerald, *Augustine through the Ages*, s.v. "Soul."

119. *Epistula* 190.1.3.

understanding the reality of man's sinful nature and our need to be "set free ... by being reborn in Christ."[120] That said, it is important to maintain that souls are created and subsequently adopted by God "by a wonderful concession of grace."[121] Faith in the incarnate son of God is the means by which one is saved, which was true for saints of the Old Testament just as it is true for believers today.[122] The value of the law therefore is to reveal one's need for God's grace in order to "heal the abundance of sin."[123]

From here, Augustine discussed the nature of God's just anger due to sin and the grace he shows in rescuing many. The question of God's election was significant and required a thoughtful reply. Augustine cited Romans 9:21-23 to emphasize the reality that "vessels of anger" receive that which they justly deserve, and "vessels of mercy" receive that which they do not deserve.[124] God's anger is no "disturbance of the mind" similar to human anger "but a just and determinate punishment."[125] Hence, God is just to punish sin and demonstrates grace when he pardons sin. This should be a cause for celebration when one learns that it was not his or her own merit which gained God's favor, but "by the glory of God's most bountiful mercy."[126] Thus, for Augustine, the working of God on the soul was clearer in Scripture than the soul's origin itself.[127]

Augustine reiterated that he was unable to find anything certain in Scripture and thus invited Optatus to send him anything he had discovered in the discussion of the soul's origin "out of brotherly love."[128] Augustine warned Optatus to avoid the opinion of Tertullian who maintained that

---

120. *Epistula* 190.1.3.
121. *Epistula* 190.1.4.
122. *Epistula* 190.2.6.
123. *Epistula* 190.2.7.
124. *Epistula* 190.3.9.
125. *Epistula* 190.3.10.
126. *Epistula* 190.3.11.
127. In *Retract.* 2.24.50, Augustine admitted that the discussion of the soul's origin created more problems than it solved, yet it continued to consume his thinking in various areas. For an extensive discussion on the soul in Augustine's thinking, see Gerard O'Daly, *Augustine's Philosophy of Mind* (Berkeley: University of California Press, 1987), 7-79. For an overview, see Teske, "Soul," 807-12.
128. *Epistula* 190.4.13.

all souls derive from Adam.[129] This is a "wild idea" that should be avoided.[130] Another idea one should avoid is the denial of original sin." This sin, which is passed down from the first man, "can be removed only by rebirth."[131] He warned Optatus to guard himself against any heresy and to avoid any line of argumentation that would lead toward the Pelagian error.[132] Augustine closed his letter by admitting that his reply was not as erudite as he had hoped yet "filled with concerned love."[133] He once again invited Optatus to share whatever insights he had gained on the topic of the soul. Friendship was thus demonstrated with an appeal to love and mutual learning.

LETTER 192 AND LETTER 209 TO CELESTINE

The first of these two letters, written at the end of 418, was penned while Celestine was still a deacon in the church at Rome. The second one came in early 423 and was written to congratulate Celestine on his appointment to bishop. In both letters Augustine revealed a strong affection for Celestine, recognizing him as a friend and cherished colleague.

LETTER 192

Augustine began Letter 192 by affirming that a "debt of love" was owed to his friend.[134] This debt, when paid in love, increased due to the ever-increasing nature of love. This debt, Augustine admitted, "is increased by being paid."[135] Christian love is the sort that increases, not diminishes, when faithfully practiced. "Love increases in us," Augustine expressed, "and we acquire it more to the extent that we pay the debt of love to more persons."[136] This sort of

---

129. Augustine's rejection of traducianism is unexplained, yet he affirmed that all were one in Adam by the *rationale seminale* in *Nupt.* 2.15. Referring to Augustine's discussion with Optatus, O'Daly notes, "Mankind's solidarity with Adam and co-responsibility for his sin, which all men willed through him, might seem to argue for the conclusion that, just as original sin is propagated by the act of generation, so also the soul may be. But such traducianism requires the explanation of how souls are actually propagated, a difficulty that does not make it more plausible: again, Augustine stresses lack of Scriptural guidance." O'Daly, *Augustine's Philosophy of Mind*, 19.

130. *Epistula* 190.4.13.

131. *Epistula* 190.4.15.

132. *Epistula* 190.6.22.

133. *Epistula* 190.6.26.

134. *Epistula* 192.1.

135. *Epistula* 192.1.

136. *Epistula* 192.1.

love also extends to enemies, though it is more fully experienced among friends. Thus, Christian love seeks to transform enemies into friends.[137] One should desire to see their enemy be good and remove all hostility. Even when one repays good with evil, love still seeks to do all it can to repay that evil action with love.

Augustine continued with the analogy of a "love" debt being paid, noting once again that this was no ordinary debt. Whereas money diminishes when paid out, "love is increased" when given and nothing is expected in return.[138] Love is increased in both the one who gives it and the one who receives it, with the goal of ongoing transformation. This is the biblical mandate of love as expressed by Paul in Romans 13:8. Hence this became one of the main biblical foundations, alongside Romans 5:5, for spiritual friendship in Augustine.[139] This sort of love set the foundation for their later exchange in Letter 209.

LETTER 209

In this second letter, Augustine wrote to Celestine, now bishop of Rome, requesting his wisdom on a matter of local ecclesiastical concern. In seeking to bring the neighboring town of Fussala into Catholic unity, many priests had been sent to convince and implore the people to leave the Donatist schism. This led to some violence, and even the death, of certain presbyters.[140] When peace and unity had been attained, Augustine moved to install a Catholic bishop, but his candidate backed out suddenly prior to ordination.[141] This led him to hastily ordain the young Antonius, who had only served as lector in the church. Augustine lamented that Antonius had not been properly vetted, and various character flaws and misdeeds appeared once he began his episcopal ministry in Fussala.[142] Augustine felt torn between the desire to have Catholic leadership established in this area, and this young bishop

---

137. *Epistula* 192.1.

138. *Epistula* 192.2.

139. Carolinne White notes, "[Both Rom 5:5 and 1 Cor 4:7] influenced his belief that love and friendship are given by God's grace rather than being instigated by man himself, a belief which is of course in harmony with the particular emphasis he placed on the need for grace in human affairs in general." White, *Christian Friendship in the Fourth Century*, 196.

140. *Epistula* 209.2.

141. *Epistula* 209.3.

142. *Epistula* 209.4.

to not be deposed and completely despised by other leaders in the church. Augustine lamented, "What am I to do?"[143]

For the remainder of the letter, Augustine repeatedly lamented and sought the intercession of his friend who now possessed episcopal authority. Augustine noted how his friend was now in "the Apostolic See [which previously] judged or upheld the judgement of others" in cases where bishops were punished for sins, yet not "stripped of their episcopal dignity."[144] Augustine's hope was that Celestine would adjudicate and uphold the decision of the leadership in this region regarding the case of Antonius. The pastoral heart of Augustine was revealed as he admitted his love both for the people of Fussala, and the bishop who stood accused.[145] His desire was to see both restored: the people to spiritual health free from wrongs, and the bishop to pastoral vitality and Christlike virtue. This episode, Augustine admitted, tempted him to withdraw from pastoral ministry altogether. He confessed that "so great a fear and sorrow" tormented him as he feared the spiritual ruin of both the church and its leader whom he "supported through imprudence."[146] Consequently, Augustine submitted himself to the possibility that he would be judged for its outcome. By writing to his friend who was now in a position of authority, Augustine leaned upon his former letter wherein love was a debt that could never be repaid yet continued to accrue for the purpose of perpetual repayment.

LETTER 245 TO POSSIDIUS

This letter to Possidius, written around 401, betrays a closeness of relationship that matches the description given in the opening of Possidius's biography. It also demonstrates a piece of practical pastoral advice from Augustine to Possidius. Possidius raised the question of proper adornment for Christians. Augustine counseled Possidius not to completely forbid women to wear "gold ornamentation or expensive clothing."[147] Augustine did forbid, however, the use of makeup in public, as it was related to the "trickery of an adulteress" and permitted only in the privacy of a marriage relationship,

---

143. *Epistula* 209.4.
144. *Epistula* 209.8.
145. *Epistula* 209.9.
146. *Epistula* 209.10.
147. *Epistula* 245.1.

but "by way of indulgence, not by way of command."[148] The "true ornament" appropriate for any Christian is the ornament related to "good morals."[149] False color and an overt display of gold, including fancy garments, do not fit the character of a Christian because they distract from the Christian's true display in the world—Christlike virtue.

Augustine adamantly decried the use of superstitious objects such as amulets. These tokens included objects such as men's earrings, which were akin to giving "service to demons."[150] While there are no specific prohibitions against the use of such objects in the New Testament, Augustine believed the universal warning against demonic activity in Scripture was enough to speak to particular instances. That said, he reminded those who wished to continue wearing such items that they should "fear to receive the body of Christ while wearing the sign of the devil."[151] In seeking to provide pastoral encouragement to his friend, Augustine revealed a certain side of his own pastoral heart. The place of adornment in the Christian life was limited to specific things for specific occasions, and anything that could be associated with the demonic should be done away with altogether. This was a pastoral matter of utmost importance, and Augustine sought to strengthen his friend's foundation of pastoral care and encourage greater Christlikeness and moral steadfastness.

SUMMARIZING AUGUSTINE AND
SPIRITUAL FRIENDSHIP WITH CLERGY

In corresponding with those in pastoral ministry, Augustine consistently exhibited specific qualities of spiritual friendship regardless of the occasion. Ministers were called to practice Christlike virtue not only for their own sake, but for the sake of their congregation. Augustine also encouraged ministers to think deeply about Scripture and theological truth. He understood the necessity of striving for virtuous living in light of God's commands

---

148. *Epistula* 245.1.

149. *Epistula* 245.1.

150. *Epistula* 245.2. From this reference, it seems that the use of amulets and talismans were common or at least a ready possibility in the pastoral context of Possidius and Augustine. For more on amulets and talismans in the ancient world, see Peter Arzt-Grabner and Kristin De Troyer, "Ancient Jewish and Christian Amulets and How Magical They Are," *Biblische Notizen* 176 (2018): 5–46. See also E. A. Wallis Budge, *Amulets and Talismans* (New York: University Books, 1961).

151. *Epistula* 245.2.

so that his congregation would follow him as he followed Christ. In some cases, Augustine was the mentor encouraging spiritual fidelity and growth, and in some cases Augustine was imploring that same kind of encouragement from his correspondents. This is because Augustine knew that ministers were not to trust in themselves for virtuous living, but in Christ who is the ultimate model of virtue. Though Augustine understood this calling to exhibit Christlike virtue, he also understood that preachers were fallen and not always worthy of imitation; yet God may still use such men. Regarding the virtues of ministers, Augustine once exhorted his audience: "Be imitators of them, as they are of Christ. A good man preaches to you; pick the grapes from the vine. A bad man preaches to you; pick the grapes hanging in the hedge. … That's what I'm saying: learn from him what's good, taking care not to fall into his bad habits."[152]

Augustine understood the trials of pastoral ministry, and therefore he sought to encourage his friends to persevere and asked them for the same encouragement. Bishops in the late fourth century were community leaders, expected to play a role in secular politics and affairs of the day. Thus, there was a heavy burden of responsibility for those in ministry. Spiritual friendship in these exchanges included the call for endurance, though not based on their own strength but based on the grace of God. While Augustine did not know all of these fellow clergy as closely as others, he understood the plight of their calling and could easily identify with the pastoral issues and theological burdens they carried. Augustine affirmed that it was God who had called these men into ministry; it would be God who would carry them through. Spiritual friendship included reminding one another of God's work in their lives for the purpose of serving others, as Augustine demonstrated with those called to ministry. Spiritual friendship with other clergy included encouraging them toward Christlike virtue and deeper theological reflection for the purpose of strengthening their own souls and the souls of those to whom they ministered.

---

152. Sermon 104.10, in Augustine, *Essential Sermons*, ed. Daniel Doyle, trans. Edmund Hill, *Works of Saint Augustine* III/Homilies (Hyde Park, NY: New City Press, 2007), 158.

CONCLUSION

In this chapter, I have demonstrated how Augustine practiced spiritual friendship with fellow clergy. He engaged these spiritual leaders on various levels pertaining to leading in the church and how to be a shepherd who followed the directives of Scripture. Augustine likewise implored others to encourage him in that same endeavor. He encouraged them toward Christlike virtue based on a deep sense of the minister's duty to model Christ to their congregation. Augustine called upon fellow clergy to reflect more deeply on Scripture in order to be more effective preachers and teachers. Based on the demands of pastoral ministry, spiritual friendship was vital for Augustine and those ministers he befriended. Thus, spiritual friendship was focused upon encouraging mutual Christlike virtue and growing in biblical knowledge together.

7

"LONG FOR THAT DIVINE AND HEAVENLY CITY"

Spiritual Friendship as Civic Counsel in Augustine's Epistolary Exchange with Roman Officials

> *No one can truly be another's friend unless he has first been the friend of truth itself.*
>
> —Augustine to Macedonius[1]

INTRODUCTION

Augustine was no stranger to the political arena. His interaction with civic officials of considerable stature is well documented in his letters and other writings. His writings to civil magistrates indicate a desire to encourage them in their role by offering his continual support and advice.[2] Augustine sought to support the work of various civic officials and to motivate them toward Christian virtue. Numerous topics arise in these exchanges, from how best to deal with the Donatist controversy, to corporal punishment and the virtues of Christian citizenship within the city of God. According to Augustine, "Only in the life, death, and resurrection of Christ ... can civic

---

1. Augustine, *Epistula* 155.1.1.

2. Peter Iver Kaufman notes, "Augustine had no interest in supplanting secular magistrates. He was terribly unhappy umpiring disputes in his church's courts, a chore he relinquished to a lieutenant late in his career. He was emphatic: rather than unseating or superseding statesmen, prelates ought to support and advise them." Peter Iver Kaufman, *Augustine's Leaders* (Eugene, OR: Cascade, 2017), 149.

virtues such as piety and courage be seen perfectly fulfilled."[3] Christ is the ultimate paragon of virtue—the only one worthy of imitation. Christ-centered encouragement infused Augustine's letters to these various individuals.

Pivotal to understanding Augustine's conception of civic virtue in Christian perspective is the idea of the heavenly commonwealth. This community, made up of the angels and saints, provides a company along the journey of life in which the faithful set their eyes upon the goal of the beatific vision—of beholding God as the fulfillment of the Christian life. This understanding of the heavenly commonwealth is most visible in Augustine's *City of God*. This conception of two cities ultimately guides Augustine's conception of mankind and his desires. This idea actually provides hope for the earthly commonwealth, even though the heavenly city was seen as primary.[4] Augustine had hope for the earthly city and its civic rulers, so long as they set their gaze on the heavenly city. This notion is woven throughout his exchanges with various civic officials and demonstrates one of the main ways in which his friendship was expressed. As a friend, Augustine sought to encourage these individuals by helping them set their sights on the eternal city so they would best perform their duties in the earthly city. Augustine's friendship in these relationships was intended to help civic officials frame their responsibilities in light of eternity. Augustine engaged these individuals so that they might see the spiritual significance of their work; hence spiritual friendship here sought to direct temporal work toward eternal outcomes.

Specifically, Augustine sought to encourage and guide these civic officials toward a better understanding of how their Christian commitments should impact their political life and decisions. These officials would best serve the common good by following the path of Christlike virtue. This chapter demonstrates that Augustine, in his exchange with various civic officials, presented a vision of the heavenly city as a foundation for serving

---

3. Augustine, *Political Writings*, ed. E. M. Atkins and R. J. Dodaro, Cambridge Texts in the History of Political Thought (Cambridge: Cambridge University Press, 2001), xvi.

4. For a recent and convincing argument regarding Augustine's hope for temporal goods, see Michael Lamb, "Between Presumption and Despair: Augustine's Hope for the Commonwealth," *American Political Science Review* 112, no. 4 (November 2018): 1036–49. See also Clair, *Discerning the Good*, 75–106.

the earthly city. His friendship took the shape of moral guidance, advising his readers toward greater understanding and appreciation of the Truth, which is Christ.

AUGUSTINE AND MARCELLINUS

Flavius Marcellinus (d. 413) was a Christian imperial commissioner in North Africa. In 411, during a conference between Donatists and Catholics, he and Augustine met and became friends.[5] The posture Augustine displayed in his letters to Marcellinus was one of a wise friend seeking to lead Marcellinus toward Christian truth and Christian virtue. Specifically, Marcellinus had the opportunity to display the virtues of Christ in his high position. As one who was simultaneously a man of imperial rank and a son of the church, Marcellinus's duty was ultimately to Christ, and Augustine called upon him to manifest his faith in the public sphere for the common good. Of particular interest in these exchanges is Augustine's view of the Donatist sect (including its various smaller factions) and the way in which governmental authorities should be involved.[6]

Marcellinus had the unique opportunity to influence civil affairs. As a son of the church, Marcellinus's first responsibility was to live in accordance with the law of Christ, though this would naturally raise questions in regards to his life as an imperial official. How could one's faith be reconciled with a secular vocation? Was one to separate the virtues of the faith from the virtues of the state? To what degree, if any, were they compatible with one another? Marcellinus was a curious soul, interested in matters of Scripture and theology, and hence established friendships with Christian thinkers like Augustine and Jerome. In their friendship, Augustine sought to guide Marcellinus through these various questions in order to provide a strong

---

5. Michael Walsh, "Marcellinus Flavius" in *A New Dictionary of Saints: East and West* (Collegeville, MN: Liturgical, 2007), s.v. "Marcellinus Flavius."

6. For a helpful overview of Augustine and the Donatist controversy, see Geoffrey G. Willis, *Saint Augustine and the Donatist Controversy* (Eugene, OR: Wipf & Stock, 2005). For a more recent overview of the Donatist controversy, see Richard Miles, ed., *The Donatist Schism: Controversy and Contexts*, Translated Texts for Historians Contexts 2 (Liverpool, England: Liverpool University Press, 2018). For recent treatments on Augustine against the Donatists, see Adam Ployd, *Augustine, the Trinity, and the Church: A Reading of the Anti-Donatist Sermons* (New York: Oxford University Press, 2015); Ployd, "The Power of Baptism: Augustine's Pro-Nicene Response to the Donatists," *Journal of Early Christian Studies* 22, no. 4 (2014): 519–40.

foundation from which this civic official could operate both as a Christian and as an effective administrator.

LETTER 133

This letter, written toward the end of 411, concerned the treatment of the Donatists and the Circumcellions, a violent offshoot of the Donatist sect. Augustine took it upon himself to encourage his friend Marcellinus toward clemency on behalf of these two groups. Though there were certain crimes that could be attributed to these groups, Augustine desired to see those within these groups "steered to the peace of good health."[7] Augustine believed that crimes should not go unpunished, but his appeal was to amend the nature of the punishment for the sake of their souls and the betterment of their society. To this end, Augustine entreated Marcellinus, "Carry out, O Christian judge, the duty of a loving father."[8] He encouraged his friend to avoid the desire for revenge and seek instead to "heal the wounds of sinners."[9] The typical instruments of cruel torture should not be used when "a form of restraint" common to parents and teachers would suffice in order to preserve gentleness.[10] Augustine asserted that Marcellinus's leadership was ultimately for the benefit of the church.[11] This allowed Augustine to speak with the authority of a bishop to one of the faithful. Augustine implored Marcellinus, "If you do not listen to a friend begging you, listen to a bishop giving you advice."[12] Marcellinus, along with his brother Apringius who served as proconsul residing in Carthage, should act as "sons of the Church" and "not forget to manifest [their] faith" in dealing with judicial matters.[13]

---

7. *Epistula* 133.1.
8. *Epistula* 133.2.
9. *Epistula* 133.2.
10. *Epistula* 133.2.
11. *Epistula* 133.3.
12. *Epistula* 133.3.
13. *Epistula* 133.3. Augustine wrote a similar letter (*Epistula* 134) to Apringius, encouraging him toward mercy in regard to Circumcellions and Donatists accused of violence.

LETTER 136

In 411 or 412, Marcellinus provided a reply to Augustine, yet did not mention Augustine's plea toward clemency regarding the Donatists and Circumcellions.[14] Instead, he insisted that Augustine answer the questions posed to him by their common acquaintance, Volusian.[15] Marcellinus's question was an apologetic one—how is Christ unique among other philosophers of his day? He notes how Volusian, a pagan, was being "held back from the stability of the true faith" because of the persuasive talk of many within these scholarly circles.[16] Having been shaken by Volusian's enquiries, Marcellinus was unsure how to understand that Christ would "take delight in the new sacrifices after having rejected the old ones."[17] Additionally, Marcellinus struggled to see the connection between the teachings of Christ and the laws of the state. Marcellinus implored Augustine to address these issues and to "present a brilliant solution to all these objections."[18] Such a response, according to Marcellinus, would benefit the entire church. Augustine would go on to do so in his Letter 137.

LETTER 138

Augustine wrote in response to Volusian in Letter 137, yet he also sent his answers to Marcellinus in Letter 138 in 411 or 412. Though the same in content, the tone differed based on their established relationship. In this reply, he continued to emphasize the role that Christian virtue should have in one's vocation, specifically as one who worked for the state and the public good. Though Christian virtue could certainly benefit the Roman state, the

---

14. The Circumcellions were a violent offshoot within the Donatist church. Their name comes from *circum cellas* meaning "those prowling around rural homes." Allan Fitzgerald notes, "The *Circumcelliones* considered violence against Catholics a pious act, especially against Donatist clergy who converted to Catholicism or against Catholic bishops who opposed them." Allan D. Fitzgerald, "Circumcellions" in *Augustine through the Ages*, s.v. "Circumcellions."

15. Volusian, a pagan intellectual, wrote to Augustine and his letter is *Epistula* 135 in Augustine's collection. In this letter, Volusian posed questions regarding the incarnation and the miracles of Christ. Volusian wrote to Augustine at the behest of various friends that had gathered in Carthage for discussions around such topics.

16. *Epistula* 136.1.

17. *Epistula* 136.2.

18. *Epistula* 136.3.

preaching of the gospel and the practice of Christian virtue were especially
for the attainment of the kingdom of heaven.[19]

Volusian took issue with the idea that the Old Testament sacrifices had
been abolished and replaced with the sacraments of the New Testament. In
his mind, if the old sacrifices were correct and prescribed by God, there would
be no need to replace them. To this Augustine quipped that "time would run
out" if he were to offer all the examples of ways in which plans change according to the season yet still remain part of a larger plan.[20] After discussing a
few examples, Augustine related this to the sovereignty of God, "who knows
much better than a human being."[21] God is like an artist who plays "a great
song" and who orchestrates all things according to his purposes.[22] He does this
not for his own sake but for the benefit of mankind.[23] God does not need any
sacrifices, regardless of when they are commanded, but rather they serve as
"signs of gifts God has bestowed either for imbuing the soul with the virtues or
for attaining eternal salvation."[24] Augustine's main point was to demonstrate
that all such signs point to Christ, whether they were pointing forward in
the Old Testament or whether they point back as in the current sacraments.

The next question dealt with the compatibility between Christian virtue
and the concerns of the state. Augustine referred to numerous examples
to prove their compatibility. He noted the absurdity that Julius Caesar was
praised for refraining from vengeance, yet a similar biblical virtue was
derided as against the state's interest.[25] The Christian way of turning the
other cheek demonstrates that evil can be overcome with good.[26] These sorts
of actions, according to Augustine, "pertain to the disposition of the heart,
which is something interior, rather than to action, which is something exteri-
or."[27] Augustine sought to demonstrate how these virtues related to the state,
encouraging Marcellinus to see how a certain internal posture would affect

19. *Epistula* 138.17.
20. *Epistula* 138.2.
21. *Epistula* 138.5.
22. *Epistula* 138.1.5.
23. *Epistula* 138.1.6.
24. *Epistula* 138.1.6.
25. *Epistula* 138.2.10.
26. *Epistula* 138.2.11.
27. *Epistula* 138.2.13.

his outward action. Mercy could be an effective weapon against wrongdoing, causing the perpetrator to give up "licentious passions" that are contrary to a just state.[28] If only the state were full of more citizens who adhered to Christian virtue it would be a "great boon for the state."[29] The reality was that the Roman state began its moral decline long before Christ, as attested by various sources. Evils were compounded among the Romans, until the "singular help against these evils" appeared in the person of Jesus Christ.[30] For this "heavenly authority" has ushered in "light-filled and powerful virtues of life" not only for the sake of the earthly city, but also for the citizens of the "heavenly and divine republic."[31] The founders of Rome introduced various civic virtues which were honorable, but in themselves they were incomplete. Only Christianity can make people citizens of another city "whose king is truth, whose law is love, and whose limit is eternity."[32]

Having adequately addressed the question of compatibility between Christianity and the Roman state, Augustine turned to assess the uniqueness of Christ's work compared to other miracle workers. This he connected to the folly of the Roman gods in general. The moral failings of the Roman state can be clearly linked to their admiration of the Roman gods who served as poor moral role models. Though demonic power was seen in magical arts, Augustine had a particular distaste for the deities of Rome. The basis of happiness and stability, therefore, should not be demons, or even miracle workers, but "him whom the angels serve and before whom the demons tremble."[33] Augustine dealt with the case of Apuleius, a second-century Latin prose writer and promoter of mystery cults. Apuleius seemed to be nothing more than a gifted speaker who was able to convince others. As such, his testimony seems to be more self-perpetuated than actually attested by observation and fact. Such "magical arts" are nothing in comparison to the holy prophets and to Christ himself, "who those prophets ... foretold would come both in the flesh that he assumed from the Virgin and the divinity in which

28. *Epistula* 138.2.14.
29. *Epistula* 138.2.15.
30. *Epistula* 138.3.17.
31. *Epistula* 138.3.17.
32. *Epistula* 138.3.17.
33. *Epistula* 138.4.18.

he is never separated from the Father!"[34] As he closed this letter, Augustine admitted that he had not said all that he had wanted regarding the person and work of Christ. Augustine asked that Marcellinus would write him back with further objections in order to address those and bring further clarity and stability to his friend's mind.

LETTER 139

This short letter, written at the beginning of 412, represents somewhat of an interruption from their previous epistolary dialogue. This letter brought the conversation back to the Donatist controversy, specifically regarding a conference at Carthage where many Donatists were present and supposedly repented of various crimes. Augustine implored his friend to demonstrate leniency toward the Donatists. The task of unification was no small one, and accomplished successfully, would verify the grace and truth of the "Catholic peace," which was "not something unimportant that God wanted to accomplish through [Marcellinus's] efforts."[35] Augustine asked that the death penalty be commuted in this case, "both on account of [Augustine and Marcellinus's] conscience and for the sake of emphasizing Catholic gentleness."[36] Though in many cases their crimes were great, commuting their sentence should not be outside the bounds for the Lord's mercy and should display the "goodness of the Church … in its exemplary brilliance."[37] Augustine entreated his friend to speak with his brother, the proconsul Apringius, and encourage leniency. Augustine insisted his letters requesting mercy be read and added to the judicial proceedings.[38] Augustine sought imperial intervention if there was any hesitancy toward clemency, citing a previous instance of Catholic martyrs whose killers were pardoned by the emperor.[39]

---

34. *Epistula* 138.4.20.

35. *Epistula* 139.1.

36. *Epistula* 139.2.

37. *Epistula* 139.2.

38. *Epistula* 139.2.

39. *Epistula* 139.2. Augustine mentions here the martyrdom of various clerics in the "Vale of Non," which is modern day Val di Non, in northeastern Italy near Trento. This instance of martyrdom refers to three clerics who were ordained by the bishop of Trent and sent out as missionaries. They were martyred by pagan villagers in 397 upon refusing to sacrifice to Saturn. For a modern assessment of this instance, see H. A. Drake, *Violence in Late Antiquity: Perceptions and Practices* (Aldershot, UK: Routledge, 2006).

In the remainder of the letter, Augustine recounted various writings that dealt with the Donatist schism and various decisions related to the afore-mentioned conference in Carthage. As he concluded, Augustine reminded Marcellinus to heed his encouragement and asked for any necessary admon-ishment. Augustine believed that such admonishment was "accomplishing something."[40] Augustine did not elaborate on what that "something" was, but it seems as if Augustine believed that admonishment from his friend was necessary to aid in his own spiritual formation. This sort of request for admonishment was typical of Augustine's relationships (one thinks specif-ically of his relationship with Jerome). In fact, this request demonstrated that Augustine saw Marcellinus's spiritual feedback as valuable for his own spiritual growth even as he was seeking to encourage him down a path of Christian virtue and wisdom.

Letter 143

This next—and final—letter from Augustine to Marcellinus had him address-ing various biblical and theological questions similar to their earlier corre-spondence. Writing this letter some time in 412, Augustine affirmed that his writings were not free from error, though he wanted to be sure they were as accurate as possible. Augustine encouraged Marcellinus to view his friend in a sober fashion, recognizing both the faults and strengths present in any friend. Additionally, Augustine directed Marcellinus's attention to the authority of Scripture in order to properly criticize human works. Any such criticism must have a solid biblical basis, as only the Scriptures are inerrant and any theological opinion must be scrutinized under the discerning light of God's authoritative word.[41]

To this end and to his critics, Augustine admitted that his thought devel-oped over the course of his life. Writings from his earlier period should be assessed in light of what he believed at a later point. This was not a point of sadness for Augustine but of gratitude. Augustine illustrated this point

---

40. *Epistula* 138.4.

41. For a thorough treatment of Augustine's views on the Bible, see Pamela Bright, ed., *Augustine and the Bible* (Notre Dame, IN: University of Notre Dame Press, 1999). For an under-standing of Augustine's spirituality connected to Scripture, particularly explained in his letters, see Coleman M. Ford, "'He Who Consoles Us Should Console You': The Spirituality of the Word in Select Letters of Augustine of Hippo," *Evangelical Quarterly* 89, no. 3 (2018): 240–57.

in terms of humility: "For a man loves himself far too wrongly if he wants others to remain in error in order that his own error may remain hidden."[42] Augustine desired correction and admonition were he ever guilty of error. Augustine argued against Cicero, who once said that he "never uttered a word that he would want to take back."[43] Augustine thought Cicero's statement foolish. Regretting any foolish or inappropriate talk is a sign of intelligence, not weakness.[44] This required humility and a knowledge of one's limitations. Augustine's self-admonition was meant to warn Marcellinus against giving undue praise to Augustine. Were he to find himself in a conversation defending Augustine, Marcellinus must be careful not to paint Augustine as "so great a man that in your opinion I would never have erred in my writings."[45] Augustine would denounce Marcellinus and not be pleased were his "dearest friends" to think of him as someone that he was not. Thus, true love for a friend would be honest in one's understanding of both his or her gifts and weaknesses.

Though Augustine was desiring of admonition, he did not wish to receive undue criticism. For this reason, he withheld the publication of both his *On Genesis Literally Interpreted* and *The Trinity*. He understood that such topics were capable of generating "dangerous questions" and wished to minimize any errors which could appear "if they were published in headlong haste and without more reflection."[46] This may have been contrary to Marcellinus's wisdom, and that of Augustine's fellow clerics, who wished him to publish and be able to defend his ideas while he was still living. It seemed to be the case that "carping enemies or less intelligent friends" were beginning to

---

42. *Epistula* 143.2.
43. *Epistula* 143.3. Augustine here cites Cicero's *Fragmenta incerta* 1.11.
44. *Epistula* 143.3.
45. *Epistula* 143.3.
46. *Epistula* 143.4. Augustine mentions the incident of the premature publication of *Trin.* 1–12 in his *Retract.* 2.15: "When, however, I had not yet finished the thirteenth Book, and some who were exceedingly anxious to have the work were kept waiting longer than they could bear, it was stolen from me in a less correct state than it either could or would have been had it appeared when I intended. And as soon as I discovered this, having other copies of it, I had determined at first not to publish it myself, but to mention what had happened in the matter in some other work; but at the urgent request of brethren, whom I could not refuse, I corrected it as much as I thought fit, and finished and published it, with the addition, at the beginning, of a letter that I had written to the venerable Aurelius, Bishop of Carthage, in which I set forth, in the way of prologue, what had happened, what I had intended to do of myself, and what love of my brethren had forced me to do."

criticize ideas that Augustine defended.[47] Augustine went on to clarify ideas from his *Free Will*. After clarifying how he viewed the relationship between the corruptible body and the soul, Augustine encouraged additional correction from his readers. He asserted, "For, if those books cannot be corrected because they have already come into the hands of many people, I certainly can be corrected since I am still living."[48] In this regard, Augustine insisted that any sort of criticism be based firmly in the authority of Scripture. As Augustine admitted, understanding the origin of the soul was difficult and the Scriptures gave multiple ways of understanding it. Augustine focused his thought on God as the creator of souls, though he admitted there were multiple ways to arrive at that understanding. Thus, he reiterated that any such argument should be grounded in the Scriptures as they have been "accepted as authoritative by the Church."[49] Augustine concluded with an affirmation of the virginity of Mary at Christ's birth. Anyone who denied this must also "deny everything that takes place miraculously in bodies."[50]

Though this letter ended rather abruptly, Augustine's point to Marcellinus was clear: all theological opinion should be filtered through the authoritative Scriptures. Augustine himself scrutinized his work in such a way, and he wished that others would do so as well. Marcellinus should be aware of the danger of making much of one's own opinion or the opinion of another. The reality of theological conversation is that one's opinion should change as they grow in their knowledge of Scripture. It was foolish to never regret one's previous thinking. In this way, Augustine encouraged his friend to understand the seriousness of theological discussion and the humility required to grow in their comprehension and articulation of truth.

AUGUSTINE AND BONIFACE

As he had done with other officials such as Marcellinus, Augustine was hoping to encourage Boniface and bring him along in the Catholic faith, being his guide in Christian virtue, all the while addressing concerns and answering questions in order to establish confidence and aid him in his calling as a civic

---

47. *Epistula* 143.4.
48. *Epistula* 143.7.
49. *Epistula* 143.11.
50. *Epistula* 143.12.

official. Boniface (d. 432 CE), or Bonifatius, was a Roman general and governor in North Africa. He was often occupied with battles against various Gothic groups, particularly the Vandals after they had invaded North Africa. Additionally, he took up arms in various campaigns against other Roman military officials, engaging in various civil wars.[51] Though we have records of events in which he was involved, no sources on Boniface exist before Augustine began his correspondence with him.[52] He would meet his end in a skirmish against his political rival Aetius on his way to Ravenna to be named *magister militum prasentalis* by Galla Placidia, daughter of Theodosius I and regent of the Western Roman Empire from 425 to 437.[53] Readers will not discern much of the military or political background in reading these letters. Augustine's primary concern with Boniface was to engage him on various points of theology, encouraging him to see his civil position in light of his faith. Readers will also see, particularly in Letter 189, that Augustine adopts a more critical tone in addressing the moral implications of Boniface's multiple marriages. The bulk of their epistolary exchange is found in the letters that follow, though two letters are not represented in this treatment. Letter 185A represents a fragment of another letter between Augustine and Boniface, and Letter 17* in the Divjak collection is a short letter describing two messengers who could not fulfill their travels based on a violent storm. In all of this correspondence, Augustine's goal remained simple: to mentor Boniface in the ways of Christ in order that he might be not only an effective ruler but a just and Christlike one as well.

LETTER 185

Augustine wrote Letter 185 around 417 in order to present in more detail the Donatist error, including some of their violent acts, and the dynamic between this schismatic group and the Catholics. Augustine treated this letter as a book and gave it the title *The Correction of the Donatists*. This short book was

---

51. For more on Boniface's engagement in Roman civil warfare, see Jeroen W. P. Wijnendaele, *The Last of the Romans: Bonifatius—Warlord and Comes Africae* (London: Bloomsbury Academic, 2015), 43–64.

52. Wijnendaele, *The Last of the Romans*, 31.

53. Meghan A. McEvoy, *Child Emperor Rule in the Late Roman West* (Oxford: Oxford University Press, 2013), 248. For more on his summons to Ravenna, see Stewart Irvin Oost, *Galla Placidia Augusta: A Biographical Essay* (Chicago: University of Chicago Press, 1968), 230–33.

dedicated exclusively to explaining the error of the Donatist schism and the reality, according to Augustine, of their lostness based on pride and a disassociation from Christ as their head.

Augustine praised his friend Boniface for his desire to know the things of God, stating, "From this it is truly evident that you serve the faith that you have in Christ even in a military setting."[54] From this desire, Augustine wished to bring further insight to Boniface regarding the key differences between groups like the Arians and the Donatists. The Donatists, unlike the Arians, agreed with Catholic doctrine, on such matters as the Trinity, for instance. These things, both doctrinal error and schism, were predicted and thus to be expected though lamented. This should cause one all the more to pray "that the Lord may open their minds and that they may understand the scriptures."[55] Though the Donatists had an orthodox view of Christ, they were lacking in the right view of his church. Forsaking the teaching of Scripture regarding the universality of the church, they had gathered as a separate sect in a small corner of the empire. For Augustine this was one of the key arguments against the validity of the Donatists. Augustine asserted, "For they prefer their contentions to the divine testimonies."[56] Though the Donatists based their argument for schism on the false ordination of Caecilian of Carthage (fl. fourth century), such a claim was difficult to substantiate, according to Augustine. The argument from Scripture for unity, however, was much stronger, for "the whole of the scriptures proclaim with one voice the Church spread through the whole world, with which the sect of Donatus is not in communion."[57]

This said, there were many who are turning back to the Catholic unity, and they "give thanks that they have been corrected and set free from that mad destruction."[58] In this regard, Augustine encouraged Boniface to not abandon hope for a fellow human or brother "lest he perish for eternity!"[59] Having been corrected, these individuals should see grace and give thanks

---

54. *Epistula* 185.1.1, in *Letters 156–210*, trans. Roland Teske, ed. Boniface Ramsey, *Works of Saint Augustine* II/3 (Hyde Park, NY: New City Press, 2005).
55. *Epistula* 185.1.2.
56. *Epistula* 185.1.4.
57. *Epistula* 185.1.5.
58. *Epistula* 185.2.7.
59. *Epistula* 185.2.7.

despite suffering persecution. Augustine desired to show good to these errant brothers, whether through "the words of Catholic preachers or by the laws of Catholic emperors."[60] In this, Augustine encouraged his friend toward the proper administration of justice. These sectarians had rebelled against the emperor's law, yet they boasted of their innocence. These individuals were not true martyrs since they participated in the "impious division of Christian unity" rather than suffering persecution "on account of justice."[61] There were two options for these people according, to Augustine: perish like the demon-possessed pigs who drown in the sea (cf. Matt 17:14-18) or be "gathered to the loving bosom of the Catholic mother."[62]

Augustine gave an additional account of a schismatic group within the Donatists led by a man name Maximian.[63] Maximian and his group had been officially condemned by a Donatist council at Bagaï in 394.[64] Augustine had even written his Letter 23 to Maximian around that time to encourage him toward unity. In providing all these details, Augustine was equipping Boniface to understand the extent of the Donatist schism and its ongoing danger to Catholic unity. So "inflamed with anger" and "aroused by such goads of hatred" were the Donatists that there was "hardly any road [that] was safe for those to travel who preached the Catholic peace against their madness and refuted their insanity with the plain truth."[65] This background and information should be important to Boniface, who was charged with upholding the law and knowing what took place within his lands. It should likewise be important for a Catholic like Boniface hoping to solidify his own faith and encourage the faithful. Augustine encouraged his civic friend by relating his calling to those of the former kings of Israel: "For ... he serves [God] by living a life of faith, but, because he is also a king, he serves him by upholding with appropriate force laws that command what is just and

---

60. *Epistula* 185.2.8.

61. *Epistula* 185.2.9.

62. *Epistula* 185.3.12.

63. For more on the context and events leading up to Maximian's break from the Donatists, see W. H. C. Frend, *The Donatist Church: A Movement of Protest in Roman North Africa* (Oxford: Oxford University Press, 1985), 213-24.

64. Maureen A. Tilley, "Anti-Donatist Works" in Fitzgerald, *Augustine through the Ages*, s.v. "Anti-Donatist Works."

65. *Epistula* 185.4.18.

forbid what is unjust."[66] Boniface, a ruler led both by faith and law, should justly promote the commands of God.[67] Augustine thought it best to convince people of error "by instruction [rather] than by the fear or the pain of punishment."[68] That said, Augustine never denied the need for the latter, for some were "guided by love," yet for others "fear corrects."[69]

To prove his point, Augustine cited numerous texts from Proverbs on discipline, as well as comparing the Lord's handling of different situations such as the calling of Paul, previously a persecutor of the church. Donatists themselves should recognize in the case of Paul how Christ used force "and afterward teaching, first striking and afterward consoling."[70] In this sense the church was justified in using force to call back "her lost children," whether they themselves were "forcing others to perish" or simply misleading, calling them "back to her bosom through fearsome but salutary laws."[71] The calling of the church was to seek out lost and wandering sheep, even through the fear of punishment. In this way, the church "imitates its Lord" who likewise forced Paul.[72] This use of force is justified as well by the fact that the Donatists, through disunity from Christ, force other toward what is evil. In the church's force, the direction is toward truth and goodness rather than schism and disunity from the head that is Christ.

Augustine continued to recount various instances of violence and oppression against Catholics from the Donatists. These included slander and other crimes. Though these sins were grievous, Augustine identified pride as the main sin of the Donatists. Their supposed sinlessness, according to Augustine, would prohibit them from praying the Lord's Prayer and asking for ongoing forgiveness. To believe that they are above the need to pray as the Lord

---

66. *Epistula* 185.5.19.

67. This idea relates to Augustine's view of civil authority in general. While Christian officials have a certain duty to act in accordance with Christian virtue, all government officials are to be viewed as acting out God's justice. Augustine recognizes that there are unjust rulers, but the burden to administer God's justice is on them nevertheless. For a helpful analysis of Augustine's view of civil authority, see Robert Dodaro, "Between the Two Cities: Political Action in Augustine of Hippo," in *Augustine and Politics*, ed. John Doody, Kevin L. Hughes, and Kim Paffenroth (Lanham, MD: Lexington, 2005), 99–116.

68. *Epistula* 185.6.21.

69. *Epistula* 185.6.21.

70. *Epistula* 185.6.22.

71. *Epistula* 185.6.23.

72. *Epistula* 185.6.23.

has commanded, and by denying a host of other texts regarding confession, the Donatists had reached the height of pride. The Donatists did not see the contradiction of their position; because they had broken off, they no longer had Christ as the head. In this way they were disconnected from the one who provided righteousness. Thus, the Catholic peace was seeking them out so that they would not remain unrighteous. All members could rejoice when the lost were found.[73] Augustine tempered the call to use force if necessary, based on the desire to seek out those who were lost for their own good. Speaking specifically to Donatist clerics, following penance, they were to be embraced and serve the church with their gifts of leadership. Augustine asserted, "We do not hate them; in fact, we embrace them, desire them, exhort them."[74] Augustine affirmed that Donatists had not committed the unforgivable sin against the Holy Spirit, so long as they repented and received forgiveness "in the unity of the body of Christ, to which the Holy Spirit gives life."[75]

Augustine closed this letter with a grave reminder that those who remain outside the church lack the Holy Spirit. Though the Donatists may have the appearance of the sacrament—that is, the Eucharist—"they do not have the reality of him whose sacrament it is."[76] The one bread of the celebration represents the unity of the body. Thus, Augustine asserted that the Spirit does not give life to anyone outside Christ's body. In fact, those who exist as enemies of unity have "no share in the love of God," meaning that they do not have the Spirit.[77] The only hope people have is inside the church, but not in pretense; one must be truly present by faith in unity "so that he may truly grow in union

---

73. *Epistula* 185.10.43.

74. *Epistula* 185.8.46.

75. *Epistula* 185.9.48.

76. *Epistula* 185.9.50.

77. *Epistula* 185.9.50. The absence of the Spirit was a pivotal point for Augustine's argument against the Donatists. Only the Catholic church could guarantee the Trinitarian work in the life of the believer because it was unified with Christ. Adam Ployd provides helpful insight to Augustine's Trinitarian vision of church unity, and specifically, his reflection on Acts 4:32 to the end. Ployd notes the biblical logic with which Augustine constructs his argument for the consubstantiality of the Godhead. Augustine demonstrates a coherence with previous pro-Nicene interpreters such as Ambrose of Milan and Hilary of Poitiers, using the "same constellation of texts." Augustine, therefore, demonstrates the thoroughly biblical argument of Trinitarian relations *ad intra* as opposed to his Arian dialogue partner. For additional reflection on Acts 4:32 and similar biblical passages in Augustine's thought, see Ployd, *Augustine, the Trinity, and the Church*, 108–9.

with the tree of life."[78] Augustine confirmed Boniface as a son of the church who needed this knowledge in order to effectively execute his duties. The goal, as previously stated, was to compel Donatists to see their error and return to the peace and unity of the Catholic church. Augustine encouraged Boniface to bring those who are in error to the "teachers of the Church."[79] By doing so, he would both fulfill his duties as an administrator and as a Christian.

LETTER 189

Augustine wrote again to Boniface in late 417, this time in a somewhat hurried manner. Boniface had desired to hear from Augustine regarding the Christian life and an encouraging word meant to build him up "for the eternal salvation that [he hoped] for in our Lord Jesus Christ."[80] Their mutual friend Faustus encouraged Augustine to reply quickly based on a sincere love for Boniface. The Christian life, according to Augustine, was founded on Christ's dual command of love for God and love for others. Boniface should "[make] progress daily in this love ... both by praying and by doing good, in order that with the help of him who commanded and gave this love to you."[81] Augustine cited Romans 5:5 and the Spirit as the agent of this love. Apart from this outpouring of love, the Christian life would be impossible. This love motivated the patriarchs, prophets, apostles, and martyrs of the faith. This love likewise motivates all believers who are seeking the kingdom of heaven, an eternal inheritance, and the vision of God, "whose sweetness and delight surpass not only all the beauty of bodies but even all the splendor of souls, however just and holy."[82]

   Augustine encouraged his friend by affirming that soldiers are just as capable of pleasing God. Numerous examples in Scripture attested to soldiers who capably served God. Boniface was called to struggle against "visible barbarians" while others "fight against invisible enemies" by praying on his behalf.[83] Because of this, Boniface was reminded that his "bodily strength

---

78. *Epistula* 185.9.50.
79. *Epistula* 185.9.51.
80. *Epistula* 189.1.
81. *Epistula* 189.2.
82. *Epistula* 185.3.
83. *Epistula* 189.5.

is a gift of God."[84] As Boniface engaged in battle, Augustine encouraged him to keep the goal of both temporal and eternal peace in perspective for the peace of God was much sweeter than human peace.[85]

As a committed Catholic, Boniface was called to both seek the peace of God, as well as live a life of purity. He was to let "marital chastity adorn [his] conduct" and not be conquered by lust nor "overcome with wine."[86] Likewise, he was not to seek after worldly riches but rather use what riches he had for the sake of heaven "by doing good works."[87] In all these things, Augustine was confident that Boniface was being faithful and was "greatly delighted by [his] reputation."[88] Therefore this letter served as a "mirror" to reflect the sort of character Boniface already possessed, though he should still seek the Scriptures to discover where he was lacking in the good life.[89] Though encouraging him toward virtue, Augustine reminded Boniface that no life was without sin. Our need for prayerful confession was always present.[90] Similarly, Boniface was to be quick to forgive others.

This letter, though short, reveals much about Augustine's desire to encourage men like Boniface toward Christlike virtue. Admittedly rushed, the bishop of Hippo was able to encourage his friend toward the life of love and help him see how his civic and military role fit into the Christian life. Augustine did not discuss issues relating to Donatism or any explicit theological error, yet the encouragement to pursue a life of love based on the power of the Holy Spirit would have addressed those issues from Augustine's perspective. To come alongside his friend in this situation simply provided a boost to further direct Boniface's heart toward Christ.

---

84. *Epistula* 189.6.

85. *Epistula* 189.6.

86. *Epistula* 189.7. As *Epistula* 220 demonstrates, this would turn out not to be the case despite Augustine's strong encouragement. See *Epistula* 220, in *Letters 211-270, 1*-29**, trans. Roland Teske, ed. Boniface Ramsey, *Works of Saint Augustine* II/4 (Hyde Park, NY: New City Press, 2005).

87. *Epistula* 189.7.

88. *Epistula*189.8.

89. *Epistula* 189.8.

90. *Epistula* 189.8.

LETTER 220

Around 427, a decade following his previous two letters, Augustine wrote again to Boniface. In this subsequent letter, he expressed concern for Boniface's spiritual state. Boniface, previously on track for spiritual growth, seems to have veered dramatically. Formerly one who hoped to live a celibate life following the death of his wife, Boniface reneged on that decision in order to marry, as well as involving himself with several concubines.[91] His spiritual disarray was matched by the disarray of his civic duties. Barbarians, once at bay, now ran amok through Africa. Hence Augustine's letter served as a heartfelt corrective for his wayward friend. It was clear that the course of Christlike virtue had been disrupted and that those who were more concerned with the ways of the world were providing counsel. Thus, Augustine stated his goal: "[To] offer you advice in accord with God, lest your soul perish."[92]

Augustine wished to provide counsel from the Lord "through the ministry of [his] weakness."[93] Augustine implored Boniface to consider his "wife of pious memory" and the reality that he had at one point wished to "become a servant of God."[94] Augustine hoped this would help lead his friend back to truth and the way of Christian virtue. In his former period, in which both Augustine and Alypius were present to encourage him, Boniface supposedly was armed "more safely and strongly with the weapons of the spirit."[95] As such, these weapons seemed to have been cast aside once Boniface took a wife, and as rumor had it, began defiling himself "by affairs with various concubines."[96]

---

91. *Epistula* 220.4. Boniface's new wife, Placida, was a wealthy Arian. Augustine also indicated that though there was an agreement for her to convert to the Catholic faith, the Arian influence remained, particularly in his daughter who was reportedly baptized by an Arian group. This Arian group was likely of the Homoian position, holding that the Son was like the Father yet still less than the Father. For more on the Homoian position see Lewis Ayres, *Nicaea and Its Legacy: An Approach to Fourth Century Trinitarian Theology* (Oxford: Oxford University Press, 2004), 133–66. See also R. P. C. Hanson, *The Search for the Christian Doctrine of God* (Grand Rapids: Baker Academic, 2006), 557–97.

92. *Epistula* 220.2.

93. *Epistula* 220.3.

94. *Epistula* 220.3.

95. *Epistula* 220.3.

96. *Epistula* 220.4.

Augustine's friendship with Boniface led him to confront Boniface outright. Noting his particular sins, Augustine asserted, "You are a Christian; you have a heart; you fear God. Consider for yourself what I do not want to say, and you will discover the great sins for which you ought to do penance."[97] Augustine knew that it was the lack of godly influence which steered Boniface toward this course. He had turned to love "the good things of this world ... [which] you ought to have held in contempt and considered worthless?"[98] Boniface was guilty of loving vanity and more fearful of short-term loss than eternal harm.[99] Proof of this came from apparent friends who seemed to protect Boniface, but for the purpose of personal gain.[100] Augustine did not provide any details regarding who these individuals were, but supposedly Augustine was informed not only of Boniface's infidelities but his current entourage as well.

Augustine connected Boniface's personal issues to the civic disruptions which arose in Africa on account of barbarian invasions. As such, he playfully jabbed at Boniface stating that no one would have dared to think that barbarians could succeed "with Boniface as the head of the imperial bodyguards and stationed in Africa as count of Africa with so great an army and such great power."[101] This seemed to no longer be the case, and therefore the "hope of the people has turned in the opposite direction."[102] Augustine did not need to remind Boniface of the military issues present within his jurisdiction, but it was clear that Boniface's about-face in spiritual matters had affected the course of his military endeavors as well.[103] Augustine entreated Boniface to return to the path of Christlike virtue by following the model of Christ, "who gave such great goods and suffered such great evils."[104] Augustine asserted, "I speak to a Christian," in contrast with "advice in terms of this world's

---

97. *Epistula* 220.5.

98. *Epistula* 220.5.

99. *Epistula* 220.5.

100. *Epistula* 220.6.

101. *Epistula* 220.7.

102. *Epistula* 220.7.

103. Augustine does not give details as to the state of the region under barbarian invasion. The Vandals were responsible for the conquest of North Africa following the fall of Rome, laying claim to the region until a Byzantine force recaptured the region in 534 AD. For more on the military history of this period, see Guy Halsall, *Barbarian Migrations and the Roman West, 376–568* (Cambridge: Cambridge University Press, 2008), 220–54.

104. *Epistula* 220.8.

standards."[105] In contrast, Augustine's encouragement was purely spiritual, guiding Boniface with biblical wisdom, specifically warning him against the triple concupiscence identified in 1 John 2:15–17.[106]

Augustine called upon Boniface to be a "man of courage," not based on military or political accomplishment, but one who could conquer his spiritual appetites. Were he to heed Augustine's advice, Boniface would see temporary goods for what they were and thereby maintain the salvation of his soul. Courage also included prayer. God would hear prayers and by them Boniface might "invisibly and spiritually conquer [his] interior and invisible enemies."[107] Boniface would then see the world as it really was, in order to bring good from the bad things of the world and continually focus upon the greatest good, which is God. Everyone possesses and uses earthly goods, but only those who have "the salvation of the soul" can have true righteousness, victory, glory, honor, and peace for eternity.[108] Earthly goods, therefore, were meant to be used in order to achieve heavenly results. Augustine concluded, "[Good] works do not perish, even when they are produced from goods that perish."[109]

As Augustine closed his letter, he reminded Boniface of the love of God over against the love of this world. Boniface's failures, spiritually and politically, arose from disordered loves fixated on his own power and temporal goods.[110] Thus, Augustine proposed a remedy. This included taking a vow of marital chastity with his wife.[111] The circumstances are unclear, but Augustine seemed to think that this relationship was somehow preventing Boniface from "performing good actions by means of the goods of the

---

105. *Epistula* 220.8–9.

106. *Epistula* 220.9.

107. *Epistula* 220.10.

108. *Epistula* 220.11.

109. *Epistula* 220.11.

110. Augustine's notion of necessity is helpful in understanding his advice to Boniface. The idea of necessity relates to the use of force or violence to maintain temporal wellbeing in society. Clair notes, "Boniface's failure to fulfill his role-specific obligations, Augustine implies, is actually rooted in the deeper problem of Boniface's soul. His preoccupation with his own needs has distracted him from his responsibility to care for both the physical and moral security of North Africa. Boniface has completely misinterpreted what *necessity* entails." Clair, *Discerning the Good*, 92.

111. Some have seen this as Augustine's only solution to such a problem regarding the conflict of obligations for those engaged in war. For example, see H. A. Deane, *The Political and Social Ideas of St. Augustine* (New York: Columbia University Press, 1963), 138–39.

world."[112] Founded upon his previous letters, Augustine hoped to see Boniface return again to the path of Chrislike virtue with the eternal city in perspective. This would be the only way in which Boniface would thrive and those under his care would flourish as well. Augustine's current admonition arose from love, which "commanded" him to write Boniface. This love was the love of "God's standards, not by those of the world."[113] Were Boniface to heed Augustine's counsel, he would prove himself to be not "a fool but a wise man."[114]

AUGUSTINE AND MACEDONIUS

Macedonius served as the imperial vicar of Africa and oversaw the entire administration of justice in Roman Africa.[115] He initiated the relationship with a letter to Augustine that is no longer extant. Augustine implored his new civic friend to consider pardoning a criminal, which led to a conversation on the duty Macedonius had toward humanity especially as a Christian who had a "duty to love."[116] Hence, Augustine's primary goal was to advise Macedonius on the function of love for a Christian which, for Macedonius, should lead to performing his civic duties out of a love for God and others.

LETTER 152

In Letter 152, written in 413 or 414, Macedonius began the exchange with affectionate language not unlike most ancient epistolary exchanges. What differed in this exchange was the spiritual authority attributed to Augustine, recognizing both his wisdom and discernment in all matters. Macedonius noted Augustine's previously expressed desire to intercede for a criminal facing the death penalty.[117] Macedonius understood that it was Augustine's priestly duty to intervene on behalf of the convicted. Concerning this priestly duty, Macedonius expressed a certain measure of confusion. The Lord's

---

112. *Epistula* 220.12.

113. *Epistula* 220.12.

114. *Epistula* 220.12.

115. For more on Macedonius in general, see J. R. Martindale, *The Prosopography of the Later Roman Empire*, 2 vols. (Cambridge: Cambridge University Press, 1980), 2:697.

116. *Epistula* 153.5.19.

117. Augustine's original letter requesting clemency is not extant, but the introduction to *Epistula* 152 reveals such a previous request.

prohibitions against sin were unambiguous, so why would he be party to any criminal act, even through intercession? Macedonius referred to the act of canonical penance within the church—the act of penance for grave sin following one's baptism—as warrant for his confusion. There was no more than one opportunity to repent, so would continual intercession not deny this teaching of the church? Macedonius posed a question to kindle further discussion with his ecclesiastical counterpart. He asked, "[How] can we claim in the name of religion that we should forgive a crime, no matter of what sort it is?"[118]

Though Augustine initiated the conversation, Macedonius maintained and cultivated the relationship. Rather than dismissing Augustine, he admired the bishop and expressed gratitude for Augustine's act of intercession.[119] However, Macedonius believed that sin should not go unpunished and that those wishing to see a guilty one go unpunished became a party to the guilty one themselves. Thus, Macedonius struggled with Augustine's request. This struggle, and the subsequent conversation, contributed to their budding friendship. As Augustine mounted a reply to the various questions posed in Letter 152, he extended the hand of friendship and encouraged his civic counterpart to walk with him in attaining knowledge and virtue.

LETTERS 153–154

Augustine's exchange with Macedonius showed him to be a capable spiritual intercessor and influential civic advisor. Commenting on Letter 153 within this exchange, Daniel Doyle notes, "This letter is replete with legal terminology and should be considered an important source for trying to determine Augustine's familiarity and proficiency in Roman law. Indeed, the bishop is seen as viewing such intercession as part of his priestly office."[120] Augustine conceded this role but extended it further into the realm of love and friendship. Marie Aquinas McNamara noted the transition from engaging their

---

118. *Epistula* 152.2.

119. *Epistula* 152.3.

120. Daniel Edward Doyle, *The Bishop as Disciplinarian in the Letters of St. Augustine* (New York: Peter Lang, 2002), 103.

help in civic affairs to "welfare of their souls [as] his primary concern" and that "Macedonius enjoyed a special place in his affections."[121]

Though Macedonius solicited Augustine to reply, Augustine recognized that Macedonius's statements in Letter 152 were meant to be gentle and inviting.[122] Augustine agreed with Macedonius's opinion that all sins seem pardonable, so long as the guilty promise to reform.[123] Augustine likewise hated the offense, yet he also pitied the person. Thus, the greater the offense, the greater the desire to see reform. Augustine noted the responsibility of one's love for humanity, based on a shared human nature and the grim reality that sin marred that basic nature. Augustine asserted, "[It] is rare and holy to love those same persons because they are human beings. Thus in one person you at the same time both blame the sin and approve of the nature, and for this reason you more justly hate the sin because it defiles the nature that you love."[124] If one had a love for humanity, then one would grieve over sin. Augustine's foundation for intercession was love for the broken and sinful because of what that sin had done to their humanity.

Augustine insisted that since reform could only take place in this life, intercession was necessary "out of the love for the human race."[125] As Joseph Clair notes, "Macedonius's obligation to public order must be reimagined within the context of his duty to love."[126] If not reformed in this world, then lives will end in punishment for eternity. Augustine corrected Macedonius's belief that intercession ought not arise out of religion. On the contrary, to intercede on behalf of the guilty was to model Christ, specifically his directives from the Sermon on the Mount (Matt 5:44–45). Augustine also recognized that God's justice was meant to drive mankind to repentance. Even so, though many offenses may go unpunished in this life, nothing is hidden from the sight of God who will punish all wickedness in the final judgment. Loving an enemy did not equate to loving impiety, according to Augustine. Citing Romans 2:4 and God's desire for repentance, Augustine stated, "We

---

121. Marie Aquinas McNamara, *Friendship in St. Augustine* (Fribourg, Switzerland: University Press, 1958), 133.

122. *Epistula* 153.2.

123. *Epistula* 153.2.

124. *Epistula* 153.1.3.

125. *Epistula* 153.3.

126. Clair, *Discerning the Good*, 100.

want to lead to this repentance those for whom we make intercession; we do not spare or favor their sins."[127] Loving in this way also recognized the gravity of sin. Augustine insisted that release from prison did not guarantee a place at the Lord's table. Only those who recognized their sin, and the weight of their crime, would also recognize their need of punishment.

Based on God's example, sparing the wicked though they may not repent, Augustine asserted that such a position was necessary in order to extend the possibility of repentance. Only God knows whether one would actually repent. Since such knowledge belongs to God alone, the best that men can do is provide as much opportunity here on earth for one to repent. Augustine uses Scripture, rather than current-day examples or civil settlements, to demonstrate the reality that pardoning the guilty can lead to repentance and restitution. He cited Zacchaeus in Luke 19 as a prime example. Again, Augustine affirms that he does not wish to pardon the guilty and thereby erase the consequences or the necessary redress which follows. Augustine closes with this final exhortation: "[We] want you to be merciful to sinners not in order that they may be loved or remain sinners but because all who become good persons become such from them and because God is pleased with a sacrifice of mercy. For, if he were not merciful to sinners, there would be no good people."[128] Here in Letter 153, Augustine provides a tangible example of "the virtues of love influencing the way a public official might fulfill his role-specific obligation to tend to the well-being of the political community at the level of the practice of punishment."[129]

LETTER 154

Macedonius received Augustine's request warmly and charitably. In his reply in 413 or 414, Macedonius remarked on Augustine's charity and frankness: "For you do not insist that you obtain whatever you desire out of some concern—something that very many men of this place do. But you advise me of what you think that you should ask for from a judge caught up in so many problems, and you use a respectfulness that among good men is most effective in difficult times."[130] Macedonius had completed the books Augustine sent him (the first three books of *City of God*) and relayed his delight in Augustine's

---

127. *Epistula* 153.2.5.
128. *Epistula* 153.5.26.
129. Clair, *Discerning the Good*, 101.
130. *Epistula* 154.1.

reflection. Macedonius demonstrated gratitude and praise for Augustine and his response, promising another letter from Italy if he had the time and if he lived that long. In this brief reply, Macedonius expressed the lingering desire to continue in this epistolary relationship, noting the earthly tasks that impeded important spiritual conversations.

LETTER 155

Written soon after letter 154, what started as a letter proved to be a small treatise on seeking true virtue founded in Jesus Christ for the good of fellow man. Macedonius demonstrated a true concern for wisdom, virtue, and a desire to honor God in his work and relationships. Augustine subsequently recognized how the love of Christ and the beauty of truth had inspired Macedonius, seeing the evidence of his love that "longs for that divine and heavenly city."[131] This commonwealth, where Christ is the ruler, is also the source of true friendship meant to be "valued as gratuitous love."[132]

Love of truth was the prerequisite for true friendship, according to Augustine. This did not discount friendship, but rather made a clear distinction between friendship that has the love of Christ as its center, and everything else. Augustine raised the question of friendship according to pagan philosophers, who in his opinion, did not have true piety because they did not know God. They sought to live in such a way so as to acquire virtue and goodness, yet Christ is the source of all these things, so anything they possessed was a mere shadow and ultimately false. Augustine asserted, "For only he who made human beings makes them happy."[133] Any such attempt to attain virtue apart from the true source of virtue was vanity. Augustine took this occasion to remind Macedonius that all wisdom and virtue proceeded from God alone. Additionally, Christian piety was found in the hopeful expectation of the life to come. Anyone seeking to attain a blessing through pride was a fool. Augustine maintained, "In the present age, however, this wisdom consists in the true worship of the true God in order that in the age to come

---

131. *Epistula* 155.1.1.
132. *Epistula* 155.1.1.
133. *Epistula* 155.1.2.

this enjoyment may be certain and complete. Here there is a most solid piety, there everlasting happiness."[134]

Augustine took a moment to clarify his own possession of wisdom. Any wisdom Augustine had came from God, and it was this God-wrought wisdom that aided his own instruction in the Christian life.[135] All praise must go to God for his gifts, not to Augustine as the steward of those gifts. Those seeking to live wisely and maintain a good life must "humbly and sincerely as God to show them the way."[136] Therefore, Augustine insisted that true blessing required holding onto the promises of Scripture, particularly those that prescribed blessing to those who remained steadfast in faith and hope. Here Augustine took pagan philosophers to task: virtue in this life was impossible apart from the supernatural grace of God, including his steady presence and divine work of changing our corruptible minds and bodies through the gift of his incorruptibility and immortality, namely the resurrection of Christ and its effects.[137]

At every turn, virtue was to be found in seeking God, both by forsaking earthly trappings and in maintaining hopeful expectation of eternal blessing. Augustine explained, "In that way both in virtue and in the reward of virtue, as the apostle says, let one who boasts boast in the Lord."[138] Augustine related this discussion to the dichotomy between the earthly and heavenly cities. This God-directed pursuit of virtue is not an individual desire but a shared vision among the citizens of heaven. Just like the earthly city in philosophical speculation, the heavenly city was populated by like-minded individuals. Thus, Christlike virtue was directly connected to Macedonius's public duties. Yet, the practice of virtue in this life alone was hollow. Governing to

---

134. *Epistula* 155.2.5.

135. Regarding Augustine on wisdom, Carol Harrison notes, "Augustine's understanding of wisdom ... changed rather dramatically during the course of his life, from an identification of wisdom with the truth of philosophy (and especially the Neoplatonists) to a conviction that a philosophical, rational quest is bound to failure. The philosophers, he later saw, lacked the necessary humility to follow the path to wisdom: there is only one way that lies in a humble following of Christ who is the one and only mediator between God and man, because he is himself the way and the life; knowledge (*scientia*) and wisdom (*sapientia*)." Carol Harrison, "Augustine, Wisdom and Classical Culture," in *Where Shall Wisdom Be Found? Wisdom in the Bible, the Church and Contemporary World*, ed. Stephen C. Barton (Edinburgh: T&T Clark, 1999), 125–37.

136. *Epistula* 155.2.5.

137. *Epistula* 155.2.6.

138. *Epistula* 155.3.9; cf. 2 Cor 10:17.

only achieve temporary peace and relieve temporary suffering could never impact true blessedness. It may be honorable in the sight of men, but it did not have an eternal perspective in mind. To govern well, according to Augustine, Macedonius must practice God-given virtues as worship back to him.[139] This was part of clinging to the good, looking forward to the day when there will be "complete and everlasting wisdom" and the happy life will be realized, having attained to the "eternal and highest good."[140] Thus, Macedonius could be a more wise and just ruler were others to see his religious life and his zeal in doing good.[141]

Augustine continued to guide Macedonius toward the life of blessing and virtue by discussing the classical virtues in light of Christian teaching. The practice of virtues such as wisdom, courage, moderation, and justice was not possible without clinging to the good, which is God. Virtue, therefore, flowed from loving God. He is the unsurpassable love. If people were to replace him as the object of their love, Augustine contended, then they would forget how to love themselves. Loving God is the best thing for people. Thus, approaching God is loving him. Human movement toward God is not physical, but emotional and spiritual. Augustine observed, "We may advance toward him who is present everywhere and whole everywhere, therefore, not by our feet but by our actions."[142]

Augustine insisted on love and humility as the most important virtues for Macedonius. Character, according to Augustine, should not be judged by knowledge but by love and action. One demonstrates character by a life well lived, and the true indication of a well-lived life is the kind of love which directs him or her. Augustine declared, "[Only] good or bad loves make good or bad actions."[143] This exertion of virtuous character was particularly important given Macedonius's position as one capable of influencing society and its members for good.[144] Donald Burt notes that for Augustine, "If a state tries to mirror the heavenly Jerusalem, its members

---

139. *Epistula* 155.3.12.

140. *Epistula* 155.3.12.

141. *Epistula* 155.3.12.

142. *Epistula* 155.4.13.

143. *Epistula* 155.4.13.

144. Clair notes, "[Virtues and living an exemplary religious life] are all things within the boundaries of the role and role-specific obligations of the judge that Augustine set forth in Letter 153." Clair, *Discerning the Good*, 103–4.

will be united by a love akin to friendship and, while seeking necessary earthly goods, will yet live as pilgrims seeking their true good in that city of God only reached through death."[145] Though Augustine recognized that a utopian scenario was impossible this side of eternity, Christian rulers nonetheless should encourage the practice of virtues that will be realized in the heavenly commonwealth.[146]

Augustine implored Macedonius to do all in his power to bring others by love to the source of love that is God. One will love others only when he or she loves the Good, and in loving the Good, truly loves their own self. No one can love God without loving their own self, but only the command to love God was necessary as all other loves should fall in line once one has God. Augustine connected this love, and other subsequent virtues, to Christ and his mediatorial work applied to believers by the Holy Spirit. Augustine encouraged Macedonius to persevere saying, "Divinely endowed, then, with these virtues, we can lead a good life now; and afterwards our reward will be paid, a blessed life, which can only be everlasting."[147]

Augustine consistently directed Macedonius to set his gaze toward eternity. The practice of Christlike virtue now would come to fruition and reward in the life to come. Eternity was the goal by which the dutiful practice of virtues would be fulfilled. Therefore, worship of God had benefits both for the present as well as the future. As an example, Augustine pointed out how a recent edict from Macedonius appeared to show pious concern for the Donatist sect, encouraging them to reconcile with the Catholic church. He exhibited heavenly virtue, though acting in the role of an earthly judge.[148]

SPIRITUAL FRIENDSHIP AS CIVIC COUNSEL

John Rist notes, "[B]efore the time of Constantine, it was not possible for a Christian to hold that Roman institutions and governmental mechanisms could in and of themselves have a role in the development of a specifically Christian life and Christian culture, let alone that the Roman Empire might

---

145. Donald X. Burt, *Friendship and Society: An Introduction to Augustine's Practical Philosophy* (Grand Rapids: Eerdmans, 1999), 120.

146. While Augustine affirmed the dependence of human law on divine law, human society is wrapped in darkness. Yet such darkness can be enlightened through heavenly virtue. See John M. Rist, *Augustine: Ancient Thought Baptized* (Cambridge: Cambridge University Press, 1996), 215

147. *Epistula* 155.16.

148. *Epistula* 155.17.

itself be a major instrument in salvation-history."[149] Unlike such Roman political authors as Scipio or Cicero, Augustine believed that a perfectly just state
was impossible in this life. Knowing the fragility of humanity and the reality of the fallen human nature, Augustine did not hold out hope for such a
society, yet still encouraged its civil magistrates to aim toward its pursuit.
While perfection is never fully achievable, the civil servant who could see the
attainment of virtue in Christ would naturally see the effects of such pursuit in their daily administration. The perfect love necessary to see perfect
justice is only secure within the eternal city of God. Even those who achieve
the heights of God's love know that this is only temporary due to human
weakness and the perpetual need for God's grace. Augustine took on the role
of civic advisor, yet his advice was more concerned with the heavenly commonwealth and seeing men and women flourish as they pursued the virtues
of Christ, rather than with the state.

Augustine, in his friendship with civic leaders, encouraged them to
extend friendship into the greater community over which they governed.
Regarding his relationship to Macedonius, Clair observes, "Throughout these
letters, Augustine exhibits great 'respectfulness' toward Macedonius and
toward his role's primary obligation to tend the *temporal* health and friendship of the political community."[150] Thus the friendship that Augustine and
Macedonius shared should be a microcosm of true friendship within a just
society. Augustine, in his civic counsel, hoped to see the secular duties of
his friends serve the purpose of building up a just community. Augustine
believed that these men might even win some to the faith through their
Christlike character and virtue. When Christlike virtue was not pursued,
as with Boniface, the spiritual and temporal effects were devastating. The
friendship shared between these men, and the subsequent friendship they
would extend to others, would be a picture of eternal friendship with God and
one another in the heavenly commonwealth. Friendship for Augustine was a
sign of the love that is to come in God's eschatological kingdom. The coming
kingdom is a realized state, not a termination, of friendship. McNamara

---

149. Rist, *Augustine*, 207.
150. Clair, *Discerning the Good*, 105.

notes, "[Augustine's] ideal was to have the unity which is an integral part of individual friendship reign among all men joined in fraternal charity."[151]

CONCLUSION

This chapter has considered the nature of spiritual friendship as civic counsel in the epistolary exchanges between Augustine and various civic officials. Augustine's civic counsel was more than just support toward effective government administration. He promoted Christlike virtue and a vision of eternity as the surest way to serve the common good. Augustine viewed public service as an opportunity to promote human flourishing based on a commitment to Christ. In order to be an effective administrator, Augustine believed one's affections needed to be properly aligned. Even though some like Boniface wavered in that responsibility, Augustine's encouragement remained undeterred: any sort of temporal prosperity will only occur when one first loves God and his heavenly city. A public official who was committed to Christ also had the responsibility to see the church flourish as well. This included promoting its unity and purity. For one like Marcellinus, helping quell and compel the Donatists was not only a civic responsibility, but a duty of love based on his commitment to the church. The love of God and his people called for one's civic responsibilities to be performed with people's eternal welfare in mind. Only then would the city of man be just, and only then would others be compelled to seek the heavenly city above all else.

---

151. McNamara, *Friendship in St. Augustine*, 221.

8

—

CONCLUSION

In reflecting on the life of his friend, Possidius wrote this about Augustine:

> Those who read what he has written on divine subjects derive profit therefrom; however, I think that greater profit was derived by those who were able to hear and see him speak when he was present in church, especially those who knew his life among men. ... [He] is likewise one of those concerning whom we read: "As you speak, so do."[1]

Augustine, as those who "knew his life" knew, befriended others for the sake of encouraging Christlike virtue. Augustine was concerned not only for his own spiritual life, but for the spiritual lives of those around him. This concern extended to numerous individuals throughout Augustine's lifetime. A careful exploration of his letters confirms that Augustine's view of friendship focused upon the spiritual transformation possible through one's friendship with another. It was this spirituality of friendship that led to a concern for the nurture of Christlike virtue in others that formed the basis of spiritual friendship. Friendship, classically defined, had temporal boundaries and terminated on the person. Plato confessed the mystery of friendship, concluding that one befriends another based on perceiving the good in the other. Aristotle concluded that the epitome of friendship was to love the virtue present in one's friend. Friendship in Augustine's perspective was extended throughout eternity and had God as its primary focus. Thus, spiritual friendship could be extended to all. It was spiritual because its focal point was "things divine," a phrase borrowed from Cicero and transformed into a

---

1. Possidius, *Life of St. Augustine* 31, in Pontius et al., *Early Christian Biographies: Lives of St. Cyprian, St. Ambrose, St. Augustine, St. Anthony, St. Athanasius, St. Paul the First Hermit, St. Jerome, St. Epiphanius, with a Sermon on the Life of St. Honoratus*, ed. Roy J. Deferrari, trans. Roy J. Deferrari et al., Fathers of the Church 15 (Washington, DC: Catholic University of America Press, 1954), 124. I modified the translation of the quotation.

distinctly Christian understanding of friendship. God's grace was responsible for changing one's heart to understand "things divine" and it was his Spirit which fueled the love needed for friendship to flourish.

Augustine's view of spiritual friendship included the desire for mutual correction and encouragement. This was evident in his relationship with Jerome, even if Jerome did not receive that correction. For Augustine, correction stemmed from love for the other and love for truth. This informed his desire to engage Jerome on topics of biblical interpretation, hoping that mutual growth in love and virtue would take place. Though some have been critical of Augustine's motives, the language of his letters demonstrates a heartfelt desire to engage Jerome as friend, which included a certain level of frankness in order to achieve his goal of growth in virtue.[2] Alongside correction, Augustine's practice of spiritual friendship included encouragement toward spiritual practices such as prayer. This was most evident within his friendships with those pursuing the consecrated or monastic life. With Paulinus of Nola, Augustine was a friend who supported his monastic calling and its related spiritual activity. Writing to Proba, a wealthy widow from Rome, Augustine prescribed a life of self-sacrificial prayer and a focus upon reading Scripture. As these men and women pursued a monastic calling, Augustine implored them to pray for him and encourage him in his own spiritual life.

As a bishop, Augustine was aware of the challenges of pastoral life. Those in ministry required additional encouragement as they engaged in various interpersonal disputes, alongside their duties of preaching and administering the sacraments. The high calling of pastoral ministry also came with the responsibility of piety. Pastors must exhibit the virtues they wish to see within the lives of their people. Effective ministry flowed from a life of holiness. Virtue is necessary for a godly life, and bishops were to model virtue based on the virtues of Christ. Commenting on Ezekiel 34:3–5, Augustine declared, "The pastor who lives a bad life openly in the sight of the people

---

2. Ebbeler, *Disciplining Christians*, 101–50. See also Ebbeler, "Tradition, Innovation, and Epistolary Mores," in *A Companion to Late Antiquity*, ed. Philip Rousseau (Malden, MA: Wiley-Blackwell, 2012), 270–84.

is killing as many people as he is observed by."[3] Thus, the need to encourage Christlike virtue among the clergy was an important task.

Augustine, in writing to civic officials, suggested how Christlike virtue should impact the common good. Christians in positions of influence have the responsibility to exercise their faith in service to the state, according to Augustine. Thus, a citizen of the heavenly commonwealth should have a significant impact on the earthly commonwealth. This included the responsibility to bring order out of chaos, especially when that chaos affected the church, as in the Donatist controversy. This aspect of spiritual friendship shows how Augustine encouraged his friends to render their vocation in love and service to God. Faith and work were clearly connected for Augustine. This was evident especially when someone like Boniface strayed from their commitment to Christ. A disordered soul led to a disordered life. Looking to Christ as the example, and loving God first, would reorder one's life in order to practice Christlike virtue for the purpose of the common good. The ideal, however, is not a perfect earthly society but a heavenly community of mutual love as members in the city of God. Only there would people be able to know one another in perfect intimacy—the true and final goal of friendship.

Augustine's letters give readers an opportunity to understand Augustine from a different perspective. While his *Confessions* provides a window into his soul and his early relationships, one needs to turn to his letters to see how these relationships blossomed and how others took shape as well. As has been discussed, Augustine engaged in friendship with numerous people as an outflow of love that had God as its center. Though he never shed his training in rhetoric and operated within an environment of specific epistolary practices in Late Antiquity, friendship was ultimately a spiritual exercise, with two souls joined together in the journey toward heaven with the desire to mutually encourage Christlike virtue. Spiritual friendship, being based on the love of God poured forth into human hearts (Rom 5:5), was a transformative relationship. Christ's love drives friends to love one another, as well as their enemies with the hope that the latter would also become friends in God. The notion that spiritual friendship hinges on the love of God in order that one could love his or her friend properly was indispensable for Augustine. For

3. *Serm.* 46.9, in Augustine, *Sermons 20–50: On the Old Testament*, ed. John E. Rotelle, trans. Edmund Hill, *Works of Saint Augustine* III/2 (Hyde Park, NY: New City Press, 1991), 268.

Augustine, the eternal reality of friendship in Christ was a fundamental component for which no classical notion of friendship could account. God was the ultimate reason that two souls could be joined together in friendship. It was by God's grace and power that friendship could be sustained, and it was only by his love poured forth in one's heart that true friendship could exist both now and for eternity.

BIBLIOGRAPHY

—

PRIMARY SOURCES

Ambrose, *De officiis ministrorum (On the Duties of the Clergy)*, in *NPNF²* 10:1–89.

Ambrose. *Selected Works and Letters*. Translated by H. De Romestin. Nicene and Post-Nicene Fathers, series 2. Vol. 10. Peabody, MA: Hendrickson, 1996.

Aristotle. *Athenian Constitution, Eudemian Ethics, Virtues and Vices*. Translated by H. Rackham. Loeb Classical Library 285. Cambridge, MA: Harvard University Press, 1935.

———. *Nicomachean Ethics*. Translated by H. Rackham. 2nd ed. Loeb Classical Library 73. Cambridge, MA: Harvard University Press, 1934.

Augustine. *Against the Academics*. Translated by John J. O'Meara. Ancient Christian Writers 12. New York: Newman Press, 1951.

———. *Confessions*. Translated by Carolyn J.-B. Hammond. Loeb Classical Library 26. Cambridge, MA: Harvard University Press, 2014.

———. *Confessions*. Translated by Carolyn J.-B. Hammond. Loeb Classical Library 27. Cambridge, MA: Harvard University Press, 2016.

———. *Epistulae*. In *Corpus scriptorium ecclesiasticorum latinorum*. Edited by A. Goldbacher. Vols. 34, 44, 57, 58. Vienna: F. Tempsky, 1895–1923.

———. *Essential Sermons*. Edited by Daniel Doyle. Translated by Edmund Hill. In *Works of Saint Augustine* III/Homilies. Hyde Park, NY: New City Press, 2007.

———. *Lectures or Tractates on the Gospel according to John*. Translated by John Gibb. In *NPNF¹* 7:7–452.

———. *Letters 1–99*. Edited by John E. Rotelle. Translated by Roland Teske. *Works of Saint Augustine* II/1. Hyde Park, NY: New City Press, 2001.

———. *Letters 100–155*. Edited by John E. Rotelle. Translated by Roland Teske. Edited by John E. Rotelle. In *Works of Saint Augustine* II/2. Hyde Park, NY: New City Press, 2002.

————. *Letters 156–210*. Edited by Boniface Ramsey. Translated by Roland Teske. In *Works of Saint Augustine* II/3. Hyde Park, NY: New City Press, 2005.

————. *Letters 211–270, 1*–29**. Edited by Boniface Ramsey. Translated by Roland Teske. In *Works of Saint Augustine* II/4. Hyde Park, NY: New City Press, 2005.

————. *Marriage and Desire*. Translated by Ronald J. Teske. In *Works of Saint Augustine* I/24:28–93. Hyde Park, NY: New City Press, 1998.

————.*Nature and Grace*. Translated by Ronald J. Teske. In *Works of Saint Augustine* I/23:217–60. Hyde Park, NY: New City Press, 1997.

————. *Political Writings*. Edited by E. M. Atkins and R. J. Dodaro. Cambridge Texts in the History of Political Thought. Cambridge: Cambridge University Press, 2001.

————. *The Retractions*. Trans. Translated by Sister M. Inez Bogan. Fathers of the Church 60. Washington, DC: Catholic University of America Press, 1968.

————. *Sermons 20–50: On the Old Testament*. Edited by John E. Rotelle. Translatedy by Edmund Hill. In *Works of Saint Augustine* III/3. Brooklyn, NY: New City Press, 1991.

————. *Sermons 306–340A: On the Saints*. Edited by John E. Rotelle. Translated by Edmund Hill. In *Works of Saint Augustine* III/9. Hyde Park, NY: New City Press, 1994.

————. *Teaching Christianity (De Doctrina Christiana)*. Translated by Edmund Hill. In *Works of Saint Augustine* I/11. Hyde Park, NY: New City Press, 1996.

————. *The Enchiridion on Faith, Hope, and Charity*. Translated by Bruce Harbert. In *Works of Saint Augustine* I/8:273–342. Hyde Park, NY: New City Press, 2005.

————. *The Excellence of Marriage*. Translated by Ray Kearney. In *Works of Saint Augustine* I/9:33–61. Hyde Park, NY: New City Press, 1999.

————. *The Trinity*. Edited by John E. Rotelle. Translated by Edmund Hill. 2nd ed. In *Works of Saint Augustine* I/5. Brooklyn, NY: New City Press, 2012.

Cicero. *On Old Age, On Friendship, On Divination*. Translated by W. A. Falconer. Loeb Classical Library 154. Cambridge, MA: Harvard University Press, 1923.

Cyprian of Carthage. *Opera Omnia II, Epistulae*, CSEL 3.2

———. Pages 5-6 in *Saint Cyprian: Letters (1–81)* trans. Sister Rose Bernard Donna, C.S.J. The Fathers of the Church. Washington, DC: The Catholic University of America Press, 1964.

Epicurus. *The Essential Epicurus: Letters, Principal Doctrines, Vatican Sayings, and Fragments.* Translated by Eugene M. O'Connor. Buffalo, NY: Prometheus, 1993.

Eusebius. *Church History of Eusebius.* Translated by Arthur Cushman McGiffert. *NPNF*² 1:81–387.

Hippolytus of Rome, *The Refutation of All Heresies.* Translated by J. H. MacMahon. *ANF* 5:9–153.

Irenaeus. *Against the Heresies.* Translated by Alexander Roberts and W. H. Rambaut. *ANF* 1:315–567.

Laertius, Diogenes. *Diogenes Laertius: Lives of Eminent Philosophers.* Vol. 2. Translated by R. D. Hicks. Cambridge, MA: Harvard University Press, 1925.

Plato. *Lysis, Symposium, Gorgias.* Translated by W. R. M. Lamb. Loeb Classical Library 166. Cambridge, MA: Harvard University Press, 1925.

Pontius, and Fathers of the Church. *Early Christian Biographies: Lives of St. Cyprian, St. Ambrose, St. Augustine, St. Anthony, St. Athanasius, St. Paul the First Hermit, St. Jerome, St. Epiphanius, with a Sermon on the Life of St. Honoratus.* Edited by Roy J. Deferrari. Translated by Roy J. Deferrari, John A. Lacy, Mary Madeleine Müller, Mary Emily Keenan, Marie Liguori Ewald, and Genevieve Marie Cook. Fathers of the Church 15. Washington, DC: Catholic University of America Press, 1954.

Possidius, *Life of St. Augustine.* Translated by Mary M. Müller. In Early Christian Biographies. Edited by Roy J. Deferrari. Fathers of the Church 15. Washington, DC: Catholic University of America Press, 1952.

Rufinus of Aquileia. *History of the Church.* Translated by Phillip R. Amidon. Washington, DC: Catholic University of America Press, 2016.

Seneca, Lucius Annaeus. *Ad Lucilium epistulae morales.* Translated by Richard M. Gummere. Loeb Classical Library 75. Cambridge, MA: Harvard University Press, 1917.

Severus, Sulpicius. *Sulpicius Severus: The Complete Works.* Translated by Richard J. Goodrich. Ancient Christian Writers 70. New York: Paulist, 2015.

SECONDARY SOURCES

BOOKS

Allen, Pauline, Bronwen Neil, and Wendy Mayer. *Preaching Poverty in Late Antiquity: Perceptions and Realities*. Leipzig: Evangelische Verlagsanstalt, 2009.

Ayres, Lewis. *Augustine and the Trinity*. Cambridge: Cambridge University Press, 2010.

———. *Nicaea and Its Legacy: An Approach to Fourth-Century Trinitarian Theology*. Oxford: Oxford University Press, 2006.

Bacchi, Lee Francis. *The Theology of Ordained Ministry in the Letters of Augustine of Hippo*. Lanham, MD: International Scholars, 1998.

Badhwar, Neera Kapur, ed. *Friendship: A Philosophical Reader*. Ithaca, NY: Cornell University Press, 1993.

Banateanu, Anne. *La Théorie Stoïcienne de l'amitié: Essai de Reconstruction*. Vestigia 27. Fribourg, Switzerland: Éditions Universitaires, 2001.

Barnes, Jonathan, ed. *The Cambridge Companion to Aristotle*. Cambridge: Cambridge University Press, 1995.

Bartsch, Shadi, and Alessandro Shiesaro, eds. *The Cambridge Companion to Seneca*. Cambridge: Cambridge University Press, 2015.

Beeley, Christopher A. *Leading God's People: Wisdom from the Early Church for Today*. Grand Rapids: Eerdmans, 2012.

Benson, Hugh H., ed. *A Companion to Plato*. West Sussex, UK: Wiley Blackwell, 2009.

Blum, Laurence A. *Friendship, Altruism, and Morality*. London: Routledge, 1980.

Bolotin, David. *Plato's Dialogue on Friendship: An Interpretation of the Lysis, with a New Translation*. Ithaca, NY: Cornell University Press, 1977.

Bourke, Vernon J. *Augustine's Quest of Wisdom: Life and Philosophy of the Bishop of Hippo*. Milwaukee, WI: Bruce, 1945.

Bright, Pamela, ed. *Augustine and the Bible*. Notre Dame, IN: University of Notre Dame Press, 1999.

Brown, Michael Joseph. *The Lord's Prayer through North African Eyes: A Window into Early Christianity*. New York: T & T Clark, 2004.

Brown, Peter. *Augustine of Hippo: A Biography*. 2nd ed. Berkeley: University of California Press, 2000.

———. *The Body and Society: Men, Women, and Sexual Renunciation in Early Christianity*. 2nd ed. New York: Columbia University Press, 2008.

———. *Power and Persuasion in Late Antiquity: Towards a Christian Empire*. Madison, WI: University of Wisconsin Press, 1992.

———. *Through the Eye of a Needle: Wealth, the Fall of Rome, and the Making of Christianity in the West, 350–550 AD*. Princeton, NJ: Princeton University Press, 2012.

Brunt, P. A. *The Fall of the Roman Republic and Related Essays*. Oxford: Oxford University Press, 1988.

Budge, E. A. Wallis. *Amulets and Talismans*. New York: University, 1961.

Burnell, Peter. *The Augustinian Person*. Washington, DC: Catholic University of America Press, 2005.

Burns, J. Patout, and Robin M. Jensen. *Christianity in Roman Africa: The Development of Its Practices and Beliefs*. Grand Rapids: Eerdmans, 2014.

Burt, Donald X. *Friendship and Society: An Introduction to Augustine's Practical Philosophy*. Grand Rapids: Eerdmans, 1999.

Caine, Barbara, ed. *Friendship: A History*. London: Routledge, 2014.

Casiday, Augustine, and Frederick W. Norris, eds. *Constantine to c. 600*. The Cambridge History of Christianity 2. Cambridge: Cambridge University Press, 2007.

Chin, Catherine M., and Caroline T. Schroeder, eds. *Melania: Early Christianity through the Life of One Family*. Berkeley: University of California Press, 2016.

Clair, Joseph. *Discerning the Good in the Letters and Sermons of Augustine*. Oxford: Oxford University Press, 2016.

Conybeare, Catherine. *Paulinus Noster: Self and Symbols in the Letters of Paulinus of Nola*. Oxford: Clarendon, 2001.

Crisp, Roger, ed. *The Oxford Handbook of the History of Ethics*. Oxford: Oxford University Press, 2013.

Cvetković, Carmen Angela, and Peter Gemeinhardt, eds. *Episcopal Networks in Late Antiquity: Connection and Communication across Boundaries*. Arbeiten Zur Kirchengeschichte 137. Berlin: De Gruyter, 2019.

Deane, Herbert. *The Political and Social Ideas of Saint Augustine*. New York: Columbia University Press, 1966.

Decret, François. *Early Christianity in North Africa*. Translated by Edward L. Smither. Eugene, OR: Wipf & Stock, 2009.

Demacopoulos, George E. *Five Models of Spiritual Direction in the Early Church*. Notre Dame, IN: University of Notre Dame Press, 2006.

Derrida, Jacques. *For Strasbourg: Conversations of Friendship and Philosophy*. Translated by Pascale-Anne Brault and Michael Naas. New York: Fordham University Press, 2014.

Divjak, Johannes, ed. *Les Lettres de saint Augustin découvertes par Johannes Divjak: communications présentées au colloque des 20 et 21 septembre 1982*. Paris: Etudes augustiniennes, 1983.

Dodaro, Robert. *Christ and the Just Society in the Thought of Augustine*. Cambridge: Cambridge University Press, 2004.

Dodaro, Robert, and George Lawless, eds. *Augustine and His Critics*. London: Routledge, 1999.

Doody, John, Kevin L. Hughes, and Kim Paffenroth, eds. *Augustine and Politics*. Lanham, MD: Lexington, 2005.

Dover, K. J. *Greek Homosexuality*. Cambridge, MA: Harvard University Press, 1989.

Doyle, Daniel Edward. *The Bishop as Disciplinarian in the Letters of St. Augustine*. New York: Peter Lang, 2002.

Drake, H. A. *Violence in Late Antiquity: Perceptions and Practices*. Aldershot, UK: Ashgate, 2006.

Dupont, A., M. A. Gaumer, and M. Lamberigts, eds. *The Uniquely African Controversy: Studies on Donatist Christianity*. Late Antique History and Religion 9. Louvain, Belgium: Peeters, 2014.

Ebbeler, Jennifer. *Disciplining Christians: Correction and Community in Augustine's Letters*. New York: Oxford University Press, 2012.

Enos, Richard Leo and Roger Thompson et al., eds. *The Rhetoric of St. Augustine of Hippo: De Doctrina Christiana and the Search for a Distinctly Christian Rhetoric*. Waco, TX: Baylor University Press, 2008.

Fear, Andrew, José Fernández Urbiña, and Mar Marcos Sanchez, eds. *The Role of the Bishop in Late Antiquity: Conflict and Compromise*. London: Bloomsbury Academic, 2013.

Finan, Thomas, and Vincent Twomey, eds. *The Relationship between Neoplatonism and Christianity*. Dublin: Four Courts, 1992.

Fitzgerald, Allan D., ed. *Augustine through the Ages: An Encyclopedia*. Grand Rapids: Eerdmans, 1999.

Fitzgerald, John T., ed. *Friendship, Flattery and Frankness of Speech: Studies on Friendship in the New Testament World*. New York: Brill Academic, 1997.

———. *Greco-Roman Perspectives on Friendship*. Atlanta: Scholars, 1997.

Frend, W. H. C. *The Donatist Church: A Movement of Protest in Roman North Africa*. Oxford: Oxford University Press, 1985.

Fürst, Alfons. *Augustins Briefwechsel mit Hieronymous*. Jahrbuch für Antike und Christentum. Ergänzungsband 29. Münster: Aschendorffsche Verlagsbuchhandlung, 1999.

Gilson, Etienne. *The Christian Philosophy of St. Augustine*. Translated by L. E. M. Lynch. New York: Random House, 1960.

González, Justo. *Mestizo Augustine: A Theologian Between Two Cultures*. Downers Grove, IL: IVP Academic, 2016.

Grayling, A. C. *Friendship*. New Haven: Yale University Press, 2013.

Gutherie, W. K. C. *Plato: The Man and His Dialogues: Earlier Period*. Vol. 4 of *A History of Greek Philosophy*. Cambridge: Cambridge University Press, 1975.

Halsall, Guy. *Barbarian Migrations and the Roman West, 376–568*. Cambridge: Cambridge University Press, 2008.

Hanson, R. P. C. *The Search for the Christian Doctrine of God: The Arian Controversy, 318–381*. Grand Rapids: Baker Academic, 2006.

Harmless, William. *Augustine and the Catechumenate* rev. ed. Collegeville, MN: Liturgical, 2014.

Harper, Kyle. *Slavery in the Late Roman World, AD 275–425*. Cambridge: Cambridge University Press, 2011.

Hauser, Alan J., and Duane F. Watson, eds. *The Ancient Period*. Vol. 1 of *A History of Biblical Interpretation*. Grand Rapids: Eerdmans, 2008.

Hennings, Ralph. *Der Briefwechsel zwischen Augustinus und Hieronymus und ihr Streit um den Kanon des Alten Testaments und die Auslegung von Gal. 2, 11–14*. Leiden, Netherlands: Brill, 1994.

Heyking, John von. *The Form of Politics: Aristotle and Plato on Friendship*. McGill-Queen's Studies in the History of Ideas 66. Kingston, Canada: McGill-Queen's University Press, 2016.

Joshel, Sandra R. *Slavery in the Roman World*. Cambridge: Cambridge University Press, 2010.

Kaufman, Peter Iver. *Augustine's Leaders*. Eugene, OR: Cascade, 2017.

Keenan, Sr. Mary Emily. *The Life and Times of St. Augustine as Revealed in His Letters*. Washington, DC: Catholic University of America Press, 1935.

Kelly, J. N. D. *Jerome: His Life, Writings, and Controversies*. Peabody, MA: Hendrickson, 1998.

Kendrick, Laura. *Animating the Letter: The Figurative Embodiment of Writing from Late Antiquity to the Renaissance*. Columbus: Ohio State University Press, 1999.

Kennedy, George A. *Classical Rhetoric and Its Christian and Secular Tradition from Ancient to Modern Times*. 2nd ed. Chapel Hill: University of North Carolina Press, 1999.

Kenney, John Peter. *Contemplation and Classical Christianity: A Study in Augustine*. Oxford: Oxford University Press, 2016.

Kolbet, Paul R. *Augustine and the Cure of Souls: Revising a Classical Ideal*. Notre Dame, IN: University of Notre Dame Press, 2010.

Konstan, David. *Friendship in the Classical World*. Cambridge: Cambridge University Press, 1997.

Kraut, Richard, ed. *The Blackwell Guide to Aristotle's Nicomachean Ethics*. Malden, MA: Wiley-Blackwell, 2006.

Lännström, Anna. *Loving the Fine: Virtue and Happiness in Aristotle's Ethics*. Notre Dame, IN: University of Notre Dame Press, 2006.

Lawless, George. *Augustine of Hippo and His Monastic Rule*. Oxford: Clarendon, 1990.

Lienhard, Joseph T. *Paulinus of Nola and Early Western Monasticism: With a Study of the Chronology of His Works and an Annotated Bibliography, 1879–1976*. Theophaneia, Beitrage Zur Religions-Und Kirchengeschichte Des Altertums 28. Köln, Denmark: P. Hanstein, 1977.

Long, A. A., and D. N. Sedley. *Translations of the Principal Sources, with Philosophical Commentary*. Vol. 1 of *The Hellenistic Philosophers*. Cambridge: Cambridge University Press, 1987.

Madec, Goulven. *Saint Ambroise et la philosophie*. Paris: Études augustiniennes, 1974.

Mariani, Goffredo. *Sant'Agostino Guida Spirituale: Lettere del Vescovo di Ippona a Proba, Giuliana e Demetriade*. Rome: Rogate, 1982.

Marrou, Henri-Irénée. *Saint Augustin et la fin de la culture antique*. Paris: Éditions E. De Boccard, 1938.

Martin, Thomas F. *Our Restless Heart: The Augustinian Tradition*. Traditions of Christian Spirituality. Maryknoll, NY: Orbis, 2003.

Martindale, J. R. *The Prosopography of the Later Roman Empire*. 2 vols. Cambridge: Cambridge University Press, 1992.

Masala, Alberto, and Jonathan Webber, eds. *From Personality to Virtue: Essays on the Philosophy of Character*. Oxford: Oxford University Press, 2016.

McEvoy, Adrianne Leigh, ed. *Sex, Love, and Friendship: Studies of the Society for the Philosophy of Sex and Love, 1993-2003*. New York: Rodopi, 2011.

McEvoy, Meghan A. *Child Emperor Rule in the Late Roman West, AD 367-455*. Oxford: Oxford University Press, 2013.

McGuire, Brian Patrick. *Friendship and Community: The Monastic Experience, 350-1250*. Ithaca, NY: Cornell University Press, 2010.

McNamara, Marie Aquinas. *Friends and Friendship for St. Augustine*. Staten Island, NY: Alba House, 1964.

———. *Friendship in St. Augustine*. Fribourg, Switzerland: University Press, 1958.

McWilliam, Joanne, ed. *Augustine: From Rhetor to Theologian*. Waterloo, Canada: Wilfrid Laurier University Press, 1992.

Meilaender, Gilbert. *Friendship: A Study in Theological Ethics*. Notre Dame, IN: University of Notre Dame Press, 1985.

Miles, Richard, ed. *The Donatist Schism: Controversy and Contexts*. Translated Texts for Historians Contexts 2. Liverpool, England: Liverpool University Press, 2018.

Morello, Ruth, and A. D. Morrison, eds. *Ancient Letters: Classical and Late Antique Epistolography*. Oxford: Oxford University Press, 2007.

Murphy, Francis X. *Rufinus of Aquileia (345-411): His Life and Works*. Washington, DC: Catholic University of America Press, 1945.

Musset, Lucien. *The Germanic Invasions: The Making of Europe, AD 400-600*. Translated by Edward James and Columba James. University Park, PA: Pennsylvania State University Press, 1975.

Nehamas, Alexander. *On Friendship*. New York: Basic, 2016.

Neil, Bronwen, and Pauline Allen, eds. *Collecting Early Christian Letters: From the Apostle Paul to Late Antiquity*. Cambridge: Cambridge University Press, 2015.

O'Daly, Gerard. *Augustine's Philosophy of Mind*. Berkeley: University of
    California Press, 1987.

Oden, Thomas C. *How Africa Shaped the Christian Mind: Rediscovering the
    African Seedbed of Western Christianity*. Downers Grove, IL: IVP
    Academic, 2010.

O'Keefe, Tim. *Epicureanism*. Berkeley: University of California Press, 2009.

Olson, Linda, and Kathryn Kerby-Fulton, eds. *Voices in Dialogue: Reading
    Women in the Middle Ages*. Notre Dame, IN: University of Notre
    Dame Press, 2005.

O'Meara, John J. *The Young Augustine: The Growth of St. Augustine's Mind up
    to His Conversion*. London: Longmans, Green, 1954.

Oost, Stewart Irvin. *Galla Placidia Augusta: A Biographical Essay*. Chicago:
    University of Chicago Press, 1968.

Pakaluk, Michael, ed. *Other Selves: Philosophers on Friendship*. Indianapolis,
    IN: Hackett, 1991.

Pangle, Lorraine Smith. *Aristotle and the Philosophy of Friendship*.
    Cambridge: Cambridge University Press, 2008.

Peachin, Michael, ed. *The Oxford Handbook of Social Relations in the Roman
    World*. New York: Oxford University Press, 2011.

Penner, Terry, and Christopher Rowe. *Plato's Lysis*. Cambridge Studies in the
    Dialogues of Plato. Cambridge: Cambridge University Press, 2009.

Percy, William Armstrong III. *Pederasty and Pedagogy in Archaic Greece*.
    Urbana: University of Illinois Press, 1996.

Ployd, Adam. *Augustine, the Trinity, and the Church: A Reading of the Anti-
    Donatist Sermons*. New York: Oxford University Press, 2015.

Price, A. W. *Love and Friendship in Plato and Aristotle*. Oxford: Clarendon,
    1989.

Purves, Andrew. *Pastoral Theology in the Classical Tradition*. Louisville, KY:
    Westminster John Knox, 2001.

Rapp, Claudia. *Holy Bishops in Late Antiquity: The Nature of Christian
    Leadership in an Age of Transition*. Berkeley: University of California
    Press, 2005.

Rebenich, Stefan. *Jerome*. London: Routledge, 2002.

Rebillard, Éric. *Transformations of Religious Practices in Late Antiquity*.
    London: Routledge, 2013.

Risseeuw, Carla. *Conceptualizing Friendship in Time and Place*. Leiden, Netherlands: Brill, 2017.

Rist, John M. *Augustine: Ancient Thought Baptized*. Cambridge: Cambridge University Press, 1996.

Rorty, Amélie Oksenberg, ed. *Essays on Aristotle's Ethics*. Berkeley: University of California Press, 1980.

Rousseau, Philip, ed. *A Companion to Late Antiquity*. Malden, MA: Wiley-Blackwell, 2012.

Schollmeier, Paul. *Other Selves: Aristotle on Personal and Political Friendship*. Albany, NY: State University of New York Press, 1994.

Smither, Edward L. *Augustine as Mentor: A Model for Preparing Spiritual Leaders*. Nashville: B & H Academic, 2009.

Spencer, Liz, and Ray Pahl. *Rethinking Friendship: Hidden Solidarities Today*. Princeton, NJ: Princeton University Press, 2006.

Stark, Judith Chelius, ed. *Feminist Interpretations of Augustine*. University Park, PA: Pennsylvania State University Press, 2007.

Sterk, Andrea. *Renouncing the World Yet Leading the Church: The Monk-Bishop in Late Antiquity*. Cambridge, MA: Harvard University Press, 2004.

Stern-Gillet, Suzanne. *Aristotle's Philosophy of Friendship*. Albany: State University of New York Press, 1995.

Stern-Gillet, Suzanne, and Gary M. Gurtler, eds. *Ancient and Medieval Concepts of Friendship*. Albany: State University of New York Press, 2014.

Stowers, Stanley K. *Letter Writing in Greco-Roman Antiquity*. Edited by Wayne A. Meeks. Library of Early Christianity. Philadelphia: Westminster, 1986.

Stump, Eleonore, and Norman Kretzmann, eds. *The Cambridge Companion to Augustine*. Cambridge: Cambridge University Press, 2001.

Taylor, Lily Ross. *Party Politics in the Age of Caesar*. Berkeley: University of California Press, 1949.

TeSelle, Eugene. *Augustine the Theologian*. New York: Herder & Herder, 1970; reprint, Eugene, OR: Wipf & Stock, 2002.

Teubner, Jonathan D. *Prayer after Augustine: A Study in the Development of the Latin Tradition*. Oxford: Oxford University Press, 2018.

Toom, Tarmo, ed. *Augustine in Context*. Cambridge: Cambridge University Press, 2018.

Topping, Ryan N. S. *Happiness and Wisdom: Augustine's Early Theology of Education*. Washington, DC: Catholic University of America Press, 2012.

Troup, Calvin. *Temporality, Eternity, and Wisdom: The Rhetoric of Augustine's Confessions*. Columbia, SC: University of South Carolina Press, 1999.

Trout, Dennis E. *Paulinus of Nola: Life, Letters, and Poems*. Berkeley: University of California Press, 1999.

Van Bavel, Tarsicius Jan. *Augustinus: van liefde en vriendschap*. Averbode, Belgium: Altiora, 1986.

Vernon, Mark. *The Meaning of Friendship*. New York: Palgrave Macmillan, 2010.

———. *The Philosophy of Friendship*. New York: Palgrave Macmillan, 2005.

Wadell, Paul J. *Friendship and the Moral Life*. Notre Dame, IN: University of Notre Dame Press, 1990.

———. *Happiness and the Christian Moral Life: An Introduction to Christian Ethics*. 3rd ed. Lanham, MD: Rowman & Littlefield, 2016.

Walsh, Michael. *A New Dictionary of Saints: East and West*. Collegeville, MN: Liturgical, 2007.

Ward, Ann. *Contemplating Friendship in Aristotle's Ethics*. Albany: State University of New York Press, 2017.

Warren, James, ed. *The Cambridge Companion to Epicureanism*. Cambridge: Cambridge University Press, 2009.

Wetzel, James. *Augustine and the Limits of Virtue*. Cambridge: Cambridge University Press, 1992.

White, Carolinne. *Christian Friendship in the Fourth Century*. Cambridge: Cambridge University Press, 1992.

———. *The Correspondence (394-419) between Jerome and Augustine of Hippo*. Lewiston, NY: Edwin Mellen, 1991.

White, Peter. *Cicero in Letters: Epistolary Relations of the Late Republic*. New York: Oxford University Press, 2012.

Wijnendaele, Jeroen W. P. *The Last of the Romans: Bonifatius—Warlord and Comes Africae*. London: Bloomsbury Academic, 2015.

Williams, Craig A. *Reading Roman Friendship*. Cambridge: Cambridge University Press, 2012.

Willis, Geoffrey G. *Saint Augustine and the Donatist Controversy*. Eugene, OR: Wipf & Stock, 2005.

Wynn, Phillip. *Augustine on War and Military Service*. Minneapolis, MN: Fortress, 2013.

Young, Frances, Lewis Ayres, and Andrew Louth, eds. *The Cambridge History of Early Christian Literature*. Cambridge: Cambridge University Press, 2007.

ARTICLES

Adamiak, Stanisław. "Unfriendly and Polemical Elements in Augustine's Correspondence with Other Clerics." *Zeitschrift für Antikes Christentum* 22, no. 1 (May 2018): 110-24.

Allen, Pauline. "Prolegomena to a Study of the Letter-Bearer in Christian Antiquity." Studia Patristica, 62 (2013):481-91.

Annas, J. "Plato and Aristotle on Friendship and Altruism." *Mind* 86 (1977): 532-54.

Annis, D. B. "The Meaning, Value, and Duties of Friendship." *American Philosophical Quarterly* 24 (1987): 349-56.

Arbesmann, R. "The Idea of Rome in the Sermons of St. Augustine." *Augustiniana* 4 (1954): 305-24.

Arzt-Grabner, Peter, and Kristin De Troyer. "Ancient Jewish and Christian Amulets and How Magical They Are." *Biblische Notizen* 176 (2018): 5-46.

Aumann, Jordan. "Saint Augustine's Theology of Ministry." *Word and Spirit* 9 (1987): 46-52.

Ayres, Lewis. "Augustine on God as Love and Love as God." *Pro Ecclesia* 5, no. 4 (1996): 470-87.

Bagnall, Roger S., ed. *The Encyclopedia of Ancient History*. 13 vols.Malden, MA: Wiley-Blackwell, 2012.

Bernstein, M. "Friends without Favoritism." *Journal of Value Inquiry* 41 (2007): 59-76.

Bonner, Ali. "The Manuscript Transmission of Pelagius' *Ad Demetriadem*: The Evidence of Some Manuscript Witnesses." Studia Patristica 70 (2013): 619-30.

Brink, D. O. "Eudaimonism, Love and Friendship, and Political Community." *Social Philosophy and Policy* 16 (1999): 252-89.

Brown, Eric. "Epicurus on the Value of Friendship (Sententia Vaticana 23)," *Classical Philology* 97, no. 1 (2002): 68–80.

Bryan, Bradley. "Approaching Others: Aristotle on Friendship's Possibility," *Political Theory* 37, no. 6 (2009): 754–79.

Burton, P. J. "Amicitia in Plautus: A Study of Roman Friendship Processes." *American Journal of Philology* 125, no. 2 (2004): 209–43.

Cain, Andrew. "Jerome's Epitaphium Paulae: Hagiography, Pilgrimage, and the Cult of Saint Paula." *Journal of Early Christian Studies* 18, no. 1 (2010): 105–39.

———. "Vox Clamantis in Deserto: Rhetoric, Reproach, and the Forging of Ascetic Authority in Jerome's Letters from the Syrian Desert." *Journal of Theological Studies* 57, no. 2 (October 2006): 500–25.

Cameron, Michael. "Valerius of Hippo: A Profile." *Augustinian Studies* 40, no. 1 (January 2009): 5–26.

Carriker, Anne P. "Augustine's Frankness in His Dispute with Jerome over the Interpretation of Galatians 2:11–14." In *Nova Doctrina Vetusque: Essays on Early Christianity in Honor of Fredric W. Schlatter, S. J.*, edited by Douglas Kries and Catherine Brown Tkacz, 207:121–38. American University Studies. New York: Peter Lang, 1999.

Cassidy, Eoin G. "Friendship and Beauty in Augustine." Pages 51–66 in *At the Heart of the Real: Philosophical Essays in Honour of the Most Reverend Desmond Connell Archbishop of Dublin*. Edited by Fran O'Rourke. Dublin: Irish Academic, 1992.

———. "The Recovery of the Classical Ideal of Friendship in Augustine's Portrayal of Caritas." Pages 127–40 in *The Relationship between Neoplatonism and Christianity*. Edited by Thomas Finan Vincent Twomey. Dublin: Four Courts, 1992.

Chadwick, Henry. "New Letters of St. Augustine." *Journal of Theological Studies* 34, no. 2 (October 1983): 425–52.

Cooper, John M. "The Magna Moralia and Aristotle's Moral Philosophy." *American Journal of Philology* 94, no. 4 (1973): 327–49.

Coyle, Alcuin F. "Cicero's De Officiis and the De Officiis Ministrorum of St. Ambrose." *Franciscan Studies* 15, no. 3 (1955): 224–56.

Curzer, Howard J. "The Supremely Happy Life in Aristotle's *Nicomachean Ethics*." *Apeiron* 24 (1991): 47–69.

Di Lorenzo, Raymond D. "Augustine's Sapiential Discipline: Wisdom and the Happy Life." *Communio* 10 (1983): 351-59.

Dodaro, Robert. "Augustine on the Roles of Christ and the Holy Spirit on the Mediation of Virtues." *Augustinian Studies* 41, no. 1 (2010): 145-66.

———. "Augustine's Secular City." Pages 231-59 in *Augustine and His Critics: Essays in Honour of Gerald Bonner.* Edited by Robert Dodaro and George Lawless. New York: Routledge, 2000.

———. "Between the Two Cities: Political Action in Augustine of Hippo." Pages 99-116. in *Augustine and Politics.* Edited by John Doody, Kevin L. Hughes, and Kim Paffenroth. Lanham, MD: Lexington, 2005.

———. "Political and Theological Virtues in Augustine, Letter 155 to Macedonius." *Augustiana* 54 (2004): 431-74.

———. "Theology of Social Life in Augustine's De Civitate Dei." *Journal of Theological Studies* 45, no. 1 (April 1994): 344-46.

Dunnington, Kent. "Humility: An Augustinian Perspective." *Pro Ecclesia* 25, no. 1 (2016): 18-43.

Dupont, Anthony. "La Doctrine de La Grâce de Saint Augustin: Aspects Pastoraux et Spéculatifs." *Revue de l'histoire Des Religions* 231, no. 1 (January 2014): 47-70.

Folliet, Georges. "La correspondence entre Augustin et Nébridius." Pages 191-215 in *L'opera letteraria di Agostino tra Cassiciacum e Milano-Agostino nelle terre di Ambrogio (1-4 ottobre 1986).* Edited by Giovanni Reale et al. Palermo, Italy: Edizioni Augustinus, 1987.

Ford, Coleman M. "'He Who Consoles Us Should Console You': The Spirituality of the Word in Select Letters of Augustine of Hippo." *Evangelical Quarterly* 89, no. 3 (2018): 240-57.

Fraïsse-Bétoulières, Anne. "Comment Traduire La Bible? Un Échange Entre Augustin et Jérôme Au Sujet de La 'citrouille' de Jonas 4,6." *Études Théologiques et Religieuses* 85, no. 2 (2010): 145-65.

Frend, W. H. C. "The Divjak Letters: New Light on St. Augustine's Problems, 416-428." *Journal of Ecclesiastical History* 34, no. 4 (October 1983): 497-512.

Fullam, Lisa. "Toward a Virtue Ethics of Marriage: Augustine and Aquinas on Friendship in Marriage." *Theological Studies* 73, no. 3 (September 2012): 663-92.

Gallagher, Edmon L. "Augustine on the Hebrew Bible." *Journal of Theological Studies* 67 (2016): 97-114.

Garver, Eugene. "The Rhetoric of Friendship in Plato's *Lysis*." *Rhetorica* 24, no. 2 (Spring 2006): 127–46.

Geerlings, Wilhelm. "Das Freundschaftsideal Augustins." *Theologische Quartalschrift* 161, no. 4 (1981): 265–74.

Haden, James. "Friendship in Plato's *Lysis*." *Review of Metaphysics* 37, no. 2 (1983): 327–56.

Hamilton, Louis I. "Possidius' Augustine and Post-Augustinian Africa." *Journal of Early Christian Studies* 12, no. 1 (March 2004): 85–105.

Harrison, Carol. "Augustine, Wisdom and Classical Culture." In *Where Shall Wisdom Be Found? Wisdom in the Bible, the Church and Contemporary World*, edited by Stephen C. Barton, 125–37. Edinburgh: T&T Clark, 1999.

———. "Marriage and Monasticism in St Augustine: The Bond of Friendship." Studia Patristica 33 (1997): 94–99.

Helm, Bennett. "Friendship." *Stanford Encyclopedia of Philosophy*. Edited by Edward N. Zalta. Fall 2017. https://plato.stanford.edu/archives/fall2017/entries/friendship/.

———. "Plural Agents." *Noûs* 42, no. 1 (2008): 17–49.

Hua, Wei. "Augustine and the Delay of Happiness." *Sino-Christian Studies* 22 (December 2016): 119–39.

Hunter, David G. "Augustine and the Making of Marriage in Roman North Africa." *Journal of Early Christian Studies* 11, no. 1 (2003): 63–85.

Jaeger, Stephen. "The Friendship of Mutual Perfecting in Augustine's Confessions, and the Failure of Classical Amicitia." Pages 185–200 in *Friendship in the Middle Ages and Early Modern Age: Explorations of a Fundamental Ethical Discourse*. Edited by Albrecht Classen and Marilyn Sandidge. Berlin: De Gruyter, 2011.

Jamieson, Kathleen. "Jerome, Augustine and the Stesichoran Palinode." *Rhetorica: A Journal of the History of Rhetoric* 5, no. 4 (1987): 353–67.

Jensen, Robin M. "Baptismal Rites and Architecture." Pages 117–44 in *Late Ancient Christianity*. Edited by Virginia Burrus. Vol. 2 of *A People's History of Christianity*. Minneapolis: Fortress, 2005.

Johnson, James Turner. "'Harsh Love' and Forgiveness." *Studies in Christian Ethics* 28, no. 3 (August 2015): 266–72.

Kamimura, Naoki. "Friendship and the Ascent of the Soul in Augustine."
    Prayer and Spirituality in the Early Church 4 (2006): 295-310.

Kilby, Maria. "Augustine of Hippo on the Bishop as Spiritual Father."
    Studia Patristica, 52 (2012): 235-45.

Kirchner, Daniel J. "Augustine's Use of Epicureanism: Three
    Paradigmatic Problems for a Theory of Friendship in the
    Confessions." *International Philosophical Quarterly* 50, no. 2 (2010):
    183-200.

Knotts, Matthew W., and Anthony Dupont. "Why Pray? Augustine of
    Hippo's Multifaceted Doctrine of Prayer." *Journal of Early Christian
    History* 5, no. 2 (2015): 49-75.

Konstan, David. "Greek Friendship." *American Journal of Philology* 117,
    no. 1 (1996): 71-94.

Krishna, Robert. "*Qui Manet in Amicitia Manet in Deo*: Friendship in a
    Latin Christian Tradition." *Pacifica* 29, no. 2 (2016): 141-60.

La Bonnardière, Anne-Marie. "Evodius et Augustin (Lettres 163 et
    164)." Pages 213-27 in *Saint Augustin et la Bible*. Edited by Anne-
    Marie La Bonnardière. Bible de Tous les Temps 3. Paris: Éditions
    Beauchesne, 1986.

Lamb, Michael. "Between Presumption and Despair: Augustine's Hope
    for the Commonwealth." *American Political Science Review* 112, no. 4
    (November 2018): 1036-49.

Lefler, Nathan. "Saint Augustine's Hermeneutics of Friendship: A
    Consideration of De Utilitate Credendi, 10-13, with Special
    Reference to Confessions, Book VIII." *Augustinian Studies* 41, no. 2
    (July 2010): 423-34.

Lienhard, Joseph T. "Friendship in Paulinus of Nola and Augustine."
    Pages 279-96 in *Collectanea Augustiniana: Mélanges T. J. van
    Bavel*. Edited by B. Bruning, M. Lamberigts, and J. Van Houtem.
    Bibliotheca Ephemeridum Theologicarum Lovaniensium 92.
    Louvain, Belgium: Leuven University Press, 1990.

———. "Friendship with God, Friendship in God: Traces in St. Augustine."
    Pages 207-29 in *Augustine: Mystic and Mystagogue*. Edited by Joseph
    C. Schnaubelt. Augustinian Historical Institute 3. New York: Peter
    Lang, 1994.

———. "Paulinus of Nola and Monasticism." *Studia Patristica* 16 (1985): 29–31.

McCann, Christine. "'You Know Better than I Do': The Dynamics of Transformative Knowledge in the Relationship of Augustine of Hippo and Paulinus of Nola." *Studia Patristica* 43 (2006):191–94.

Merdinger, Jane E. "Conversations and Peregrinations of Augustine with His Closest Friends." *Studia Patristica* 49 (2010): 39–44.

———. "On the Eve of the Council of Hippo, 393: The Background to Augustine's Program for Church Reform." *Augustinian Studies* 40, no. 1 (2009): 27–36.

Miller, Richard B. "Evil, Friendship, and Iconic Realism in Augustine's Confessions." *Harvard Theological Review* 104, no. 4 (October 2011): 387–409.

Mommsen, T. E. "St. Augustine and the Christian Idea of Progress: The Background of *The City of God*." *Journal of the History of Ideas* 12 (1951): 346–74.

Murphy, Francis X. "Melania the Elder: A Biographical Note." *Traditio* 5 (1947): 59–77.

Myers, J. A. "Law, Lies and Letter Writing: An Analysis of Jerome and Augustine on the Antioch Incident (Galatians 2:11–14)." *Scottish Journal of Theology* 66, no. 2 (2013): 127–39.

Nadjo, Léon. "Desiderantissimo Fratri Chez Saint Augustin." Pages 285–97 in *Chartae Caritatis: Études de Patristique et d'antiquité Tardive En Hommage à Yves-Marie Duval*. Edited by Benoît Gain, Pierre Jay, and Gérard Nauroy. Collection des Études Augustiniennes. Paris: Institut d'études augustiniennes, 2004.

Nawar, Tamer. "Augustine on the Dangers of Friendship." *Classical Quarterly* 65, no. 2 (December 2015): 836–51.

Nichols, Mary P. "Friendship and Community in Plato's 'Lysis.'" *The Review of Politics* 68, no. 1 (2006): 1–19.

O'Connell, Robert J. "When Saintly Fathers Feuded: The Correspondence Between Augustine and Jerome." *Thought: Fordham University Quarterly* 54, no. 4 (1979): 344–64.

O'Connor, David K. "The Invulnerable Pleasures of Epicurean Friendship." *Greek, Roman, and Byzantine Studies* 30 (1989): 165–86.

O'Donnell, James. "Augustine: His Times and Lives." Pages 8-25 in *Cambridge Companion to Augustine*. Edited by Eleonore Stump and Norman Kretzmann. Cambridge: Cambridge University Press, 2001.

Paño, Maria Victoria Escribano. "Bishops, Judges, and Emperors: CTh 16.2.31/CTh 16.5.46/Sirm. 14 (409)." Pages 105-26 in *The Role of the Bishop in Late Antiquity: Conflict and Compromise*. Edited by Andrew Fear, José Fernández Urbiña, and Mar Marcos Sanchez. London: Bloomsbury Academic, 2013.

Perälä, Mika. "A Friend Being Good and One's Own in *Nicomachean Ethics* 9.9." *Phronesis* 61, no. 3 (2016): 307-36.

Petit, Jean-François. "Sur Le 'Phénomène Amical': L'expérience de l'amitié Chez Saint Augustin." *Transversalités* 113 (January 2010): 47-63.

Pizzolato, Luigi Franco. "L'amicizia in Sant'Agostino e il Laelius di Cicerone." *Vigiliae Christianae* 28, no. 3 (September 1974): 203-15.

Ployd, Adam D. "The Power of Baptism: Augustine's Pro-Nicene Response to the Donatists." *Journal of Early Christian Studies* 22, no. 4 (2014): 519-40.

Radvan, Iain. "Spiritual Direction, Experiential Focusing and the Examen of St Ignatius." *The Way* 57, no. 1 (January 2018): 101-10.

Rist, John M. "Epicurus on Friendship." *Classical Philology* 75, no. 2 (1980): 121-29.

Robinson, Bernard P. "Jonah's Qiqayon Plant." *Zeitschrift für die Alttestamentliche Wissenschaft* 97, no. 3 (1985): 390-403.

Russell, D. A. "On Reading Plutarch's 'Moralia.'" *Greece and Rome* 15, no. 2 (1968): 130-46.

Schoeman, F. "Aristotle on the Good of Friendship." *Australasian Journal of Philosophy* 63 (1985): 269-82.

Sellner, Edward Cletus. "An Inclination of the Heart: Jerome and His Female Friendships." *Spiritual Life* 47, no. 3 (2001): 161-77.

Smither, Edward L. "Pastoral Lessons from Augustine's Theological Correspondence with Women." *HTS Teologiese Studies/Theological Studies* 72, no. 4 (2016): 1-6.

———. "Unrecognized and Unlikely Influence? The Impact of Valerius of Hippo on Augustine." *Irish Theological Quarterly* 72, no. 3 (2007): 251-64.

Vander Valk, Frank. "Friendship, Politics, and Augustine's Consolidation of the Self." *Religious Studies* 45, no. 2 (June 2009): 125-46.

Williams, Joe. "Letter Writing, Materiality, and Gifts in Late Antiquity: Some Perspectives on Material Culture." *Journal of Late Antiquity* 7, no. 2 (2014): 351–59.

DISSERTATIONS AND THESES

Bonner, Alison Clare. "The Scale, Context, and Implications, of the Manuscript Transmission of Pelagius' *Ad Demetriadem*." PhD diss., University of Cambridge, 2012.

Congrove, Joshua Jay. "Authority, Friendship, and Rhetoric in the Letters of St. Augustine of Hippo." PhD diss., Indiana University, 2011.

Ebbeler, Jennifer. "Pendants in the Apparel of Heroes? Cultures of Latin Letter-Writing from Cicero to Ennodius." PhD diss., University of Pennsylvania, 2001.

Kreidler, Mary Jane. "The Pastoral Theology of Augustine of Hippo as Found in His Letters." PhD diss., Marquette University, 1987.

Osseforth, Matthieu Hendrikus Johannes Gemma. "Friendship in Saint Augustine's *Confessions*." PhD diss., Vrije Universiteit Amsterdam, 2017.

SUBJECT INDEX

—

SCRIPTURE INDEX

—